THIRD DOWN
AND A WAR TO GO

Also by Terry Frei
Horns, Hogs, and Nixon Coming

THIRD DOWN
AND A WAR TO GO

THE ALL-AMERICAN
1942 WISCONSIN BADGERS

TERRY FREI

Wisconsin Historical Society Press
Madison, Wisconsin

Published by the
Wisconsin Historical Society Press

Publication of this book was made possible in part by grants from the Alice E. Smith fellowship fund and the D.C. Everest fellowship fund.

Quotes from The Associated Press, *United Press International, Wisconsin State Journal, Columbus Dispatch,* and *Daily Cardinal* used with permission.

Photographs identified with PH, WHi, or WHS are from the Society's collections; address inquiries about such photos to the Visual Materials Archivist at the above address.

Publications of the Wisconsin Historical Society Press are available at quantity discounts for promotions, fund raising, and educational use. Write to the above address for more information.

Printed in the United States of America
Designed by Jane Tenenbaum
Composition by Timothy O'Keeffe

09 08 07 06 05 5 4 3 2 1

Frei, Terry, 1955–
  Third down and a war to go: the All-American 1942 Wisconsin Badgers / Terry Frei.
    p. cm.
  Includes bibliographical references and index.
  ISBN 0-87020-360-6 (alk. paper)
  1. Wisconsin Badgers (Football team)—History. 2. University of Wisconsin—Football—History. I. Title.
GV958.U5867F74 2005
796.332'63'0977583—dc22

                    2004000786

∞ The paper used in this publication meets the minimum requirements of the American National Standard for Information Sciences—Permanence of Paper for Printed Library Materials, ANSI Z39.48-1992.

To my mother, Marian Frei, who was in on this from the start—in so many ways.

"I keep picturing the boys who are playing for me as they may be a year from now, battling a Jap or a Nazi with a bayonet. We've always wanted our football players tough. Now we want them tougher than ever."
—*Wisconsin Coach Harry Stuhldreher, October 1942*

Contents

Acknowledgments

My wife, Helen, again tolerated and supported my passion for a project I often buried myself in.

My mother, Marian, was a guiding spirit in this work, as she has been all my life. A Wisconsin native herself, she pointed me in the right direction, proofread the manuscript, and gently made suggestions.

The folks at the Wisconsin Historical Society—including Kent Calder, Margaret Dwyer, John Nondorf, Michael Stevens, and editor *par excellence* Kate Thompson—were helpful and encouraging long before we agreed the WHS would publish the book.

The staffs at Wisconsin libraries—including the University of Wisconsin–Madison Archives, the Madison Public Library, the Schreiner Library in Lancaster, Wisconsin, and the Grant County Historical Society—never winced at my requests and didn't kick me out when I broke microfilm and copying machines.

UW Sports Information Director Justin Doherty and his staff welcomed me and gave me access to the department's rich archives.

Terry Murawski, executive director for the National W Club, and his staff helped locate surviving 1942 Badgers.

Father Stan Drongowski and the other priests, brothers, staff members, and parishioners at Madison's Blessed Sacrament Catholic Church made me feel at home during my stay in Madison. It was a fortuitous coincidence that many in the Dominican religious community also have been posted to Saint Dominic's, our Denver parish.

Fellow journalists Neal Rubin and Jim Beseda read drafts of the manuscript and offered astute feedback and help, as did my four siblings: David Frei of New York; Judy Kaplan of Wilsonville, Oregon; Susan Frei Earley of Tulsa; and Nancy McCormick of Wadsworth, Illinois; as did two history professors and authors: Tom Zeiler, chairman of the University of Colorado–Boulder history department, and Nick Sarantakes of Texas A&M–Commerce.

Literary agent John Monteleone believed in this book from the start, and entertainment agent Jeanne Field, a Cheesehead herself, has kept the faith.

My day-job editors, Kevin Dale and David Wright at *The Denver Post* and Sherry Skalko at ESPN.com, were understanding when my mind sometimes seemed to be off in Madison or in the Pacific and European battle theaters.

Former Marine and *Orange County Register* reporter John Gunn provided important background information in his book about the Corps and football, *The Old Core*.

This will become clear to readers, but I can't thank enough the surviving 1942 Badgers and their families for their cooperation and trust. In particular, Judy Corfield went above and beyond the call of duty. Also, numerous surviving members of the Sixth Marine Division and Don Esmond, veteran of the 26th Photo Reconnaissance Squadron, responded to my requests for help with invaluable memories and insight.

So before we move on:

On Wisconsin!

And *Semper Fi.*

1942 Wisconsin Badgers Roster and Schedule

Note: Roster includes those who were on the squad during the season. Several players listed on the preseason roster and shown in the team picture left the squad before the season started, for various reasons. Others joined the team after the beginning of fall practice.

1942 Roster

Number	Name	Position	Year	Height	Weight	Hometown
22	ANDERSON, Ashley	QB	Jr.	5-11	182	Milwaukee, Wis.
74	BAUMANN, Bob	T	Sr.	6-2	210	Harvey, Ill.
54	BOORMAN, Harry	C	So.	5-11	190	Chicago, Ill.
61	BOYLE, Pat	G	Jr.	6-0	183	Duluth, Minn.
45	BREITENBACH, Otto	HB	So.	5-9	173	Madison, Wis.
33	CALLIGARO, Len	FB	Sr.	5-11	190	Hurley, Wis.
76	CRABB, Jack	T	So.	6-3	210	Milwaukee, Wis.
64	CURRIER, Ken	G	So.	5-10	190	Rice Lake, Wis.
—	DAVIS, Ralph					
68	DEAN, Bob	G	So.	5-11	193	Tomahawk, Wis.
23	DIERCKS, Bobby	QB	Sr.	5-8	181	Antigo, Wis.
78	DONNELLAN, Dave	T	So.	5-11	195	Eau Claire, Wis.
65	FREI, Jerry	G	So.	6-1	190	Stoughton, Wis.
24	GALLAGHER, John	QB	So.	5-8	189	Eau Claire, Wis.
83	HANZLIK, Bob	E	Jr.	6-1	195	Chippewa Falls, Wis.
34	HARDER, Pat	FB	Jr.	5-11	193	Milwaukee, Wis.
72	HEKKERS, George	T	So.	6-3	197	Milwaukee, Wis.
71	HIRSBRUNNER, Paul	T	Sr.	6-2	212	Darlington, Wis.
40	HIRSCH, Elroy	HB	So.	6-1	185	Wausau, Wis.
11	HOSKINS, Mark	HB	Sr.	6-1	185	Lancaster, Wis.
89	JOHNSON, Farnham	E	So.	6-0	191	Neenah, Wis.

Number – Name – Position – Year – Height – Weight – Hometown

—	KING, Tom					
16	KISSLING, Erv	HB	So.	5-8	187	Monticello, Wis.
67	KLINZING, Vern	G	So.	5-10	187	Fond du Lac, Wis.
26	LITCHFIELD, Don	QB	So.	5-11	184	Eau Claire, Wis.
52	LYNCH, Lawrence	C	Sr.	6-0	187	Waukesha, Wis.
—	LYONS, Pat	E	Sr.			Horicon, Wis.
62	MAKRIS, George	G	So.	5-10	185	Rhinelander, Wis.
35	MAVES, Earl	FB	Sr.	5-10	187	Stanley, Wis.
15	McFADZEAN, Jim	HB	Sr.	5-10	178	Winnetka, Ill.
53	McKAY, Bob	C	So.	6-0	192	Sioux Falls, S. Dak.
51	NEGUS, Fred	C	So.	6-2	201	Martin's Ferry, Ohio
69	NEPERUD, George	G	So.	5-9	195	Chippewa Falls, Wis.
86	OLSHANSKI, Hank	E	So.	6-1	189	Wausau, Wis.
46	OMELINA, Bob	HB	So.	5-10	178	Cudahy, Wis.
14	PFOTENHAUER, Don	HB	Sr.	5-9	185	Escanaba, Mich.
31	RAY, Bob	FB	So.	5-11	187	Eau Claire, Wis.
18	RAYACICH, Dan	HB	So.	5-11	178	Superior, Wis.
44	REGAN, Jim	HB	So.	5-11	181	Berwyn, Ill.
75	REICH, Herbert	T	So.	5-11	215	Chicago, Ill.
87	RENNEBOHM, Bob	E	Sr.	5-11	187	La Crosse, Wis.
60	ROBERTS, John	G	Sr.	5-10	185	Des Moines, Iowa
80	SCHREINER, Dave	E	So.	6-2	198	Lancaster, Wis.
17	SCHROEDER, Bill	HB	Sr.	6-1	190	Sheboygan, Wis.
43	SEELINGER, Bud	HB	Sr.	5-11	178	Great Falls, Mont.
84	STUPKA, Bob	E	Sr.	6-0	181	Watertown, Wis.
77	THORNALLY, Dick	T		6-3	210	Chicago, Ill.
—	UTEGAARD, John		Jr.			
63	VOGDS, Red	G	Sr.	5-11	194	Fond du Lac, Wis.
70	WASSERBACH, Lloyd	T	So.	6-0	210	Bailey's Harbor, Wis.
25	WINK, Jack	QB		5-10	190	Milwaukee, Wis.

Head Coach: Harry Stuhldreher
Backfield Coach: Guy Sundt
Tackles and Ends Coach: George Fox
Guards and Centers Coach: Russ Rippe

1942 Schedule

Saturday, September 19   vs.   Camp Grant at Madison

Saturday, September 26   vs.   Notre Dame at Madison

Saturday, October 3   vs.   Marquette at Madison

Saturday, October 10   vs.   Missouri at Madison

Saturday, October 17   vs.   Great Lakes at Chicago

Saturday, October 24   vs.   Purdue at Lafayette, Indiana

Saturday, October 31   vs.   Ohio State at Madison

Saturday, November 7   vs.   Iowa at Iowa City, Iowa

Saturday, November 14   vs.   Northwestern at Evanston, Illinois

Saturday, November 21   vs.   Minnesota at Madison

Prologue

As Veterans Day 2000 approached, my father was struggling. Jerry Frei was seventy-six, and heart, knee, and circulation problems limited his mobility. That was bad enough, but he also felt himself slipping away from the football community.

The sport was his occupational passion. After playing for the University of Wisconsin, he served as a high school and college coach, primarily at the University of Oregon; then, he was a longtime offensive line coach in the National Football League with the Denver Broncos, Tampa Bay Buccaneers, and Chicago Bears. Finally, he became a scout for college talent with the Broncos.

In my travels as a sportswriter, whether for *The Denver Post, The Oregonian,* or *The Sporting News,* football coaches and executives would frequently respond whenever we'd meet with "Oh, you're Jerry's boy!" It helped.

In his sixties, after he moved into scouting, he picked up computer skills as if he were a twelve-year-old raised on Windows and a mouse. When Dad was in his seventies and serving as the Broncos' college scouting director, a reporter for the *Colorado Springs Gazette Telegraph*, Mike Burrows, struck up a conversation with him during the team's training camp at the University of Northern Colorado in Greeley. Burrows was a student of the World War II air war, and a team official had told him he should ask Jerry Frei about his war experiences. *He was a fighter pilot, after all.* But it's really all anyone who worked with him knew. The few who knew more didn't know very much. As Dad told Burrows about flying the F-5 version of the Lockheed P-38 fighter plane on photo reconnaissance missions over Japanese targets, those within earshot were transfixed.

The next summer, when the Broncos media guide came out, Jerry Frei's biography for the first time in his long NFL career disclosed that he was a former World War II pilot. For years, the press guides noted that Jerry Frei played college football at Wisconsin in 1942, 1946, and 1947, but nobody thought to explain that three-season gap.

After taking his official NFL retirement, he remained a consultant for the Broncos. But, Jerry Frei step completely away from football? Unthinkable. Even my mother, Marian, knew that would have driven him nuts, so she went along with his determination to continue working part-time. By 2000, he stopped making road trips with the Broncos and found it difficult to get to the Mile High Stadium press box to sit in the second row with his buddy Jack Elway, quarterback John Elway's father and the Broncos' director of professional scouting. For years, Jerry and Jack were office pals, drinking buddies, and roommates during the team's training camp at UNC. They were considered the veteran voices within the organization.

A pacemaker helped my father's heart, but he had trouble catching his breath and moving around. When he felt up to it, he would go to the Broncos' offices, watch tape, and act as a cross-checker for draft-eligible college players. During the season, he sat on a bench near the dressing room and watched practice.

One day, a KUSA-TV reporter, Blake Olson, who had read that press guide biography, decided to pursue a feature about "the man on the bench." With the tape rolling, the two discussed my father's life in football. But Olson was spellbound after he asked my father about his World War II flying experiences.

Olson, whose path had crossed mine on various assignments, later asked me to pick out pictures to complement the video. I went to my parents' house, gathered numerous photos, made copies, and took them to the TV station. When the feature aired, those still shots—some of young Jerry Frei standing outside his plane and sitting in the cockpit—were interspersed with the video. Olson's feature was moving, and I was chagrined to realize that I had never heard some of the information in the story. For example, Dad told Olson that a P-38 reconnaissance pilot carried a .45-caliber pistol as his only means of self-defense. My father laughed and said he probably wouldn't have been able to get the pistol to work, much less hit anything. Olson's television story prodded me to find out more.

In late 2000, I mentioned to my father that I wanted to talk with him about his war service for a column to run the Sunday before Veterans Day. He was reluctant. I emphasized that I would portray him as a representative of a generation we hadn't thanked enough and that it would be a "nice, little article."

I brought a tape recorder and a notebook to my parents' home in Englewood, near the Broncos' headquarters. My father and I went into his den. We began by talking about the start of the war, which came when he was a UW freshman, and of the interim time he spent at UW before entering the Army Air Forces.* Throughout our conversation, a point of reference was the 1942 Badgers team picture on his wall. The photo was mounted on a large plaque that UW had presented in recent years to members of the 1942 team. The 1942 results, also engraved on the plaque, made it clear that this had been a glorious season for the Badgers. Jerry Frei was Number 65 in the fourth row, the eighteen-year-old sophomore guard from Stoughton, Wisconsin.

I had known for years that this Badgers team included famous players. Elroy "Crazylegs" Hirsch had visited our home in Eugene, and during a vacation we had visited him at the Wisconsin athletic department offices in Camp Randall Stadium. Dad had coached Hall of Fame players, but he sounded like an awestruck eighteen-year-old when he talked about Dave Schreiner, the '42 team's senior All-American end. Fullback Pat Harder, the Badger next to my father in the team picture, became an NFL star and then an NFL umpire, and I knew that offensive line coach Jerry Frei thought Harder called too darned many holding penalties. (Dad thought that about all NFL umpires.)

I also realized that many of the players in the picture, like my father, had gone off to serve in World War II—and that not all of them had returned. And I knew that one of my father's lifelong close friends was Ken Currier, another Wisconsin guard, and that when they got together, the intervening years disappeared.

That was pretty much all I knew.

That day my father told me that after the Japanese attacked Pearl Harbor, Wisconsin coach Harry Stuhldreher helped arrange for him, then a freshman, to sign up for an Army Air Forces reserve unit because it was based in Madison. My dad's induction notice came in February 1943, just after that successful '42 season. He was eighteen, and he had been in college for three semesters.

"At that point, we all wanted to go," he said. "All your friends were going, and you were not going to stay in school."

His teammates scattered, and he was among the handful of Badgers entering the Army Air Forces.

"I had no inclination, no great desire to be a pilot," my father said.

As I asked questions, he kept reaching into the closet for material. He showed me pictures, many more than the few I had borrowed for

---

*Although many veterans, including my father, preferred to call the branch by its older name, the Army Air Corps—which remained in widespread use—the AAF was founded in early 1941. Some functions remained under the Air Corps name for a while, but for simplicity's sake I will use the term Army Air Forces in this book.

The Badgers on September 1, 1942, the first day of practices. Several players pictured here left the squad before the season started. Three important members of the team weren't in the photo: halfback Bud Seelinger, because of travel problems, plus end Bob Hanzlik, and fullback Bob Ray, who were taking Marine physicals. In many cases, players in the photo were wearing jersey numbers that didn't coincide with their game numbers. (Some players didn't have numbers at all, and in a couple of cases the number is obscured.)

Front row, left to right: 17 Bill Schroeder, 72 George Hekkers, 64 Ken Currier, 33 Len Calligaro, 53 Bob McKay, 60 John Roberts, Dick Thornally, 13 Lloyd Wasserbach, 71 Paul Hirsbrunner.

Second row: 67 Vern Klinzing, 89 Farnham Johnson, Frank Granitz, 23 Bobby Diercks, 62 George Makris, 42 Mark Hoskins, 15 Jim McFadzean, 74 Bob Baumann, 80 Dave Schreiner, 84 Bob Stupka.

Third row: 45 Otto Breitenbach, 85 Jim McClellan, 69 George Neperud, 27 Bob Omelina, 44 Jim Regan, 24 John Gallagher, 16 Erv Kissling, 35 Bob Rennebohm, 51 Fred Negus, 40 Elroy Hirsch, Hank Olshanski, Jack Crabb.

Fourth row: 26 Don Litchfield, 25 Jack Wink, 35 Earl Maves, 66 Gene Walgenbach, 61 Pat Boyle, 52 Larry Lynch, 67 Gene Hahn, 65 Jerry Frei, 34 Pat Harder, 78 Dave Donnellan, Bob Owen, 68 Bob Dean.

Fifth row: Assistant coach Russ Rippe, head coach Harry Stuhldreher, assistant coach George Fox, 75 Herb Reich, 54 Harry Boorman, 14 Don Pfotenhauer, Jack Mead, 22 Ashley Anderson, 63 Red Vogds, assistant coach Guy Sundt, assistant coach Dynie Mansfield, trainer Walter Bakke, manager Eugene Fischer.

PHOTO COURTESY OF UNIVERSITY OF WISCONSIN SPORTS INFORMATION DEPARTMENT

Olson's story. We looked at unit yearbooks, scrapbooks, and letters. I had seen some of it before, but most of it was new to me.

He went through basic training in Wichita Falls, Texas, and then went to Santa Ana, California, for a battery of tests designed to help the AAF decide what kind of role suited each new soldier—pilot, bombardier, navigator, or something else. Waiting out the training backlog, Frei and other potential pilots—many of whom would "wash out"—briefly studied at Union University in Jackson, Tennessee, and then took primary flight training near Phoenix. "We were flying an open-cockpit Stearman biplane, and it was an exciting little airplane," my father said. "It was probably the most fun we ever had flying."

It amazed me that the first time he was ever in an airplane, he was piloting it by the end of the flight. Dad shrugged. "Mechanically, Terry, flying then was not very mysterious," he said.

Other flight training took him to California and Colorado, and he still didn't know what kind of plane—or duty—he would draw. Then he was sent to Coffeyville, Kansas, where he was trained to fly the Lockheed P-38 for reconnaissance flights. The single-pilot, twin-engine fighter was usually outfitted with guns; the F-5 version replaced the guns with cameras. "That was a very popular airplane at that time," he said. "They taught us the mechanics of the cameras, and of taking pictures."

My father and his buddies were assigned to a photo recon group in Europe, loaded onto a troop train, and sent to Savannah, Georgia, which was their stopping-off point for Europe and the air war against Hitler. When they got to Savannah, they were told they would be going to the Pacific instead—and they were put right back on the train and sent back across the country to San Francisco. (A classic example of a military SNAFU: Situation Normal, All . . .)

By then, a four-man group of buddies from his training class had grown tight, having been assigned together because of a quirk of the alphabet—Jerry Frei; Ed Crawford, from Texas; Madison Gillespie, from Iowa; and Don Garbarino, from Oregon. They traveled to a replacement center in New Guinea. "Then they put maybe a dozen of us on a plane and went up to Biak Island, another island off New Guinea," Dad said. "They put us in the back of a truck. We were all excited about this whole thing. We were carrying our guns and thinking, 'God, we're going to be in the middle of this war.' The truck went to the 8th Photo Squadron and dropped off three or four guys, went to the 17th Photo Squadron and dropped off some more, and then it was just the four of us."

They climbed out of the truck at the 26th Photo Reconnaissance Squadron.

Each pilot's tour would be one year or three hundred combat flying hours, whichever came first. If he stayed alive that long.

On September 18, 1944, three months after his twentieth birthday, Dad flew the first of sixty-seven combat missions. Usually, two planes were on the mission in case one plane's cameras failed.

"You could get anti-aircraft fire, but as you looked out the back window, you could see it behind you," he said. "Most of the time, we were coming in high and staying for such a short period of time. You went down one direction, back over the target in the other direction, and got out of there.

"As soon as you got back into radio range, you would tell 'em, 'Yeah, I got pictures, I'm on the way home, I'll be there about such-and-such time.' You'd get back and you'd buzz the home area, saying, 'Here I am, come and get me at the airstrip and get my pictures out of the cameras.' The newer you were and the younger you were, the harder you buzzed, because you didn't think you were going to live, anyway. But as soon as you got halfway through, you said, 'My God, I'm going to make it, maybe I'm going to last.' That's when you started flying more conservative, straight and level. One of the guys who came over with us and went to another squad got killed buzzing. He hit a palm tree with his tail, and that calmed down a lot of people."

Like all P-38 pilots, Jerry Frei was alone in his twin-engine, one-person plane.
PHOTO FROM THE AUTHOR'S COLLECTION

Dad pulled out an old hanging folder from his desk. It was his flight record, and I could picture a sweaty clerk typing information onto the sheet after every mission more than a half-century earlier, lining it up on the correct line and making sure the carbon paper was in place. The sheets listed my father's sixty-seven missions and targets with names such as Davao, N. Halmeras, Mindanao, Lianga Bay, Babuyan Island, Cape Bojeador, Solvec Cove, Cagayan Valley, even Wenchou, China.

Twice, my father was sent to Australia for rest and rehabilitation. The second time, the squad moved from Biak Island to Lingayen, on the Lingayen Gulf to the north of Manila. When he finally caught up with his squadron, he got off the transport plane at Lingayen and noticed one of the 26th's planes taking off.

"I asked one of our people, 'Who's that?'" Dad said. "He said it was Madison Gillespie, and he was going on a low-level mission to Ipo Dam. I went over to the squadron area, to the others' tent. It always was Ed Crawford, Don Garbarino, Madison Gillespie, and me. But while I was gone, they'd moved another pilot in with them when they got to Lingayen, so I was going to go get a cot and be the fifth."

He didn't have to get the cot.

"Madison Gillespie never came back," Dad said. "No one ever knew what happened, but we lost two planes over Ipo Dam."

Dad flipped through the commemorative 26th Photo Reconnaissance Squadron book, pointed to pilots' pictures, and counted, slowly, from one to eight. That represented eight killed in action from a group that numbered twenty at any one time and about thirty-five in rotation over the time covered by my father's combat tour. The dead were the victims of anti-aircraft fire or mechanical failure or . . . who knows? Sometimes, like Gillespie, they just didn't make it back. After the war, salvaged dogtags and wreckage provided some answers. Other pilots' deaths were never explained.

Yet my father said, "We did not consider it a very dangerous profession. When I think of what people went through down on the ground, and how they lived, and how they ate, and how they slept, and how they were in combat, we weren't in a dangerous profession."

Only later did I figure out that he was talking about what some of his Badger teammates, among others, went through "on the ground."

His toughest days were March 22, 1945, when he flew missions to northwest Manila and to the Cagayan Valley (the squadron received a group citation); and April 15, when he flew an eight-hour mission from Lingayen to a guerrilla airstrip for refueling; then to Wenchou, the harbor port across the East China Sea from Japan. (The Battle of Okinawa, involving some of his teammates, began on April 1, between those two missions.) The reconnaissance missions were important work, mostly in support of the 6th Army.

"But again," he said, "I emphasize the point that mine was a nice war, if there was such a thing. I didn't hurt anybody. I didn't kill anybody or shoot anybody. I didn't get shot at a lot, although we did go through bombing raids when we were on the ground. But I also know what other men were going through, and it was a lot worse."

After horrific fighting, Major General Roy S. Geiger declared Okinawa secure on June 21, 1945. The 26th Photo Squadron was ticketed to shift to Okinawa, one step closer to Japan. Before the move, though, Jerry Frei crossed the three-hundred-hour threshold on a two-plane mission to the Batan Islands, north of Luzon. (The islands aren't to be confused with the Bataan Peninsula.)

After the two P-38s successfully flew over the target, took pictures, and turned back to Lingayen, the pilot in the other plane used the cameras to take a picture of my father in the air on his final mission.

Soon, his war—America's war—was over. He and so many other veterans went on with their lives. "I think everyone was looking at it like, 'I did what I had to do,'" he told me as we talked in his den. "Everyone who survived gave a big sigh of relief, and felt sad for those who didn't." He emphasized that he was "sheepish" about talking about this, especially for a story. "I'm proud," he said, "but I don't claim a lot of credit for winning World War II."

The day before Veterans Day 2000, my mother, Marian, retrieved the paper off the porch in Englewood, took a look at my column, and reported to my father: "It's not just a 'nice, little story.'" Okay, if I ever had intended it to be a nice, little story, I junked that plan the minute I sat down at the computer to write it. The column ran with a handful of pictures, and the shot on the cover of the sports section showed my father facing the camera in his flying helmet and raised goggles, peering into the distance.

I included in the preface that I considered my father a representative of his generation, and I closed with the thought that we hadn't sufficiently thanked World War II veterans. It was sincere . . . and, in my case, long overdue.

The response was heartening. Many wrote to me, politely telling me that my father had been too modest in downplaying his own ability as a flyer and minimizing the danger he had faced as a reconnaissance pilot. The message: If you flew a P-38, an assignment coveted by pilots, you had to be damn good. I was lectured that flying over Japanese targets, alone, was perilous, period, before one even factored in the issue of the entire mission—getting to the target and getting back. At the Broncos' offices, players and staff members let Dad know they agreed with the sentiment of the column and thanked him. (Later, while I was researching my book about the 1969 Texas-Arkansas football game, *Horns, Hogs, and Nixon Coming,* I talked with former Arkansas congressman John Paul Hammerschmidt, who had attended the game with his close friend Texas Representative George Herbert Walker Bush and the Nixon party. I asked Hammerschmidt about his decorated World War II stint, when he flew 217 missions with the Third Combat Cargo Group "over the hump" in the China-Burma-India Theater, and I mentioned that my father had flown a P-38. "Oh," Hammerschmidt exclaimed, "we all wanted to fly that plane!")

By early 2001, a couple of months after the column ran, Dad was doing most of his Broncos work at home. Walking for more than a few steps at a time was difficult. The team sent over a video system and ferried tapes between the offices and his home. In early February, he lost his breath and briefly blacked out, and my mother rushed him to the hospital. Doctors insisted he stay for a week of tests and treatment. He was told he would have to be hooked up to an oxygen supply for at least the foreseeable future.

One night near the end of his stay, I walked down the hall at the hospital. His door, at a corner of the wing, was open, and I could see him the entire length of the hall. He was sitting on the side of the bed, with his food tray table over his legs. His Broncos Super Bowl satchel was on the bed next to him. On the tray table, he had strewn sheets of lined yellow legal paper, and with the hospital ID bracelet still on his wrist, he was leaning over and writing out his final ratings of offensive line prospects for the upcoming 2001 draft. He was doing it that way because we hadn't let him have his laptop computer in the hospital room. He told me he had promised Ted Sundquist, his successor as the Broncos' director of scouting, that he would get his ratings in, and, by God, that's what he was going to do.

We took him home the night of February 15, with a temporary oxygen supply. The next morning, I went back to my parents' home to see how he was doing and to be there when the larger oxygen system was delivered. After the man made the delivery and showed us how to use the system, Dad went back to his desk and, with the clear tubing connecting him to the oxygen tank, resumed his work on the scouting reports. He took a break to talk on the phone with Jack Elway, who was by then living in Palm Springs. They laughed a lot, as they always did.

He was working on a report about Michigan tackle Jeff Backus. He thought Backus was a great player, and his report declared that Backus "could come in and play for us immediately."

He didn't finish the report. His raves about Backus were still on the screen when his heart finally gave out.

For the memorial services in Denver and Eugene—the latter put on by his former Oregon players, including Hall of Fame quarterback Dan Fouts, longtime NFL receiver Bob Newland, and former kicker Ken Woody—we assembled booklets of remembrance, including pictures of him in the P-38 and that Veterans Day column.

Fouts, who attended the service in Denver and helped organize the one in Eugene, was a champion. He praised my father to everyone who called him for comment on February 16, and he repeated the sentiments at both services. "Jerry was more than a coach," Fouts said on the day of my father's death. "He was a friend and a man I could look up to. At that time, Oregon was kind of an off-Broadway version of Cal-Berkeley.

After Denver's victory over the Atlanta Falcons in Super Bowl XXXIII, veteran Broncos executives Jack Elway and Jerry Frei quickly donned championship hats in the raucous dressing room and celebrated the Broncos' second-straight NFL title.

PHOTO FROM THE AUTHOR'S COLLECTION

Things got pretty crazy on campus. But he was always so non-judgmental. He was willing to treat us all as individual, mature young men."

Fouts told me that he was astounded by the details of his coach's wartime flying. The coach, he said, never mentioned any of that to his players. And they hadn't known about it.

The letters poured in from former players from both his high school and college teams—from stars and scrubs alike. In a letter to me, former Oregon Ducks star Ahmad Rashad wrote, "I always felt like one of his sons and I felt it was so important to represent him well." And that was a typical sentiment.

It also got to me when I read Ron Bellamy's column in the Eugene *Register-Guard*, that quoted, among others, Ken Woody. Woody said he thought of what my father had taught him every day at his job as principal of Oregon's Lebanon High School. For years, my father kept on his den wall a plaque that Woody had given him. It has a picture of Woody and Dad on the sideline, and beneath the photo is a poem Woody wrote about his coach. The final line: "A great man touched me once."

I went back and listened to the tape of my interview with my father. I came across an exchange I hadn't used in my story, from when we were looking at that picture of his plane in the air on what he knew was his final mission. I asked what he was thinking after he landed in the Philippines that day. "I wanted to get home, I wanted to get married, and I wanted to get back in college and play football," he said decisively.

After his death, that response made me think of one phrase.

Missions accomplished.

He got married in December 1945. He re-enrolled at Wisconsin, played two more seasons, and got his degree. He spent more than fifty years as a husband, father, grandfather, player, coach, scout, and administrator, and he was still working and sharp when he died.

Missions accomplished.

The cynical sportswriter was reminded. Done right, sports teach. Sports bond. Sports enrich. Sports are about lessons and unbreakable friendships that can last through one man's lifetime.

And longer.

My mother moved into a retirement community apartment, but she put some of my father's den pictures on her walls. One of them was that 1942 Wisconsin team picture. I kept looking at it, reading the names, and matching them with faces, marveling at how young all of them looked.

Finally, I decided.

I wanted to know more about what it was like for the players to go through that 1942 season, knowing that they, like so many of their contemporaries, soon would be in another uniform, risking their lives for their country.

I set out to learn more about that team, about that season, about the men, about their fates in the war and in later life.

I knew that World War II–era values—and certainly, his own service experiences—were critical foundations in my father's life and philosophy, in combination with lessons he learned in athletics. "I was still sixteen when I graduated from high school, and I was nineteen when I got my wings," he said that day in his den. "I had kind of come off the farm. Really, I didn't have very many social graces. I'm sure that between football and World War II, those things had a lot to do with me growing up, maturing, and facing the world."

I suspected that it was the same for his teammates.

As I set out to research this story, regret and curiosity combined to create powerful motivation. Those emotions helped shape in me a prideful perspective. What follows is a story I took too damn long to seek, involving questions I didn't think to ask—or never got to ask at all. My father could have provided many answers and fascinating remembrances. I didn't ask him enough questions early enough. So I say to you now, if you're in the position I was in a few years ago, I implore you to ask. Ask before it's too late.

After I completed my research, I came to view these men—both the survivors and those who had passed on before I could talk to them—as my extended family, and not just because they were part of my father's life.

The 1942 Wisconsin Badgers were a terrific football team. As young men of that era, they were extraordinary, yet typical. Among other reasons, that's why theirs is an All-American story.

ONE

The Lancaster Boys

The B-17 bomber was on fire. Copilot Mark Hoskins could see the flames, smell the cordite, and sense the crew's time running out. From the seat to Hoskins's left, the captain yelled the order to abandon the plane. Hoskins scrambled down to the nose, joining the navigator and bombardier, expecting to follow them out the opened hatch.

They were struggling with the little door. The navigator and bombardier yanked and shoved and twisted but couldn't get it open. The flames burned and the smell grew stronger. If they didn't get out soon, they wouldn't get out at all, and their frenzy showed they knew it.

Hoskins pulled them away from the door.

The twenty-two-year-old airman told himself he was a blocker again, leading a sweep for Elroy Hirsch or Pat Harder in Camp Randall Stadium. Against Notre Dame or Ohio State, it didn't matter. He backed up, charged at the little door, and crashed into it with his shoulder.

Not only did the hatch open, but Hoskins flew through it and found himself in the skies over Hungary. Stunned, he managed to pull his parachute ripcord and began to drift to the ground, where he would take his chances.

Then he saw the German fighter plane, presumably the one that had nailed the B-17.

The pilot, his guns at the ready, was flying toward Hoskins, a floating and defenseless target.

It was June 27, 1944.

★ ★ ★

The sad news that Lieut. Mark Hoskins is missing in action threw a pall of gloom over Madison and particularly the [fraternity row], where Mark was a friend of hundreds. . . . He was playing

*in the biggest game of all, as a member of Uncle Sam's team. He was
the same quiet, efficient officer as he had been a football star. He gave
his all on every play. We'll never forget Mark Hoskins, a fighter, a gentleman and a grand guy.* — HANK CASSERLY, *CAPITAL TIMES,* JULY 1944

★ ★ ★

Dave Schreiner was trying to get ready for the much-anticipated game.
Around him, as kickoff approached, the frenetic wagering continued
among the thousands of Marines—attendance estimates ranged from
2,500 to 10,000—ringing the so-called field. Money was thrown out and
matched, involving a day's pay, a week's pay, a month's pay, all risked as
if the thrill of the wager and the bluster behind it were the attractions. The
game was touch football—officially, anyway—because the brass had ordained it, reminding the Marines that they had best save their most ardent aggression for the upcoming island fighting. Everybody knew it
would be fierce and ugly and—well, they didn't talk much about the rest.
Schreiner and many of the others had already been through other battles and had been fortunate to have made it this far.

It was Christmas Eve, 1944.

The game pitted two regiments of the Sixth Marine Division—the
4th versus the 29th. The gridiron was the 29th's parade ground on
Guadalcanal, an open space with as much coral and gravel fragments
as dirt, and no grass at all. Schreiner mused that the site wasn't even as
conducive for football as that vacant lot back in Lancaster, Wisconsin,
where as a kid he played football and other games with his buddy, little
Mark "Had" Hoskins.

Wearing a green T-shirt, khaki pants, and boots, Schreiner surveyed the
field. He saw many familiar faces—ones he had seen under leather helmets during his playing days at Wisconsin. He could argue again with
George Murphy—the former Notre Dame captain he had greeted at midfield at Camp Randall Stadium less than three years earlier—about which
team really got the best of the other in that much-discussed 1942 game in
Madison. He could tease Rusty Johnston, the fine back from Wisconsin's
in-state rival, Marquette, about the way the Dairyland battle turned out in
'42—except maybe *battle* no longer seemed an appropriate term for a game.

Schreiner's Badger teammate, big tackle Bob Baumann, would be
on his side again in this game. Good ol' silent, lady-killer Bob. But Badger
halfback Bud Seelinger, the wavy-haired cowboy from Montana who
threw such a nice pass, was set to play for the 29th—partly because he
had caught such hell when he played on the same side with his Badger

buddies from the 4th in previous pickup games. If Seelinger played with the 4th in this game and cost his fellow Marines in the 29th some money . . . hell, he'd be better off facing the Japanese.

On a day Schreiner thought about Mark Hoskins, as he did every day, he shook hands with the 29th's team captain, Chuck Behan, who had come to the Marines straight from the Detroit Lions. Halfway around the world from Lancaster and Madison, Schreiner was the captain of his team once again. This time Hoskins wasn't around to be Schreiner's cocaptain.

★ ★ ★

Lancaster, the seat of predominantly rural Grant County, was tucked in Wisconsin's southwest corner. In the early years of the Great Depression, it had a population of about 2,600. The majestic county courthouse was in the middle of the downtown square, and too often the legal dealings involved deeds and foreclosures, with farmers either attempting to hold onto their land or giving up and allowing the stamped paperwork to take away their dreams. For those who could afford them, the closest "big-city" shopping or dining alternatives were in Dubuque, Iowa, twenty-five miles to the south, across the Mississippi River.

Herbert Schreiner, gray-haired, bespectacled, and dignified, was from a family that for years had owned the general store a block from the courthouse. He had Jewish ancestors, but the family hadn't practiced the faith for generations. His wife came to Lancaster in 1916 as young schoolteacher Anne Virum. (Although variously referred to as Anna or Ann, she preferred Anne.) She married thirty-nine-year-old Bert and had two children, Betty and David, who were raised and baptized in the Congregational Church. By the '30s, the Schreiners were out of the department store business, and Bert was a stockbroker and investment counselor, trying to survive troubled times. He also served multiple terms as the town's mayor.

Mark Hoskins, another of Lancaster's leading citizens, was raised in the nearby town of Bloomington before he went across the state to the University of Wisconsin in Madison, where he earned a W letter as a catcher on the Badgers' baseball team. Back in Bloomington, he followed his father into the furniture and undertaking businesses (often linked in small towns) and eventually moved to Lancaster. He and his wife, Doris, had three sons, Mark Hadley ("Hadley" honored a family name on the maternal side), Billy, and Charles.

Dave Schreiner was a year older than the junior Mark Hoskins, who in those days was called Had, in part to differentiate him from his father. Although Dave and Had attended different grade schools, they gravitated to one another. The Hoskinses owned a vacant lot near their home, and

Dave and Had were among the kids who used it as a playground. It was a football gridiron, a rough baseball diamond, and, in winter, a hockey rink after the city firemen flooded the lot.

When the Hoskins family played host to bridge games, the adults grew accustomed to hearing the screaming from the basement, a part of the house that had been converted into a neighborhood gym.

"Davey! Had!" the parents hollered from the top of the stairs. "They can hear you in Dubuque!"

One day when Had was over at the Schreiners' house, Anne Schreiner took a photo of young Dave, wearing vertically striped pants and towering over Had, in overalls. It looked as if the two boys had just come from the fishing hole or from convincing someone to whitewash a fence.

At Lancaster High, they were the stars for young coach Fausto Rubini,

Young Dave Schreiner and Had Hoskins, circa 1932.
PHOTO COURTESY OF THE HOSKINS FAMILY

only a few years removed from having been a reserve halfback for coach Clarence "Doc" Spears and a boxing-team star at Wisconsin. Dave played fullback, and the smaller Had was halfback for the coach they affectionately called Rube. In Schreiner's senior season, the fall of 1937, Lancaster was 6–0 and won the Southwest Wisconsin League. That was exciting enough, but then the town was abuzz with the news that University of Wisconsin coach Harry Stuhldreher was going to speak at the team banquet.

> *The coach is coming all the way over from Madison!*
> *Harry has his eye on our boys!*
> *Somebody ask him about Rockne!*
> *Think he really can ride a horse?*

Stuhldreher had just finished his second season in Madison after moving from Villanova, but he was still best known as the quarterback of Notre Dame's famed Four Horsemen. Legendary sportswriter Grantland Rice christened them in print after the Fighting Irish—with Stuhldreher, Elmer Layden, Don Miller, and Jim Crowley in the backfield—walloped Army 13–7 in 1924, only thirteen years earlier. (If the score of that game had been more decisive, Lord knows what Rice would have called them besides Famine, Pestilence, Destruction, and Death.)

Like his Notre Dame coach and hero Knute Rockne, Stuhldreher was a stirring orator, and he considered himself Rockne's spiritual successor. After Rockne's death in a March 1931 plane crash, Stuhldreher wrote the popular book about his former coach, *Knute Rockne, Man Builder.* (In some later printings, the dust jacket carried a different title, *Knute Rockne, All-American.*)

Four days before Christmas 1937, Stuhldreher took Lancaster by storm, and the *Grant County Independent* reported that the speech "has been generally commented on as the finest ever given at a similar affair in Lancaster. He mixed humorous incidents of his football career at Notre Dame, as one of the Four Horsemen, with the serious side of life, issuing his charge to the boys on the football team and their elders alike."

Stuhldreher told Dave Schreiner and Had Hoskins, the Lancaster stars, that he would be glad to have them on the Badger practice field someday, but there was nothing approaching serious recruitment. That didn't bother either of the boys, because they didn't expect to be handed anything. They knew financial aid for athletes involved lining up jobs of varying legitimacy and pay for the players or "sponsors" paying the players' college costs.

When they met Stuhldreher, Schreiner was sixteen and Hoskins fifteen. Hoskins already had a steady girlfriend, Mary Carthew, who was the daughter of a Lancaster attorney. Hoskins, also a musician and a thespian, had more eclectic interests than did Schreiner.

"Had and I were in a couple of plays together," says Constance Sherman Smyth, who was raised with the boys in Lancaster and graduated first in Hoskins's high school class.*

"At one point, he was supposed to kiss me, but he wouldn't, and I felt quite rejected. But he and Mary loved each other from the time they were little kids, so he was always spoken for."

Smyth says a large group of Lancaster friends that included Schreiner, Mary Carthew, Had Hoskins, and herself was called The Gang. Mary Carthew's parents and the Schreiners were close, so Mary knew Dave before she met Had. "I didn't know Dave well, though," Mary says. "He was always involved with things." She began dating Had in ninth grade, and they were considered a serious couple by their sophomore year of high school.

After his Lancaster High graduation in spring 1938, when he still was only seventeen, Schreiner was sent to Shattuck Prep School in Minnesota. Many boys, especially those who began school early in the accelerated approach of rural communities, took the prep school interim step if their families could afford it. But Schreiner hated Shattuck from the start. In a letter home on September 25, 1938, he declared:

> I am punting, placekicking, running and passing for Shattuck, and if that doesn't make me like a school, nothing will. I am not homesick and if you wish I would go to the university this year although I would rather stay at home and get a lot of football experience from Rube who is 10 times the coach this fellow is. He smokes in the dressing room between halves, a fine example.
>
> The real thing of it is the school, not homesickness. We will make the best of this folks and come through it high.

He dropped out and came home. His parents told him he could work for the rest of the school year before heading to Madison and UW the next fall. Schreiner toiled on a road crew while Hoskins finished up at Lancaster High.

Though the UW Athletic Department's publicity office later portrayed their simultaneous arrival on campus in the fall of 1939 as a case of

---

* Hereafter, quotations attributed in the present tense—e.g., "says"—are from the author's contemporary interviews. Quotations attributed in the past tense are from archival sources or are reconstructed from the author's contemporary interviews.

Schreiner waiting for his friend, that was an exaggeration. It also was typical of publicity departments. Hyperbole and "close-enough" artful creativity were accepted, encouraged, and even expanded upon by scribes seeking colorful angles.

Hoskins decided he would go straight to college after his graduation at seventeen, but he wasn't certain he would attend Wisconsin until the last minute. The family visited Colorado in the summers, because of his mother's allergies, and Had was fascinated by both the Boulder campus and former Colorado halfback Byron "Whizzer" White, who exemplified the scholar-athlete ideal.

In Madison, Hoskins and his father—the Wisconsin baseball letterman—stopped in to see an assistant football coach, and Had again was told he was welcome to come out for the football team. The coach also said Hoskins would get help finding a job if he needed one. That wasn't an issue for Hoskins, whose family was affluent for the times, and he decided to go to Wisconsin and join Schreiner.

When he showed up in Madison, he started going by Mark. But that

The Lancaster Boys ham it up in a publicity shot. In games, of course, Dave Schreiner, the end, never handed off to Mark Hoskins, the halfback.
PHOTO COURTESY OF JUDY CORFIELD

didn't stop those who had known him in Lancaster, including Schreiner, from continuing to call him Had. You could tell the old friends from the new by what they called him.

The boys from Lancaster moved into a room in the new dormitory along Lake Mendota, on the northwest side of the campus, in September 1939. They started classes the same month that Germany invaded Poland, which led to declarations of war by England and France. Like most college boys, they wondered if they, too, might be drawn into the maelstrom.

Hoskins and Schreiner settled into life in Madison, where the downtown, including the State Capitol, was on an isthmus between the two lakes, Monona and Mendota. The social centers were fraternity and sorority row and, even more so, the tavern- and store-lined State Street, which ran from the capitol to the eastern edge of the campus. The taverns were beer joints, where eighteen-year-olds could drink legally and with socially embraced enthusiasm, then stumble back to their rooms. The minimum age was twenty-one for liquor bars, which were more common away from the campus.

On campus, the Memorial Union's back terrace stretched to the banks of Lake Mendota, and many a romance began over meals and discussions against the panoramic view. Hoskins was devoted to Mary Carthew, but Schreiner didn't have a girl back home and had his eyes wide open.

That fall, the two Lancaster boys eventually stood out among the freshmen football players. But it wasn't immediate. In a September 25 letter home, Dave gently chided his father for coming to Madison for a freshman team scrimmage as if it was a major deal. He added:

> I have to make my own chances out there, and once I do, watch out. The coach doesn't even know my name. . . . But really the guys up here ain't tough. All they've got over me is reputation. (And that ain't nothin'). Just wait.

Freshmen couldn't play for the varsity, though, and didn't have formal games as a team, so the only way fans could see them play was to attend practice. Quarterback Ashley Anderson, from Milwaukee, was also in the dormitory complex. "I met them the first day I was in Madison," Anderson says. "I had never heard of them, and they had never heard of me, and that's the way it was then. We walked over to try out for football. Every night, we'd walk back to the dorms after practice, so I got to know them pretty well. Dave was just one great gentleman. He was easygoing and shy almost to a point of having it be painful. I mean, extremely shy. Hoskins was the same way. They were country boys, but real gentle-men from day one."

Often the freshmen were practice fodder, operating as a "scout" team and imitating upcoming varsity opponents. But they were also drilled in the Wisconsin system.

Schreiner, the high school fullback, was switched to end. In one-platoon football and Stuhldreher's beloved Notre Dame Box formation, a Wisconsin end made his mark primarily with blocking and playing the flank defensively. Schreiner's extraordinary abilities soon became obvious. Away from the field, he was hanging around with Hoskins and Ashley Anderson. In mid-November, all three pledged fraternities, with Hoskins and Schreiner signing on with Phi Delta Theta and Anderson go-ing with Alpha Delta Pi. Schreiner sheepishly passed along that news to his parents, but—as he would in many letters home over the years—he brazenly lectured his mother about not telling everyone his affairs. He was conscious that in a small town in which everyone had a three-digit phone number, and where the operator—who came into play on every call—knew where everyone was and what everyone was doing, the boys off at Madison often were the topic of conversation. In the letter, he in-sisted: "Don't, **PLEASE**, blow it around though. Don't tell your busybody friends." Similar admonitions appeared in his letters all through college.

> The drinking up here is terrible. Really awful. I've never seen anything like it in my life. The fraternities are especially bad with drinking parties at least once a week. They have parties and to be a good fellow, you have to drink, but you can count on me as not even drinking beer.

In the same letter, he disclosed that Helen Godfrey had asked him to a formal dance and that he would need to either rent or borrow a tuxedo. He added:

> This fraternity business costs too much and I'll be darned if I'm going to lay out so much money. Now, I'm sort of sorry I joined. Don't tell the Lancaster busybodies about this social business or that Helen is asking me to go out with her.

Many of his teammates assumed that he came from a convention-ally struggling family in the Depression years, because like most of them, he worked—eventually, in his case, as a waiter in the dining area of Ann Emery Hall, a girls' dormitory. Later, though, his teammates understood that the Schreiners were comfortable enough financially to allow Dave to avoid working. Still, he watched his money, painstakingly keeping track of a checking account. In letters home, he repeatedly enclosed what he called his "expense accounts," and apparently his father demanded those detailed reports of how much he spent—and for what.

Schreiner was tall, dark, and handsome, and a scar that started near the corner of his mouth and curved upward seemed to add to his movie-

Dave Schreiner, All-American.
PHOTO COURTESY OF THE UNIVERSITY OF WISCONSIN SPORTS INFORMATION DEPARTMENT

star allure. His parents hoped he would become a doctor and encouraged him to take pre-medicine classes. He was intelligent and quietly charismatic, but he neither enjoyed nor sailed through the heaviest of the science-related courses. Over the next three years, his agonizing over wanting to please his parents by taking pre-med courses, while not feeling comfortable or confident about it, was unrelenting.

Hoskins, the better student of the two Lancaster boys, also emerged as a major prospect as a freshman, playing left halfback, the showcase position in Stuhldreher's system. But the boys' success didn't completely satisfy Schreiner. During spring practices in early 1940, when he was preparing for his first varsity season, Schreiner was having misgivings about sticking with the sport. He wrote his parents:

> I'm getting awfully tired of football. It takes so much time and is no fun. I don't know if I'll keep on with it or not. What do you think I should do?

He stuck with it.

Late that semester, he and Hoskins went through their Phi Delta Theta initiation. They reported to the fraternity house wearing long underwear and carrying flashlights. Schreiner told his parents he couldn't disclose all that happened but said the rite included being taken into the country to the west of Madison and walking back, from 1:00 to 7:30 a.m.

The next fall, when Hoskins and Schreiner were on the varsity, the Phi Delts were congratulating themselves for making wise choices. Schreiner broke into the first-team lineup when senior Al Lorenz needed to take some time off from practice for academic reasons. Schreiner never left the first unit. By the time the season started, though, he had also started working at Ann Emery Hall.*

> I have a very nice setup at present although I had to change my schedule so to not include any 8 o'clocks. In the morning, I work from 7:30 to 8:45. I get my breakfast and dinner. Then Rex Hoffman is working for me until football season is over at supper from 6:30 until 8:00. This way I get all my meals free and Rex gets his evening meal. In the morning I clear away the girls tables and at night wipe silverware. The food is swell, too.

---

* Subsequent Schreiner indented quotations are from his letters to his parents, unless otherwise noted.

After their first game with the varsity as sophomores in 1940, the Lancaster combination seemed destined for three seasons of collaborative greatness. Hoskins threw a key touchdown pass to Schreiner in a victory over Wisconsin's in-state rival, Marquette.

Hoskins was quoted in the Madison newspapers the next day. Player quotes rarely were used in newspaper stories, and when they were, they were often sanitized or punched up by scribes who didn't take extensive

While still getting used to being called Mark instead of Had in Madison, Hoskins at first played left halfback in Harry Stuhldreher's Notre Dame Box.

notes and who considered word-for-word accuracy neither important nor desirable.

"It sure was a big thrill for me when Dave hooked the ball in," Hoskins was quoted as saying. "I never tossed to him in a game before. Oh, he has caught them all right, but not from me."

Wisconsin played Columbia in New York City that season, losing 7–6 to the Lions. The Badgers attended the Broadway musical *Hellzapoppin* as well as another show in the Waldorf-Astoria Hotel's Empire Room. Wisconsin officials let it slip that three Badger players—Hoskins, plus upperclassmen Fred Gage, and John Tennant—often performed for their teammates or entered talent shows as the harmonizing "Singing Firemen Trio." Musically inclined, Hoskins also played the saxophone. Called on to sing a number in the Empire Room, the Badgers gladly obliged. The Wisconsin publicity department later put out the word that the performance had been at *Hellzapoppin* and that the Badgers had brought down the house.

Neither was true.

At the Empire Room, the trio sang:

*"Oh, what will you have, the waiter said, casually picking his
     nose.
"Hard boiled eggs, you son of a gun,
"Cause you can't get your finger in, you can't get your finger in,
     you can't get your finger in those."*

They were met with absolute silence.

That sophomore year, when the Badgers went 4–4, Hoskins was living in the Phi Delta Theta house. Schreiner wouldn't move in for another year. As a sophomore, Schreiner shared a room in a house with another buddy from Lancaster, apparently thinking it was cheaper. He got his meals for free, and he was still a little queasy about the amount of beer-drinking at the fraternity. He continued to work at Ann Emery and told his parents he had met "an awfully nice bunch of girls." He was dating Barbara Nelson, also known as B. J., but didn't feel attached or unable to date others, especially because the sorority dances encouraged the girls to ask out the boys. Though he was still shy, he was asked often. Constance Sherman, the Lancaster classmate who also attended the university, remained a platonic friend in Madison.

By the second semester of his sophomore year, when he had established himself as a football star, Schreiner was struggling academically in the pre-med sequence. He was continuing to write home virtually daily, either in postcards or letters, and he was capable of pouting when his parents didn't reciprocate. In February 1941, he wrote:

> I was kind of disappointed to have only a postcard from both of you so far this week as I wrote a nice letter to you. I suppose you are holding off though so that you can write me a real long letter concerning my standing at the university. Although I am on probation, it doesn't mean a thing. Almost everyone goes on probation before they are through. So don't let it worry as so far my studies are coming fine and there isn't anything to worry about.

As time went on, it seemed obvious he was remaining in the pre-med sequence only to please his parents. Even on his tight budget, he had a vibrant social life, and he joked that before going to one dance with B. J. Nelson, neither his roommate nor anyone else in the boarding house could help him tie his bowtie, so he ran to the clothing store and bought a pre-tied one. Schreiner's penchant for self-deprecation was showing in his letters, and he often teased his parents, both about his mother's propensity for gossip and his father's insistence on accounting for every penny.

That spring, he alarmed his parents when he explored the possibility of signing up to be a Naval flyer and leaving school. He told his parents a Badger unit would be organized from among University of Wisconsin students in June and that the fifty men would be elite. His scholastic struggles and the sense that he was disappointing his parents undoubtedly were contributing factors, as well as his awareness of the war in Europe that might eventually draw in the United States and American boys. In April, he explained:

> They give you one month of preliminary training in which they find out if you are good officer material. About 20 percent wash out at this preliminary base and the others go to Pensacola for three years of training. The pay is $54 the first month, plus food and equipment, $75 the next seven months, and then you are an ensign receiving $245 a month. After you are out there is no obligation to the navy except to fly so much each year for which you get paid. There are really fine opportunities in aviation and if I didn't want to stay with aviation I wouldn't be very old anyway. I could still come back and finish college if that is what I wanted. If after the first month I found that I didn't like it I could also come back and start school again in the fall. I

think this is a wonderful opportunity for young men like me. We really do need a fine air corps to prevent Hitler from even challenging a country like the U.S. and that is the idea, rather than actually equipping for war. I believe that a young man is performing a fine service if he does this for his country as well as equipping himself for the future. Remember, only the highest type of boys are taken. Let me know what you think of it. If I am drafted, which I certainly will be in a year, there will be no deferments and I will be yanked right out of school. The air corps then may have their quota and I would have only a measly $21 a month with the worst part of the whole army. I think it's a fine opportunity.

His parents convinced him that he should wait and keep his options open.

In the summer of 1941, Schreiner went back to work on a state road crew and took Hoskins with him. They were cement puddlers on the highway being built between Madison and Milwaukee. They stirred the cement with vibrating tools and then shoveled it, making sure it didn't settle with air pockets. The older men on the crew respected the boys' work ethic but told them they better beat archrival Minnesota next season. When they could, Schreiner and Hoskins tossed around a football Stuhldreher sent them.

That fall, as the Roosevelt administration negotiated with the Japanese government, Schreiner and Hoskins were fraternity brothers and reunited roommates after Dave moved into the Phi Delta Theta house. In their junior football season, when the Badgers were a disappointing 3–5 and lost to the consensus national champion Minnesota Gophers for the ninth consecutive season, Schreiner was named an Associated Press All-American and continued to work at Ann Emery Hall. The fact that he was chosen as one of the nation's top players while performing on a losing team underscored his one-field dominance.

Opponents virtually gave up trying to get around his end and called most plays to go the other way. The team's other star was fearsome sophomore fullback Pat "Hit 'em Again" Harder, the Big Ten's leading rusher and scorer. Although there was considerable grumbling around Madison (and the state) about the Badgers' lackluster record, optimism was warranted. The '41 freshman crop was exceptional, led by a lean and pale left halfback from Wausau, Elroy Hirsch, and center Fred Negus. The '41 freshmen group didn't just run through plays to test the varsity. "We generally *beat* the varsity," Negus says. Stuhldreher didn't know whether to be infuriated or encouraged. The word had gotten around campus: The "kids" were good.

The '41 football freshmen immediately regarded Schreiner, then a junior, as a leader. In two years, he had gone from being a shy freshman who wasn't even sure he wanted to play football to a still-quiet yet decisive and self-assured All-American. By then, he was neither a teetotaler nor a saint, but he was less obvious—and far less enthusiastic—about his beer-drinking than the others. Many of the Badgers worked in bars, frequented them often, or did both. "Wisconsin was a big drinking school, and a lot of guys on Saturday night after football games were pretty heavy drinkers," says halfback Jim McFadzean, who played three varsity seasons with Schreiner. "I never saw Schreiner take a drink. He was just a real gentleman."

George Hekkers was a tackle on that '41 freshman squad, and he came from the same Milwaukee high school as Pat Harder. Hekkers recalls taking a lot of punishment from upperclassmen, a few who even reacted to the freshmen's success with dirty play. "Dave came all the way over from the varsity side to the freshman side, and everyone saw this," Hekkers says. "He came up to me and said, 'You know, George, you don't have to take that if you don't want to. He thought I was lying back and taking it because I was a freshman. From then on, I didn't back up, I went after them."

Otto Breitenbach, a freshman halfback in '41, says Schreiner "was the emotional and spiritual leader of the team. Everybody looked up to him. As a freshman, when we were scrimmaging the varsity, if I had a blocking assignment, I would rather block him than someone else. He always treated you correctly and didn't take advantage of you. He was an all-around good guy, a very smart guy, both on the football field and on the campus."

Bob Omelina, another halfback who would be a sophomore in 1942, noted that "every once in a while, the upperclassmen would get on somebody. And Dave always seemed to be right there to quell it."

Jerry Frei, a seventeen-year-old freshman guard in '41, later liked to say that Schreiner would "hit you so hard, your head would ring, and then he'd apologize to you."

After the Badgers closed out the disappointing '41 season with another loss at Minnesota, their followers knew that in '42 Schreiner and Hoskins would be back for their senior seasons, serving as the quiet leaders. Harder, the team's most outgoing character and roughest personality, would be only a junior. And the bright array of youngsters would move up from the freshman team.

Then, suddenly, America was at war, too.

TWO

Day of Infamy

Rennebohm's Pharmacy was at the west end of State Street, at the edge of the campus. On Sundays, many students passing through the doors of "The Pharm" nursed hangovers after a night of carousing at the taverns along the same street. They could get headache remedies from the shelves or risk making things worse by ordering greasy eggs and bacon served at the counter.

Around 1:30 in the afternoon of December 7, 1941, Erwin Kissling strolled into the Pharm to pick up a newspaper. The stocky halfback from nearby Monticello had just finished his freshman season, and he was proud to be considered one of the athletes on campus. Only his parents and his professors called him Erwin. A few called him Erv. Almost everyone else knew him as Booby.

As Kissling paid for his paper and headed out, another student rushed through the door. Kissling had never seen him before and never would again. But this guy had to tell somebody. He settled for Booby.

"Hey," he breathlessly informed Kissling, "the Japs just bombed Pearl Harbor!"

"What are you talking about?" Kissling asked.

"The Japs just bombed Pearl Harbor!"

Kissling squinted. "You just coming from a party or something?" Then he knew, as he had feared, that the kid was right.

This was war.

The student probably had heard the terse flash from CBS Radio a few minutes earlier: "Flash, Washington. The White House has announced a Japanese attack on Pearl Harbor."

Students streamed out of apartments above the stores on State Street.

17

"The Japs bombed Pearl Harbor!"

"We're in it now!"

After the other kid moved on, Kissling stood there, stunned, holding his newspaper.

"Holy mackerel," he said.

Kissling hadn't noticed that at the lunch counter two other Badger freshmen—halfback Jim Regan and quarterback Jack Wink—were having coffee after finishing their meals. As they talked, the clerk in the white shirt behind the counter suddenly turned up the radio.

The Japs bombed Pearl Harbor!

As other students crowded behind them to hear the radio, Regan and Wink looked at each other. It was a look exchanged across America that morning. It meant: "Our lives have just changed."

Freshman guard Jerry Frei had worked all night as a prep cook and hasher at Toby and Moon's, the restaurant owned by a couple of former Badger athletes, Dave Tobias and Moon Molinaro, who considered it their duty to employ Wisconsin football players. Frei was living in one of the Madison firehouses, as many of the football players did, and his roommate woke him.

"The Japs just bombed Pearl Harbor!"

"Huh?"

"The Japs just bombed Pearl Harbor!"

Still in a fog, Frei asked, "Where's Pearl Harbor?"

Mark Hoskins's girlfriend Mary Carthew was attending the National College of Education, a teachers' school in Evanston, Illinois. Burley Jacobs, Hoskins's fraternity brother, had wanted to visit his girlfriend, a Northwestern student, so that weekend Hoskins and Jacobs drove down to Evanston together, and Mark took Mary to her school's Saturday night dance. That was part of their routine. When it was Mary's turn to visit Madison, she stayed with Connie Sherman or other friends at a sorority house. On this trip, as Mark and Burley were on their way back to Madison, they stopped in Wauwatosa, near Milwaukee, to have lunch with Jacobs's family. And that's when they heard.

The Japs bombed Hawaii!

At the Alpha Delta Pi fraternity, the boys quickly gathered around the radio in the second-floor living room. Ashley Anderson sat silent as his fraternity brothers around him let loose about the "damn Japs!" And worse.

"A lot of the fellows were ready to enlist right then and there," Anderson says.

A few blocks away, Badger freshman halfback Otto Breitenbach was at his brother's house. As they visited, the Breitenbach brothers had the radio tuned to Chicago Bears–Chicago Cardinals football game. A newscaster broke in with the bulletin.

Tackle Dick Thornally, a junior on the Badgers '41 team, visited his girlfriend, Barbara Appleton, at her sorority every Sunday afternoon. Sometimes, they remained at the sorority; other times, they went out for a bite to eat. This time, he was confused when he walked through the big front door and saw the sorority girls gathered, crying.

"I couldn't imagine what was going on," Thornally recalls.

Red-eyed, Barbara spotted her boyfriend and noted his confusion. "The Japanese have attacked Pearl Harbor!" she sobbed.

At Toby and Moon's, the day shift of football players was on duty. Freshman tackle Dave Donnellan was a counter hop. As the radio reports started coming in, the restaurant quieted and customers and workers bunched up around the radio.

"Then everyone went outside," Donnellan says. "We had it figured out that we were going to war."

Freshman quarterback John Gallagher had driven to Minneapolis for the weekend with some buddies, and on the way back they heard the news on the radio. Gallagher looked at one of his pals, Al Kaylor.

"We both said, 'Well, I guess we're going to have to go,'" Gallagher says. "And when we got back to the campus, that was all the talk. 'Everybody's going to have to go.'"

Many of the Badgers weren't aware of the events of the morning until they heard excited newspaper hawkers scrambling down the Madison residential streets. Four freshmen players—Elroy Hirsch, Bob Rennebohm, Hank Olshanski, and Russ Schultz—lived on the upper floor of the house at 812 West Johnson Street, renting rooms from the kindly Mr. and Mrs. Hanley.

"We didn't have our radios on," says Rennebohm, a distant relative of the family that owned the drugstores. "We were studying. We heard a guy yelling 'EXTRA!' on the street. So we ran out, bought a paper, and turned on the radio. We knew we'd be going somewhere by the time it was over."

Don Litchfield, a freshman quarterback from Eau Claire, was in his room at 204 North Murray. He and his roommate heard the yelling about Pearl Harbor. While Litchfield hustled out to buy a paper, his roommate looked for a map. Like Jerry Frei, neither Litchfield nor his roommate had any idea where Pearl Harbor was.

Freshman center Fred Negus also heard the fuss and ran down to the street for a paper. The Madison papers sold a lot of "extras" that day.

Business at the bars was brisk, especially for a Sunday, but the customers were unusually quiet as they listened to the reports on the turned-up radios. Staffers in the sports departments at the two newspapers were flabbergasted when they got the usual calls, including repeated requests for the Bears–Cardinals score. The Green Bay Packers, Wisconsin's NFL team, didn't play that day and had already finished their regular-season schedule. The Bears needed a victory to tie the Packers for the Western Conference title, at 10–1.

As the callers were told, the Bears won 34–24, setting up a Green Bay–Chicago playoff the next Sunday.

THREE

What Now?

In the remaining days of 1941, Madison's recruiting stations were jammed. Often, potential recruits were told to come back after backlogs cleared. On campus, uncertainty prevailed. Some men abandoned their studies, planning to enter the Army or other branches of the service. Most settled in to see how everything would sort out.

On Thursday, December 11, Dave Schreiner called his parents during the lunch hour and had a brief conversation, then wrote them later in his fraternity room.

> The war situation doesn't bother me especially. It makes me a little bit disgusted though that so many boys up here are doing everything they can to get deferred. I don't like to leave my normal way of life, but I'm not going to sit up here snug as a bug, playing football, etc., when others are giving their lives for their country. I'm not going to foolhardily rush into it, but I am going to do more than sit up here and do nothing but go to school. If everyone tried to stay out of it what a fine country we'd have! We'll talk about it Xmas.
>
> In such trying times I'm certainly glad I have such fine people behind me as you two. I'm afraid I don't appreciate you nearly enough at times, but I hope you know that I'm really very proud and fond of my two swell parents.

Between Pearl Harbor and the beginning of spring practices—none of the Badgers recall the exact timetable—Harry Stuhldreher called several team meetings and discussed, among other things, the players' military choices.

Boys, the coach first told the Badgers, who knows what the Lord has in store for the country. He recommended that the boys not do anything rash, but stay in school and, in the meantime, enlist in the reserves, which he said was especially important for the boys who would be sophomores and juniors in the fall of 1942. They could pick their branch, begin the paperwork, and signal their intention to serve when called up. Initially, many of the Badgers enrolled in the on-campus, for-credit Army Reserve Officers Training Corps, or ROTC, and also enlisted in the off-campus Army Enlisted Reserve Corps, beginning the move into the military. They could switch branches later, but they were marked as officer material. At the time, the draft age was twenty.

Eventually, in behind-the-scenes discussions with university president Clarence Dykstra, Stuhldreher was told that the Marines were likely to post a unit for underclassmen on the Wisconsin campus. During the year of classroom study that would be part of the program, the Marines could play on the football team.

Quarterback John Gallagher remembers Stuhldreher saying, "Fellas, if you're going to join any service, I suggest you join the Marine Corps because there's going to be a unit here." Gallagher adds, "So everybody said, 'OK, let's go in the Marines.' It really was that simple."

After the United States entered the war, various new military programs evolved on the fly. Gallagher and a handful of the '41 season freshmen eventually signed up for the Marines, hoping their year of study after induction would take place on the Madison campus. The others included halfback Elroy Hirsch, quarterback Jack Wink, center Fred Negus, fullback Earl Maves, plus ends Bob Rennebohm, Hank Olshanski, and Farnham "Gunner" Johnson. "I must say I was responsible for some of the guys coming in because I had found this picture of a Marine captain in dress blues," Rennebohm says. "You never saw a nicer looking military man in your life. I was circulating that, and everybody wanted to be one of those. And I think there was a tendency for football players to want to be in a challenging thing like the Marines."

Not all of the '41 freshmen who wanted to be Marines were accepted. Jack Crabb, a tackle from Whitefish Bay High School in the Milwaukee area, tried to become a leatherneck, but he had 20/40 vision in one eye, and that wasn't good enough for the Marines—he ended up in the Army.

Fullback Pat Harder and end Bob Hanzlik, both sophomores in '41, also signed up for the Marines, hoping they would be considered young enough for the V-12 program. "In those days, we thought that was the best group to be in," Negus says. "But after we got into it, we knew that the Marines were the first ones to get off the ship."

Although they were too old for the V-12 program, a group of Badger '42 seniors-to-be also signed up for the Marine Reserves before the season started. They included tackles Bob Baumann, Dick Thornally, and Paul Hirsbrunner, along with guard George Makris and halfback Bud Seelinger.

"We wanted to go into what we thought was the toughest branch of the service, and the Marines had the reputation," Makris says. "We were looking forward to going overseas and fighting, which was stupid."

Jerry Frei, who wouldn't turn eighteen until June 1942, and several teammates joined the Army Air Forces Reserves, another Stuhldreher recommendation because Madison's airport, Truax Field, was being upgraded as an Air Forces technical training facility. Others who signed up for the AAF included Frei's buddy guard Ken Currier, halfback Otto Breitenbach, quarterbacks Don Litchfield and Ashley Anderson, tackle George Hekkers, guard John Roberts, and halfback Mark Hoskins. All would be sophomores in the '42 football season except Hoskins and Roberts, the seniors-to-be. Most of them had never been in an airplane. Like the Marines, the AAF represented a means of serving in a role other than Army foot soldier.

Young quarterback Don Litchfield, one of the boys from Eau Claire, enrolled in the Army ROTC and abhorred it "because it was climbing around Bascom Hill with a gun over our arms." He and a buddy "went down to the vocational school for the Air Forces, right down by the capitol, and took the tests." They passed. Excited, they looked forward to being pilots and even signed up for civilian flying lessons.

"I thought flying would be fascinating, and I didn't have any great desire to be an infantryman," recalls Otto Breitenbach, who signed up and settled in for the wait. "It was a case of being put on hold. That was before they had enough planes and when they had more enlistments than they could handle."

A year earlier, Dave Schreiner had stepped away from his plan to become a Navy flyer, but he still wanted to be a pilot and perhaps even follow Mark Hoskins into the AAF. But he discovered he had trouble distinguishing colors and was told—most likely at that Air Forces vocational facility—that he wouldn't qualify for pilot training. He didn't give up easily, though. That spring, he wrote to his parents that he was drinking carrot juice because the vitamin A might help his color vision, and he said he hoped to take the test again over the summer. At the same time, he hadn't given up on medical school, and the Lancaster draft board had that on record and had him classified 2-A, a pre-med student deferment. He had filled out medical school application forms in January, but because he was still a year and a half away from graduation, that was only a tentative first step.

Schreiner and Hoskins were riding around in a shared Model A Ford they called "Tin Lizzy," and Mary Carthew visited often. Schreiner cooled on B. J. Nelson in mid-February and told his parents he wouldn't be bringing her to Lancaster for a visit after all.

Although the Badgers were distracted as they faced their military choices, the spring practices further convinced Stuhldreher that his 1942 sophomores would significantly strengthen his squad that fall and be the core of great teams for the next two seasons, if they remained on campus.

The spring workouts concluded with a public intrasquad game on May 2. Rather than use colors—cardinal versus white, for example—as the squad names, Stuhldreher got in the spirit of the times by designating one team "Army" and the other "Navy."

The player the Badger fans were most eager to see, Hirsch, was injured and couldn't play. End Pat Lyons caught a touchdown pass for the Navy team, and Harder's extra point turned out to be the winning margin. Army's only score came on a pass from John Gallagher to Gunner Johnson. Navy won 7–6.

A total of seventy-six players went through the 1942 spring practices. Attrition over the summer was inevitable, but it also was a winnowing process: Stuhldreher issued invitations to fall practice, and the initial 1942 roster listed fifty-four men. Most of them thought it would be their final football season. At least for a while.

FOUR

Hirsch and Harder

Joseph "Roundy" Coughlin's sports columns in the *Wisconsin State Journal* could read as if they were satires, given his unabashed cheerleading and inattention to the rules of grammar and syntax. He and his copy could have stepped right from the pages of a Ring Lardner or Damon Runyon tale. But Roundy was for real, once poor and uneducated, brought onto the newspaper staff as a sort of Everyman. Copy editors didn't try to edit him into something he wasn't. Coughlin considered his style unvarnished candor. English professors considered it disgraceful. However, some called him the Dean of the College of Common Sense, and he was an institution in Madison. Roundy's Fun Fund, which benefited underprivileged children, was one of the area's most popular charities.

As the 1942 season approached, Roundy—his column "Roundy Says" listed neither his real first nor last name—had to get something off his chest. Coughlin watched the spring practices, before sophomore-to-be Elroy Hirsch was injured and couldn't play in the intrasquad scrimmage, and he was excited.

"A lot of people asked me what kind of football player this new man Wisconsin has got this year, Elroy Hirsch in the backfield will be,"

Sportswriter Roundy Coughlin, the "Sage of Mendota," was one of Wisconsin's most beloved journalists.
WHi Image ID 11956

Roundy wrote. "Don't ask me all my advice is buy a ticket and hold onto your seat. That baby can really step. . . . We haven't had a runner like that since you used to wear stiff hats and button shoes going to class."

If Roundy said it, it must be so.

Elroy Hirsch was the son of Mayme Hirsch and Otto Hirsch, an iron-worker in the northern Wisconsin town of Wausau. The family lived across

Even as a Wisconsin sophomore, Elroy Hirsch had crazy legs. It just took a while for someone to spot them and come up with the nickname that stuck.
PHOTO COURTESY OF JOHN GALLAGHER

the street from the Wausau Brewing Company. Elroy, a skinny kid with a stutter, was eventually nicknamed Goldie because of his prominent gold crown in front. As one of the most athletic kids in town, he could often be spotted running through one of the local parks with a football under his arm.

"I'd go at top speed heading straight for a tree, then shift the football as I dodged right or left just in time to miss it," Hirsch was quoted in *Crazylegs: A Man and His Career.* "I never pivoted, just dodged. It's hard to fake a tree. Sometimes I plowed right into it."

He was a star for the Wausau High Lumberjacks, playing for coach Win "Brock" Brockmeyer.

"When he came into Wausau, Wausau had been the doormat of the conference up there for years," Hirsch told interviewer Barry Teicher for the University of Wisconsin–Madison Oral History Project.*

Hirsch continued, "Brock came in and immediately turned it around and started winning. I was very, very fortunate to play under him because he was a sound fundamental coach—the blocking, the tackling, all the things you needed to go on to be a good football player.

"We played single wing, and I always played tailback. One thing I could always do was run fast. I was cowardly as a child. I ran away from everything. To not fight, I ran. I learned to run fast and learned to dodge. When I went to high school, I couldn't make it my sophomore year. I wasn't big enough. I weighed only 125 pounds. But over that next year, I grew to 160. I was one of the bigger guys and fortunately retained the speed—and, still, the fear."

Hirsch started dating a local Methodist minister's daughter, Ruth Stahmer, and considered his college possibilities. Brockmeyer had coached in Minnesota and had contacts at the University of Minnesota. He took Hirsch and another Lumberjack, Hank Olshanski, to Minneapolis to look at the campus and laughed when his two players staged a mock radio interview of each other in the car on the way back.

"I was torn between Minnesota and Wisconsin," Hirsch told the Oral History Project interviewer. "But a group of businessmen in Wausau, very prominent businessmen who were Wisconsin people, got a pool together for my tuition and my room and board. They sent me to school, so to speak."

There was nothing untoward about that arrangement, but it was exceptional. Most star players got some kind of help, but it usually came in the form of jobs rather than direct subsidy. Hirsch was expected to work

---

*The Oral History Project began in 1971 and is conducted by the UW Archives. As of this writing, it includes more than six hundred interviews with experts on the university's past.

for his spending money, and he held several jobs in Madison over the years, including a stint as a radio station receptionist five nights a week. Hirsch also worked at the Bancroft Dairy with center Fred Negus and tackle Dick Thornally. Oh, the perks of being a star.

"We swept and mopped the floor every night," Negus recalls. "The route people would come in and do their paperwork, and there would be paper all over the place. We would pick up and sweep the floor and drink all the milk we wanted. We got fifty cents an hour."

Tackle George Hekkers, a freshman with the Hirsch group, laughs about the first time the first-year players practiced together in the fall of '41. During the running, Hekkers says, "I took off and I'll never forget it, I heard what sounded like a 'swish-swosh,' 'swish-swosh.' This guy passed me like I was standing still. I said, 'Who the *hell* is that?' I was pretty fast, too. That's when they said, 'It's Elroy Hirsch from Wausau.'"

Erv Kissling, the halfback from Monticello, says Hirsch was so great as a freshman that the rest of the first-year players "were just trying to hit him, because if you hit him, you'd be noticed by the coach."

Tom Butler, a Madison native who was a senior at Madison's East High School when Hirsch was a UW freshman, was a huge sports fan and was already planning to enroll at the university and study journalism. "We used to hear the stories about how Hirsch would run wild against the varsity in the scrimmages and everything, and how they just couldn't wait to see this kid from Wausau," Butler recalls.

Challenged to describe his running style for the University of Wisconsin Oral History Project, Hirsch said, "My left foot points out farther than my right when I run. When I take that step, the toe points out. When the foot comes back behind my body, I have to swing it way out and around to get it in front of me again. It's a natural movement for me. People just notice it. I wobble when I run. I was never a sprinter. I could never run the 100-yard dash because I could run the first 30, 40 yards quick in a straight line, but then I start to wobble, side to side, and I lose my speed."

Early in his Wisconsin stay, he was called several nicknames in the papers, including Ghost, because he was so pale, and Wausau Wiggler, because of that running style. But neither of those became universal, though Hirsch himself liked and used Ghost.

During '42 spring practice and the fall drills, Hirsch settled in at left halfback, the position that usually took the tossed snap in Harry Stuhldreher's Notre Dame Box. The offense was becoming archaic, with more teams going to the innovative T formation, in which the quarterback lined up right behind the center and—as strange as this looked—

reached between his legs and took the snap directly from the center's hands. In the Badgers' system, the left halfback, who often shifted into the equivalent of the single wing's tailback position, did much of the throwing, and Hirsch never was more than an average passer. But the most exciting prospect was Hirsch running behind the blocking of fullback Marlin "Pat" Harder.

The Badgers are careful to try to keep what they say from coming off as a lack of respect for Dave Schreiner and Hirsch, but the consensus is that Harder was their best player—when he was healthy, which wasn't often in 1942. In the one-platoon, no-facemask, little-padding game, Harder kept coming at opponents, and sometimes even at his teammates.

But, boy, was Harder—also called The Mule—a handful. Many of the Badgers saw the film *Knute Rockne, All-American* after its 1940 release, and they wondered if Pat Harder was Harry Stuhldreher's George Gipp without the pneumonia. Of course, a tougher actor than skinny Ronald Reagan would have had to play Harder.

"The Mule drank his share of beer," says Dick Thornally. "But when the chips were down, he could do everything—block, back up the line, carry that ball. He was one hell of a football player."

Pat Harder was well known from the time he led the Washington High Purgolders to great seasons in inner-city Milwaukee. At Wisconsin, he had

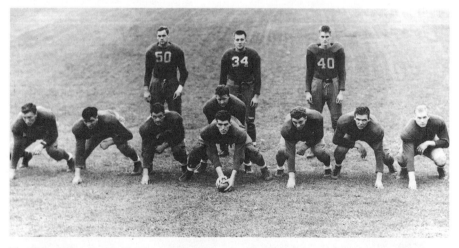

The T formation looked better in pictures, as in this shot of the usual 1942 starting lineup, but the Badgers more often ran out of the Box. The line, from left to right as the players face the camera: RE Dave Schreiner, RT Paul Hirsbrunner, RG Ken Currier, C Fred Negus, LG Red Vogds, LT Bob Baumann, LE Bob Hanzlik. QB Jack Wink takes the snap in front of RH Mark Hoskins, FB Pat Harder, and LH Elroy Hirsch.
PHOTO COURTESY OF THE UNIVERSITY OF WISCONSIN SPORTS INFORMATION DEPARTMENT

a crewcut, he smoked, and he was a regular in the State Street taverns. In other words, although they considered each other friends, Schreiner and Harder didn't hang out together. Harder's hell-raising belied his upbringing in a strict Mormon household in Milwaukee. He paid only passing attention to the classroom, and it was a challenge to keep him eligible. Also, Harder acted as if he acknowledged nobody's authority—not even Harry Stuhldreher's. His brothers in the Sigma Alpha Epsilon fra-

Pat Harder was his own man, and his teammates both loved and feared him.
PHOTO COURTESY OF JOHN GALLAGHER

ternity considered Harder their resident rebel. Jack Crabb, the reserve tackle from Whitefish Bay High in the Milwaukee area, was a year behind Harder and shared a fraternity room with him for a semester. "That was enough," Crabb says, laughing. "He was my friend and I liked him a lot. What a good guy! But I didn't get a hell of a lot of sleep. He sure was a hell of a football player, though."

Indeed, everyone on the Badgers' roster respected Harder. Many also feared him.

"If anyone could get into trouble, it was Pat," says Ashley Anderson. "He wouldn't always do things the way Harry wanted him to. But he could run, I tell you. He was surprisingly fast."

Quarterback John Gallagher calls Harder "a roustabout, a real character. He was always pulling some kind of a joke, something in the locker room. He was a hell of a player when you got him on the field."

Harder drove around Madison in his Model A Ford. It had a rumble seat, and he often gave lifts to teammates.

"He would park down at the extension of State Street, by Bascom Hall, where all the classes were," recalls halfback Otto Breitenbach. "First day of classes, he got a ticket, and from then on, he parked there every day and got away with it by changing the date on the ticket. And he got away with it for a long, long time."

The heat and humidity were sweltering during the 1942 preseason practices. One day, between the morning and afternoon workouts, a group of Badgers went to a movie at the Orpheum Theater to cool off. Harder was driving the Model A. When the boys left the theater, they realized they probably wouldn't be on time for the two o'clock practice. Harder shoved the accelerator down, and his teammates on the running board and in the rumble seat held on.

A police officer pulled them over and gave Harder a ticket. To passenger Erv Kissling, Harder seemed surprisingly unconcerned. As the officer began a lecture, Harder snapped, "Just write the ticket and give it to me." Then he resumed the drive to the practice field, which was adjacent to Camp Randall Stadium.

"So we all get out at Camp Randall, and we're all late and panicking," Kissling says. He and the others—all but Harder—hurriedly dressed for practice and charged out onto the field, a couple of minutes late. Stuhldreher strutted over and barked, "Take five! Take five!"

That meant five laps, so Kissling and the other tardy moviegoers began running. Harder walked onto the practice field and approached Stuhldreher. The other late Badgers, running their laps, wondered, *Was he going to ask for forgiveness?* Kissling says, laughing: "He walks up to

Harry and says, 'Here, take care of this, coach!', hands Harry the ticket, and then goes to practice his kicking."

Other times, when Harder gave teammates lifts to the stadium for practice, he thought nothing of pulling over at a firehouse—the player-friendly residences of some of the Badgers—and going inside for a couple of minutes to have a cigarette. "We just sat there and waited," end Bob Hanzlik says.

Tackle Dave Donnellan notes that Harder "was one guy who could do just about anything he wanted to do. He had that much ability. Everything came natural. I can recall Harry asking him, 'Pat, should we scrimmage today or not?' Really, he asked him that. Pat said, 'No!' He never wanted to scrimmage. But I guess Harry knew that."

Like most Badgers, Harder had a job to earn spending money, but he turned even that into a racket. Each State Street business had a keyed lock on the outside of the building, and Harder's job was to go down the street at ten o'clock each night and turn the key, which would turn out the lights inside. But Harder gave a cut of his salary to a local high school athlete to do the job for him.

The star fullback could also be a charmer, and Stuhldreher's wife, Mary, was enamored of him. Years later in her book *Many a Saturday Afternoon*, she wrote of going on the train rides with the Badgers for road games and having Harder tell her, "You're my girl, not my coach's wife." She added, "No wonder I was so fond of him. He made me feel so young."

On the field, Harder was a terror. He didn't much care if he was carrying the ball, blocking, or tackling, because all he wanted to do was run over or hit somebody. "Pat Harder was a killer in blocking," says center Fred Negus. "If he couldn't hit somebody, he'd get mad. He'd just run over you. He was that type of ballplayer. I didn't know of a tougher guy than he was."

In the spring of '42, Harder carried on a vendetta against halfback Bud Seelinger, the small passing specialist known for his skill and finesse. Harder believed football was meant to be played with anger and bloodied noses, and Seelinger rubbed him the wrong way. Harder hated Seelinger's Western wardrobe of a buckskin shirt, dungarees, and moccasins and, frequently, a cowboy hat. He didn't care that Seelinger, raised on his family's ranch near Great Falls, Montana, came by the wardrobe naturally. "Now there's a cowboy," recalls Arlie Mucks, Jr., a 1941 Badger who entered the Army Air Forces after that season. "He rode in from Montana and never took off his boots. He just put cleats on them."

In a scrimmage, Harder broke through the line and, instead of heading for the goal line, ran down Seelinger, who was playing in the defensive backfield. He was determined to run over the cowboy, even if he had to go twenty yards out his way to do it. He chased Seelinger, calling him a "panty-waist." (Nobody else thought that, and the Badgers assume the fun-loving Seelinger must have angered Harder by turning the tables on the jokester. Subsequent events proved that Seelinger was anything but cowardly.)

Montana cowboy Bud Seelinger was a fine passer ahead of his time, so the halfback was underutilized in the Notre Dame Box.
PHOTO COURTESY OF JOHN GALLAGHER

As a sophomore in 1941, Harder led the Big Ten in rushing, and that was difficult to do as a fullback in the Notre Dame Box. In '42, Stuhldreher was contemplating having Harder carry the ball less and block more, mostly for Hirsch. But if the coach expected rebellion from Harder, it didn't come. It was as if Harder said, "I'll take care of it."

FIVE

The Little General

Harry Stuhldreher's former Four Horsemen compatriot Elmer Layden departed Notre Dame to become commissioner of the National Football League after coaching the Irish to a 7–2 record in 1940. Layden's replacement was Frank Leahy, who had played for Rockne's 1929 national championship squad and coached Boston College—another Catholic school—to an undefeated record in 1940. Stuhldreher liked Leahy, and he invited the new Notre Dame coach to address the Wisconsin football banquet after the Badgers' disappointing 1941 season. Leahy, who had just guided the Irish to an 8–0–1 record in his first season in South Bend, so vigorously praised Stuhldreher as a football genius and a man of honor that some in the audience wondered if Leahy had just saved Stuhldreher's job.

Despite a lackluster 16–22–2 record in four seasons, Stuhldreher had consolidated power as the Badgers' athletic director and head football coach. His more irreverent players called him The Little General—when he wasn't within earshot. Stuhldreher had a slight lisp but an otherwise commanding voice. On the sidelines, he usually had a cigarette between his fingers, and players often coughed through his one-on-one exhortations because he blew smoke on them. (Schreiner, who was so offended by his smoking prep-school coach, liked Harry and didn't seem to mind his smoking.) Stuhldreher's players generally considered him a football genius, but many hated his unwillingness to adapt to the changing standards of the game.

In the summer of 1942, the word out of South Bend was that even Leahy was abandoning Knute Rockne's Notre Dame Box and going to the T formation with Angelo Bertelli, who was previously the left halfback and now the quarterback in the newfangled alignment. When critics questioned the change, Leahy snapped, "If Rockne was here, he'd be the first to try it. Besides, material, coaching, blocking, and tackling—not systems—win football games."

Stuhldreher was more stubborn. He loved the Notre Dame Box, in which the quarterback was a step back from the center and directly in front

Harry Stuhldreher (kneeling) with his 1942 coaching staff: from left, backfield coach Guy Sundt, tackle and end coach George Fox, center and guard coach Russ Rippe.
PHOTO COURTESY OF THE UNIVERSITY OF WISCONSIN SPORTS INFORMATION DEPARTMENT

of the three other backs, who were lined up straight across. The alignment indeed was roughly a "T," but it wasn't what became known as the T formation, and the backs usually shifted before the snap. In the Box, after the quarterback surveyed the field and literally called out the play in a numeric code, the backs moved, usually to the right. When that happened, the right halfback moved over and up, parallel to the quarterback, primarily to serve as the lead blocker for a run to the right, and the fullback and left halfback moved straight to their right. The result was a box in the backfield. The snap from center could fly through the air to any one of the backs. For years, in line with that Notre Dame tradition, Stuhldreher also insisted that the backs swing one arm in a huge loop as they shifted. The Badgers hated that so much, they derisively imitated the move years later— especially after a few beers. The left halfback threw the majority of the passes, but any of the backs might put the ball in the air.

As the '42 season approached, Stuhldreher installed a few T formation plays and greatly pleased his players by dropping the hated arm swing during the shift, but the bulk of the Badgers' offense remained the Notre Dame Box. His system still called for the quarterback usually barking out signals in the open, without a huddle. The cadence was a series of four numbers. Dave Schreiner once explained the signal system to his parents.

> The first number the quarterback calls is meaningless. If the first digit of the second number is even it goes to the right. The second digit of the second number is the first digit of the play. The next number's first digit is the last digit of the play and the last is meaningless. The last number's first digit is meaningless and its last digit is the number of the variation. Most plays have a variation.

Schreiner ran through an example, then concluded the section of his letter with another admonition, "Don't forget to destroy this!"

The system required the quarterback to think quickly and for everyone else to pay attention and decode the call. When Stuhldreher was looking for quarterback material, he sought players who reminded him of himself under Rockne. During the season, the quarterbacks met with the coach daily after the team's "training table" dinner in the Memorial Union and for long recap sessions on game mornings.

Ashley Anderson started his Badger career as a freshman halfback. He also had two freshman years, in effect, after he was injured in the fall of 1939 and decided to leave school and start over the next fall. "When Harry saw my grades my freshman year, he said, 'You're going to be my quarterback.'" Anderson says. "Nobody called your plays for you; you called your plays yourself. We spent a lot of time in those meetings going over strategy, and what to look for, and even which of our guys to ask about how their defensive men were reacting."

Stuhldreher made it clear that even the play-calling would be done with the coach's guidelines in mind. "I don't want to say he was a tyrant," says halfback Otto Breitenbach, "but he certainly was dictatorial. Of course, he was very wedded to the Notre Dame Box and the shift, and I have to say our passing attack was not very sophisticated—even for that time."

The Badgers were impressed with one of Stuhldreher's assistants, Howie Odell, but he left after the '42 spring practice to become the head coach at Yale. They generally believe Odell's departure hurt, because the three assistant coaches on the staff that fall—Russ Rippe, Guy Sundt, and George Fox—didn't inspire confidence, in part because of the way Stuhldreher treated them. Sundt was an athletic department administrator pressed to go back into coaching after Odell's sudden departure. The assistants usually ran to Stuhldreher for orders, but when the assistants did try to take initiative, Stuhldreher often jumped in and made them look bad, contradicting what they had just told the players. So the assistants became gun-shy.

At the beginning of practice, Stuhldreher identified the first and second teams for the day, even if they hadn't changed in weeks. After that, he watched and coached, often with that cigarette in his hand.

"He always had bloodshot eyes," says fiery end Bob Hanzlik, who didn't get along with his coach. "He looked to me like he'd been drinking every night. It's like you'd come out of the shower or out of the ocean. My eyes get red, too, when I come out of the water. But he never had clear eyes. His eyes to me were threatening eyes."

Tackle George Hekkers says he "always felt Harry had a sense of the game that nobody else had. I think he could call every play the opposition was going to run. He had that sense of the science of football, but I always questioned his ability to relay it to me."

Hekkers laughs. "That probably was because I was a big dumb tackle."

Stuhldreher often talked about his days at Notre Dame and more than once reminded the Badgers that he had played the final half of his senior season for Rockne with a cracked bone in his leg. (That was the story, anyway, and who were the Badgers to question Irish lore?) Many Badgers aggravated minor injuries because they were trying to prove their toughness to their coach.

Ashley Anderson suffered a broken collarbone in a 1941 game. "Harry came up to me and said, 'Anderson, you're not hurt, shake it off!'" Anderson says. "And of course, when we went into our box, we shifted and swung our arm. So when we shifted, I couldn't swing my arm and that really got Harry mad. He said, 'Why didn't you swing your arm?' I said, 'I can't lift it.' Then [trainer] Doc Bakke came out, felt it, and said, 'No wonder, it's broken!' Harry didn't think you should get hurt."

In some spring drills early in 1942—before the weather was good enough for the Badgers to go outside—Hekkers earned the gratitude of his teammates when he stepped back from the line and his spikes landed on Stuhldreher's toes. The Little General yelped and jumped and cussed, and his players fought to keep from laughing. *This was the man who played with a broken leg and doesn't believe any of us can get hurt?*

Halfback Bob Omelina nailed his coach once, too. "We were in the stock pavilion, and we used to say they took the cows out and brought us in," Omelina says. "Harry was telling me I wasn't stepping off, cutting, and going into the line. He would say, 'Step and drive off that foot!' So I did it and he was there and I stepped right on his foot. He jumped in the air and he howled, and he jumped around and he said that was the end of practice. I didn't want to get near him, but the guys were going, 'Way to go, Bob!' I got a hero medal for that one."

Generally, though, the players respected their coach as a firm, fair man. Fred Negus, the '42 team's star sophomore center, offers a common sentiment: "Well, nobody liked his system too much. But I liked Harry."

When *State Journal* sports editor Henry J. McCormick was leaving for Naval duty in 1942, he composed an ode to Stuhldreher:

> Harry was a perfect example of the fact that a man can play savage, all-out football while still being a thorough-going gentleman. He's the same as a coach. . . . Winning football games is important to Stuhldreher. He doesn't like to lose. Yet he thinks that developing traits in boys that will help them after college is just as important. That's why he coaches his boys to play right up to the hilt but to abide by the rules. He'll never censure a boy who does his best, and any criticism he makes of the players is to them and not to the public. In fact, I've seen Stuhldreher tell falsehoods about his boys in public to protect them, and even when it shifted the blame to his shoulders.

McCormick had that right: Stuhldreher never targeted specific players for criticism to reporters or the public, but that was in large part because reporters rarely, if ever, asked sharp-edged questions and usually allowed the Badgers' coach considerable control over what information reached the public. That situation wasn't unique to Madison; it was the norm around the country.

One problem Stuhldreher had in 1942 was an abundance of young talent coming onto the varsity from the freshman team, which forced him to break the news to a lot of upperclassmen that their playing time probably would be cut from the previous season. But that was a good problem for a coach to have.

SIX

The '42 Badgers

In the summer of '42, still without military responsibilities, Dave Schreiner and Mark Hoskins decided they wanted no part of a return to cement work on the highway construction crew.

At first they remained in Madison and worked at Truax Field, the Madison airport, which was being upgraded for the Army Air Forces. There they dug ditches, which wasn't much better than being cement puddlers. After a Lancaster buddy who was working at the Dubuque Country Club offered them jobs as lifeguards, they headed for Dubuque.

Hoskins spent most of the summer playing golf and watching others swim. Schreiner, reaping spoils of his All-American '41 season, quickly got another offer to work as a counselor at a youth summer camp, Kooch-I-Ching, at International Falls, Minnesota. In the early days at the camp, Schreiner confessed to his parents:

> So help me I'm really homesick. This is a healthy life up here, but I miss all my old friends. . . . Please write me daily until I get over this nostalgia.

The pay was good, and many of the counselors were college players, including Minnesota's stars, halfback Bill Daley and tackle Dick Wildung. Schreiner begged his parents to send him all the Wisconsin T-shirts in his room so he could make some trades, and he and the two Gophers struck up a friendship that survived their teasing about the annual rivalry game at the end of each team's schedule. Wildung and Daley kept pointing out that Minnesota had easily won the 1941 game, 41–6, and had been named the national champion in the Associated Press poll for the second straight year. The Badgers hadn't beaten the Gophers since 1932.

"That's going to change," Schreiner kept saying. Wisconsin would have

a bunch of great sophomores, he told the Gophers, declaring that the Badgers were going to be a much tougher team in 1942. He knew Stuhldreher
faced difficult choices in selecting the starting lineup.

In the era of one-platoon football, the rules discouraged anything
beyond occasional substitution. The accepted coaching convention was
to keep the stars on the field until a bone was showing through the skin
or the outcome was decided. Though Wisconsin would have better depth
than in any previous season of the Stuhldreher tenure, most players going through practices and suiting up for games knew they wouldn't play
much, if at all. "I played a lot of football at Wisconsin," '42 sophomore
tackle Dave Donnellan says, smiling. "But most of it was during the week."
The reserves were important for more than practice fodder, though. They
were critical to the development of an *esprit de corps,* providing support
in the locker room, during practices, and on the sidelines on game days.
Everyone on the roster was part of the team, sharing in dreams, triumphs,

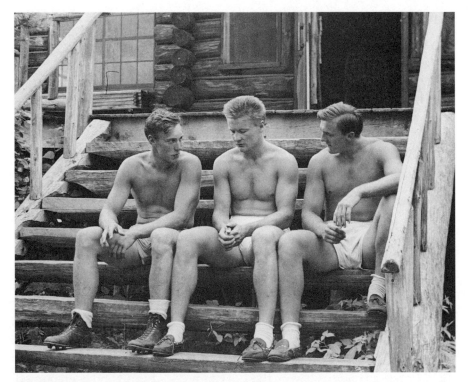

Dave Schreiner, wearing football cleats, takes a break during summer camp to chat with
Minnesota stars and fellow camp counselors Bill Daley and Dick Wildung. The three All-
Americans would meet again in the last game of the 1942 season.
PHOTO COURTESY OF JUDY CORFIELD

and disappointments. And in 1942, they all knew that down the road, Uncle Sam wouldn't be asking whether they had started or rarely played for the Badgers.

★ ★ ★

With Schreiner locked in at one end, the other spot was up for grabs among junior Bob Hanzlik, sophomore Bob Rennebohm, and senior Pat Lyons. Lyons took himself out of the running when he told the coaches in mid-August that he was going to skip football because of a tough class load in mining engineering.

The fiery Hanzlik didn't seem to differentiate between practice and games or between teammates and opponents, so the Badgers had to be especially wary of him on the practice field. Nobody doubted his competitiveness, which showed up in his exhortations on the sideline and on the field. He also had quirky ideas about staying in shape, especially because he often followed a night on State Street (where he liked to play pinball for hours with Bob Baumann) with a training regimen that raised eyebrows. Baumann, George Makris, and Dave Schreiner often joined him. Hanzlik climbed ropes and lifted weights. The coaches frowned on that because they believed weightlifting made players muscle-bound, less flexible, and slower. Hanzlik kept lifting all spring and summer and showed up for fall practice weighing a rock-solid 195 pounds.

Hanzlik's hometown of Chippewa Falls was near the Minnesota border, and he had strongly considered attending the University of Minnesota. But one of Stuhldreher's assistants kept working on Hanzlik, telling him if he came down to Madison right after he graduated from high school, he could work at a brewery all summer and stockpile money. Eventually, that's what Hanzlik did. He played most of '41 as the starter ahead of Pat Lyons, but in the early stages of the fall workouts, sophomore Bob Rennebohm was running with the first unit.

The young Rennebohm's name was familiar because of the chain of Rennebohm drugstores around the state, including "The Pharm" on State Street. The scion of the chain, Oscar Rennebohm, "was my second cousin," Bob says. "But for purposes of ease, he always called me his nephew and I called him my uncle. That's the way they reported it when I played, too."

Bob's wing of the family lived in La Crosse. "When I was a little kid I used to pray that the world wouldn't end before I had a chance to play for the Badgers," he says.

A football and baseball star at La Crosse's Central High School, Rennebohm was one of the few Badgers who drew a recruiting visit from

Bob Rennebohm, the sophomore end from La Crosse, was challenging for a starting position in the early days of preseason practices.
PHOTO COURTESY OF JOHN GALLAGHER

Stuhldreher. "They got me out of class and told me to go to the principal's office," Rennebohm says. "I thought I had done something wrong."

Instead, Stuhldreher and assistant coach Russ Rippe were waiting to see him. Rennebohm said he would love to be a Badger but that he also wanted to wait a year, work, save his money, and add to his 180-pound frame. "Harry said that would be fine," Rennebohm says. "I waited a year up there and worked at the Trane Company."

Sophomores Hank Olshanski, Elroy Hirsch's buddy from Wausau; Gunner Johnson from Neenah; Jim McClellan from Chippewa Falls; and senior Bob Stupka from Watertown were also hoping to get in some varsity games at end.

★ ★ ★

The number-one tackles heading into fall practice were both seniors. Bob Baumann was from Harvey, Illinois, abutting Chicago's southern border, and he had been a star and multiple-sport captain at his high school. It amazed his teammates that though he was rugged-looking, round-faced, and usually silent, women were drawn to him.

Once, in the stadium catacombs, Stuhldreher came across Baumann in some heavy romantic scrimmaging with a female student. The extent of the "action" varied widely in the retelling as the story got passed around the locker room and campus. But there was no disputing that his coach had caught him at the stadium in the throes of passion. "Bob Baumann

Bob Baumann didn't say much—but he didn't need to talk to make his case as a star tackle.
PHOTO COURTESY OF THE UNIVERSITY OF WISCONSIN SPORTS INFORMATION DEPARTMENT

was a quiet, unassuming individual, but he was entirely different on the football field, and he was a ladies' man," halfback Erv Kissling says.

The other starter, Paul Hirsbrunner, had a dark complexion and a heritage that caused everyone to call him Indian. Hirsbrunner had been one of twelve siblings working the family farm in Darlington before he came to Madison. He had played high school games against Lancaster's Schreiner and Hoskins, and a respect and friendship developed among the three even before they were Wisconsin teammates.

Hirsbrunner had an infectious, enthusiastic attitude and a droll sense of humor that sneaked up on those who didn't know him. He would say something, and it wouldn't register until a moment later, even longer, that, hey, this guy is funny. One of the most studious players on the team, Hirsbrunner learned the plays at both tackle and end, and he so loved to stick his nose into an opponent, either blocking or tackling, that his face always seemed to be torn up.

Backup Dick Thornally came from the Morgan Park area on Chicago's south side. He started out at the University of Washington after graduating from high school in the middle of an academic year. "Washington recruited a bunch of us guys out of Chicago," Thornally recalls.

He didn't like Seattle, though, and bailed out, returning home before even going through spring practices. "There was a Wisconsin alumnus in Chicago, a businessman named Mike Agazim, who recruited a bunch of guys for Harry, and I was one of them," Thornally says.

As part of his Wisconsin deal, Thornally was lined up with a summer job working as a "hooker," maneuvering giant girders on chains for a Chicago steel company that also made railroad cars. One of his friends

Tackle Paul Hirsbrunner was one of the smartest Badgers.
PHOTO COURTESY OF THE UNIVERSITY OF WISCONSIN SPORTS
INFORMATION DEPARTMENT

Tackle Dick Thornally couldn't stand the rain in Seattle and soon returned to the Midwest to play for Wisconsin.

was killed on the job when a girder fell on him.

Senior Lloyd Wasserbach, from Bailey's Harbor, Wisconsin, and sophomore George Hekkers were also pushing for playing time. Hekkers had been a year behind Harder at Washington High. He also wrestled, and George Martin, the successful coach of the UW wrestling program, wanted him, too, making it an easy decision for Hekkers to enroll at Wisconsin.

Dave Donnellan, the reserve tackle who got all that playing time during the week, was one of the three Badger sophomores from Eau Claire.

"My dad was in the real estate business in Eau Claire at a time when if you sold one house a year, you were creating a record," Donnellan says. "Times were tough. He became a farm home loan appraiser. Then he went to work at the rubber company. We had a good life, very quiet, and I guess the only excitement I can remember is the time the airplane flew into the grocery store roof.

"In the meantime, I worked for a sausage company. My uncle owned it, and when I graduated from high school, he wanted me to work for him. I said no, I was going to college."

★   ★   ★

The two top guards from that freshman team, Ken Currier and Jerry Frei, were inseparable. Their teammates called them Roughie and Toughie, respectively. Frei's hometown of Stoughton was only

Tackle Dave Donnellan philosophically accepted his reserve role.

PHOTO COURTESY OF JOHN GALLAGHER

fifteen miles away, and Currier had come down to Madison from Rice Lake in the northwest part of the state.

Currier didn't talk about it much, and few knew, but he was adopted. His adoptive parents were terrific to him but didn't have much money, and college seemed out of the question. He said he at least wanted to try it, so in the late summer of 1941, his adoptive father drove him to Madison, gave him ten dollars, shook his hand, and said good luck. Currier was going to have to earn money for his tuition and other college expenses.

For a time, Currier slept outside on the campus or in Madison parks, wherever he could. Once it was clear that the 5-foot-10, 190-pound fireplug of a guard was a fine football player and a voluble, funny guy, his teammates watched out for him. Before long, he was living in a rooming house and working. His enthusiasm and sense of humor made him one of the most popular players on the team.

Currier had the inside track at the right guard spot, but Frei—barely eighteen—didn't expect to beat out senior Evan "Red" Vogds for the other starting guard position. Vogds was raised on a dairy farm near Fond du Lac, seventy miles northwest of Madison, and one day at Fond du Lac High School, football coach Mike Calvano spotted the stocky redhead and asked him why he wasn't out for the team. Vogds said he had to milk cows, but the coach arranged for him to come in from the country, live in the YMCA, and work for his meals—all so he could play football. That was more organized than the process that brought him to Madison; he just showed up, tried out for the team, and played.

Two other guards were the stars of other Wisconsin sports teams. After playing two seasons of varsity football in obscurity, George Makris was coaxed into going out for the boxing team in early 1942 and won the NCAA championship in his weight class. John Roberts, meanwhile, was a Big Ten champion wrestler.

In Rhinelander, where Makris was raised, his father, Bill, owned a Greek restaurant in partnership with George's uncle, Thesackos. George spent much of his youth toiling in the restaurant, refereeing disputes between his father cooking in the back and his uncle working in the front. When Makris went out for boxing, the Wisconsin sports publicity department declared in a release: "His relatives are the kind of people that resisted Axis aggression in such fine style for such a long time with so little to work with. If there ever was a young warrior to whom the Greek war god, Ares, could point with pride, it is this affable, black-haired lad who becomes a keg of human dynamite whenever he enters the ring."

Makris was a hero to his football teammates, not only because he was a national boxing champion and a good guy, but because he and his closest friend, tackle Bob Baumann, made them some money.

When weather permitted, Makris took Baumann along on training runs around Lake Mendota. The boxing team's student manager was a fat boy named Maury who was jealous of the attention paid Makris and Baumann, especially by the women on campus. Maury belittled their training regimen as all show and bet Makris twenty-five dollars—roughly the tuition bill for a semester—that Makris and Baumann couldn't start from State Street, run all the way around the lake, and make it back to the starting point without stopping or walking. Word of the wager got around, and the other Badger football players got in on the action, backing Baumann and Makris.

The bettors on both sides of the proposition waited on State Street. Soon, the two big football players, winded but still running, chugged down the street to the designated finish line. The winning bettors cheered. The losers cursed.

Makris and Baumann celebrated winning another wager. They had bet Maury that he couldn't stick with them on his bicycle as he tracked the football players' progress. Sure enough, Maury had to dismount and walk the bike and then pedal quickly to catch up.

"We had trouble collecting the money," Makris recalls. "We threatened to beat him up. We wouldn't have done that, of course. But he finally paid us."

John Roberts, the wrestler, was aggressively recruited by wrestling coach George Martin, who along with an assistant football coach visited Roberts at his high school in Des Moines. "They got me a job for that summer, which paid my tuition for the year, and it was out-of-state, too." Coach Martin was having a house built, and the contractor—what a co-incidence—hired the young wrestler to work on the project. "I was just a humpty dumpty, carrying boards, picking up wood chips, and things like that," he says. "That was all, but I had enough money then to pay tuition."

By his senior year, Roberts was Wisconsin's best wrestler and a backup right guard. He liked Currier, so he had a hard time staying mad about not starting.

Football was backup guard John Roberts's second-favorite sport. He was one of the top wrestlers in the country.

"Roughie did a good job, so it was hard to keep him out of there," Roberts says. Sophomore George Neperud, part of the team's Chippewa Falls contingent, was another backup guard hoping for a chance.

★ ★ ★

After Fred Negus's impressive spring practices in '42, everyone connected with the Badgers knew that the sophomore was going to be the starting center and linebacker. At 6-foot-2 and 201 pounds, he was lean, rugged, and fast. The youngest of four sons, Negus was raised on a dairy farm outside Martin's Ferry, Ohio. "My parents were Quakers because it was Quaker territory, but they kind of grew out of it," Negus says. "I milked a few cows in the morning and some-times in the evening. There wasn't much money in selling milk to dairies, so we started our own retail routes and had two or three trucks on the road."

A star at Shreve High School, he visited the Ohio State campus on his own and considered attending school in Columbus but was wary of the huge campus. After Shreve, he went to Kiski Prep for a year. While Fred was at Kiski, his brother, Al, a dairy equipment salesman, was trans-ferred to Madison.

One day, Harry Stuhldreher got a visit from Al Negus. The Wisconsin sports publicity office's version of the encounter had Al telling the Badger coach about his brother: "He's interested in agriculture, and I'd like to have him come up here and play football for you." Fred came to Madison that September, moved in with his brother, and enrolled at the UW. The pub-licity release continued with "Stuhldreher, never one to pass up a bet, but making allowance for natural brotherly pride, investigated the lad when he arrived for the fall term and found he had played center and fullback in high school and guard at Kiski. That meant adaptability and speed, so Stuhldreher assigned the lad to center on the Badger frosh squad. Sud-denly, previously unknown Fred Negus became an outstanding prospect."

In the summers, Fred Negus still worked in the family dairy business, so a part-time job at Madison's Bancroft Dairy during the school year was a natural fit. When he returned for the fall of '42, he lived in the Phi Delta Theta fraternity house, joining Hoskins and Schreiner.

Negus had a tendency to end every sentence with a nervous chuckle, whether in the dressing room, in the frat house's living room, or during card games in the Memorial Union. The other card players learned that he laughed over good hands and bad hands.

★　★　★

Stuhldreher's public posture was that the left halfback job was wide open. Henry J. McCormick of the *State Journal* parroted the coach's view, writing, "People who already have consigned the left halfback job to soph-omore Elroy Hirsch should think twice. Beyond the shadow of a doubt Hirsch is a brilliant prospect. But Hirsch has yet to gain a yard for Wis-consin at passing or carrying the ball. Until he does the logical thing to assume is that the inside track for that post belongs to the soft-spoken Bud Seelinger."

Seelinger, the Montana cowboy, came to Madison because his uncle was on the Wisconsin athletic department staff, and everybody except Pat Harder respected and liked him. "He was a free spirit," says Arlie Mucks,

Jr., Seelinger's 1941 teammate. "He was like a little kid with a ball. He enjoyed life."

He was also unlucky and miscast in the Notre Dame Box. After missing most of the 1940 season because of a kidney injury, he was limited again in '41 by a bad knee and spinal meningitis. Despite Seelinger's problems, Stuhldreher knew that if he went to the T formation full-time, the cowboy could be a great passing quarterback.

Hoskins was set at right half, as the back who most often shifted up to a wing spot and led the blocking. The other backup halfbacks were going to be sophomores Jim Regan, Otto Breitenbach, Bob Omelina, and Erv Kissling, plus senior Jim McFadzean.

Regan was from Berwyn, Illinois, near Chicago, and had been all set to go to Notre Dame. His uncle, a priest at Our Lady of the Sacrament in downtown Chicago, took him to Notre Dame for a visit and introduced him to new Fighting Irish coach Frank Leahy, who offered Regan financial help to come to South Bend. But, there was a catch: Leahy's plan was that Regan would work for the Chicago Street Company, gain weight,

The Box formation meant that the ball carrier could have three backfield escorts. Here, Pat Harder (right) carries as (left to right) Jack Wink, Mark Hoskins, and Elroy Hirsch lead the way.

PHOTO COURTESY GEORGE NEPERUD

then sit out a year and work. The common strategy of taking a year off didn't appeal to Regan.

"When I got home," Regan says, "there was a telegram from Harry Stuhldreher, saying, 'Are you going to come up here or aren't you?'"

Sure am, Regan declared in an answering telegram.

In the heavily Swiss Wisconsin towns of Monticello and Monroe, Erv "Booby" Kissling spoke Schwyzerdeutsch, or Swiss-German, as a child. His tiny high school didn't even have a football team, and he was a sparkplug basketball guard who drew interest from Wisconsin coach Bud Foster. But before he could go out for basketball, he was detoured. "At the end of the registration line, there was a big table with a sign: 'Sign up for football,'" Kissling says. "I decided what the hell, I'd try it to get into shape to play basketball."

The former player at the table asked Kissling where he played high school football. "I said I hadn't. He gave me a little card that had 'D' on it. I didn't know what the hell 'D' was. I went up to the equipment room, and after they issued the equipment, I knew what 'D' meant. I had a green shirt that must have been sewed fifty times. I could stand it on end. I had a pair of pants that could stand up by themselves, too, and I had a pair of shoes that were size 11. I wore 8."

After Kissling showed flashes of speed and talent in the first workouts, when the freshman scrubs were used as "cannon fodder" for the varsity, Stuhldreher approached the stubby player.

"Can you run like that all the time?"

"Yeah, but I can run a lot faster if you get me a pair of shoes that fit."

Stuhldreher gave him a card with "A" on it, and he got better equipment.

Jim McFadzean, the senior backup, was the son of a Scottish immigrant and the product of New Trier High in Winnetka, north of Chicago. He was one of the fastest players on the team but remained a backup. Roundy Coughlin kept pumping him up in print, but that didn't convince the coach.

Bob Omelina, from Cudahy, played a benefit basketball game as a high school student against some Wisconsin athletes, including football player and Singing Firemen Trio member John Tennant. Tennant talked Omelina into committing to go to Wisconsin on the spot.

Otto Breitenbach was raised in Madison, about five blocks from the state capitol, and attended Edgewood High School, which was run by the Catholic Church's Dominican order. His grandfather had started a neighborhood grocery store and passed it down to Otto's father. Otto was only sixteen when he got his Edgewood diploma, and he "never gave any thought" to going anywhere other than Wisconsin. "I hardly knew any others existed at the time," he says.

★ ★ ★

At fullback, nobody was going to beat out Harder. Seniors Bob Ray, from Eau Claire, and Len Calligaro, from Hurley, would have started for a lot of teams, but they weren't going to play unless The Mule couldn't make it on the field.

★ ★ ★

That left Harry's old position, quarterback.

The left-handed Ashley Anderson had the inside track, because as an upper-echelon student able to think quickly on his feet, he reminded Harry of himself. He came to Madison after playing at Milwaukee's Riverside High and then at nearby St. John's Military Academy for a year.

Several sophomores looked as if they could step up to challenge Anderson. One was Jack Wink, from Boys Tech in Milwaukee. The other was John Gallagher, who threw a touchdown pass in the spring game. Of the Badgers' three sophomores from Eau Claire, Gallagher had taken the most roundabout way to get to Madison. After high school, he worked briefly as a machinist and then decided to go to college. His father was incredulous.

"How the hell can you go to college?" he challenged.

"Well," John responded, "I don't have any money, but I can work."

John traveled to Minneapolis and visited with football coach Bernie Bierman, who lined up a job for Gallagher on a highway crew near the North Dakota border. Gallagher did that for a summer, saved his money, and started out at Minnesota. His Eau Claire buddy Dave Donnellan was rooming at Wisconsin with Bob Hanzlik from nearby Chippewa Falls, and they successfully lobbied Gallagher to transfer and join them in the middle of his freshman year.

Don Litchfield was the other quarterback from Eau Claire. His father owned the local Chrysler dealership, where Don says he and his brother, Tommy, did all sorts of menial chores. Don finally got out of the work by heading to Madison.

"That freshman year, we were playing against the hotshots down here," Litchfield says. "There were a hundred freshmen out. Stuhldreher walked around saying 'cut, cut, cut,' and pretty soon they had us cut down to thirty-six guys. I think I was going to be the next cut if they hadn't stopped there."

That freshman team gave the '41 varsity fits. And by the time the Badgers were approaching opening day in 1942, more than half the players were sophomores.

SEVEN

Getting Ready

The *Wisconsin State Journal*'s Henry J. McCormick expressed a sentiment common among most preseason stories assessing the Big Ten race, writing in mid-August that it "still has that same familiar look of Minnesota against the field." *Street & Smith*'s magazine, prestigious and virtually uncontested as a preseason national preview, made Michigan the pick, followed by Minnesota, Northwestern, Ohio State, Wisconsin, Iowa, Indiana, Purdue, and Illinois.

The major question about the Badgers was whether they would be improved defensively after giving up an average of 26 points a game in 1941—a scandalous total, especially for a team with All-American Dave Schreiner shutting down one flank. The players were optimistic, but even they had limits. "We had a bad team the year before and Wisconsin hadn't won much for a few years," says center Fred Negus, "so I don't think anyone really knew."

Quarterback John Gallagher notes, "After we had the first couple of scrimmages, we all felt we were going to have a real ball club. The spirit was high, and the team was cohesive. Because I was a backup quarterback, I worked a lot of the scrimmages against the first team." He laughs. "They were good."

Stories noted that roughly half of Big Ten players were at least twenty, the minimum draft age. A mid-August *Capital Times* story declared that Harry Stuhldreher "does not expect that his personnel will be affected by the national emergency this fall, as practically all those men of active draft age are already enlisted in the reserves of various armed forces and will probably not be called until they are graduated."

Not even the players believed that. The season was setting up to be their final football fling. Even the teenagers on the team were coming around to that view.

"At first, I think we felt like a lot of others, that we'll take care of this in a matter of months," says halfback Otto Breitenbach, who turned eighteen in June 1942. "But how wrong can you be? It wasn't long before we caught on and knew we would be in."

The Badgers reported for fall workouts on September 1, nearly three weeks before the beginning of the fall term. Stuhldreher invited fifty-four players to the workouts. He said perhaps twenty would play on the B team in a limited schedule but would also suit up for the Badgers' varsity games.

On the day they reported and had their physicals, the Badgers posed for team pictures. Three prominent players weren't in the pictures—end Bob Hanzlik and fullback Bob Ray were having their Marine Corps physicals, and halfback Bud Seelinger had cut it too close getting back to Madison from Montana and was stuck in St. Paul waiting for a train. The next day, the team started practices. Schreiner wrote home between the two practices, saying that most of the Badgers lost five or six pounds in the heat at the first workout.

At the time, something was weighing on Schreiner's mind. He had stopped in Lancaster only briefly between working at the Minnesota youth camp and reporting for practices. He was in great condition, thanks to the workouts and the long canoe trips at camp. Yet he was gently breaking the news to his parents that he wanted to give up on pre-med studies and switch to economics. Even more significant at that time, because students on track to go to medical school generally could be shoved to the back of the line by their draft boards, the move could make Schreiner more vulnerable to being called into the service. He used his struggles in zoology to help explain to his parents why he wanted to change majors.

> I'm not very good in it, and don't especially like it. I believe also that I'd rather be in something but pre-med as courses in it don't fit me too well. Will talk all this over when I come home after the [season-opening] Camp Grant game. I do think I will transfer out of pre-med and that I will tell the draft board I am doing this. After last summer I know I have the ability and ambition to become successful if I'm in work that I like. If they don't want to keep me in school, that's perfectly OK with me. I'm quite sure I can get a commission of some kind in the Army, and if not I'll do a good job as private. I really am serious about dropping pre-med however. Don't think I'm a quitter though.

In the same letter, Schreiner assured his parents the practices were going well. "My blocking is good especially," he wrote.

As the season approached, Stuhldreher made Elroy Hirsch learn both halfback spots, theorizing that he could switch the sophomore star over to the right and use Bud Seelinger, the better passer, at the featured left half when the situation warranted.

In the first Saturday scrimmage that fall, Pat Harder suffered a severe bone bruise on his leg, as well as an ankle injury, when he was tackled at the end of a 40-yard run. That was the beginning of injury problems that would plague Harder all season. Before he was hurt, Harder went 78 yards for one touchdown. Hirsch ran 44 for another, causing spectators to excitedly tout the two "H" boys as backfield mates.

"We sputtered," Stuhldreher told the *Wisconsin State Journal.* "We weren't consistent, but we did move well in spots. For a first scrimmage, it wasn't bad."

The Badgers' schedule involved two distinct segments. The first five games were against nonleague opponents, the final five against Big Ten Conference teams. The Big Ten had only nine football-playing members after the University of Chicago dropped football in 1939, and not all teams played the same number of conference games. The league was often called the Western Conference, and the two names were interchangeable. And some even called it the Big Nine during football season.

Whatever the league was called, the Badgers finally seemed to be shaping up as a significant threat to win their first championship since 1912.

EIGHT

Gainful Employment

Without formal athletic scholarships, the Badgers generally earned their way through school. They had help lining up part-time jobs, and understanding employers were flexible in scheduling the players' hours, both during and after the season.

Pat Harder had the job turning out the lights in the downtown stores, which he subcontracted out to the local high school athlete. One other duty came close to being a racket, or perhaps it even crossed that line. Many of the Badgers "worked" for the Madison Business Association, clocking in whenever they wanted, walking around the downtown square area and writing down automobile license numbers, and turning them in at the association's office in the Park Hotel.

"That was kind of our version of the scholarship," says end Bob Rennebohm. "We'd copy down license plate numbers and then come back and look them up to see where the shoppers were coming from. That was supposed to help Madison choose the right method of advertising and so forth. We used to get seventy-five cents an hour, and you could only work enough to get the equivalent of your room, and in our case, it was fifteen dollars a month." That meant twenty hours per month of copying down license numbers. It was a semi-legitimate means of allowing businessmen to sponsor players and get them extra money.

As many as ten Badgers, including George Makris, Bob Baumann, Jerry Frei, and Ken Currier, had free rooms in Madison firehouses, earning their way by closing the big doors when the engines departed. Several others were among the many Wisconsin athletes who worked at Madison restaurants and taverns. Toby and Moon's, near downtown, led the way, with enough Badgers on staff to field a full eleven-man lineup. Quarterback John Gallagher worked there as a freshman in the 1941–42 school year. "My first job there was working in the tank, boiling hot water and rinsing off the spoons and the dishes," Gallagher says. "We had spaghetti coming out of our ears. That was a popular meal there. We could get a cheese sandwich for twenty-five cents and a bottle of beer for fifteen."

(Eventually, after moving up to a better position as a bartender at The Pub on State Street following the '42 season, one night Gallagher heard a soldier call him a draft-dodger. Especially after a few beers, some soldiers posted to Madison considered able-bodied college men to be soft, pampered, and privileged. "He was from Truax Field," Gallagher says. "I pulled him out half over the bar and said, 'You son of a bitch!' I just picked him up and shook him and said, 'I should take you outside and beat the shit out of you.' I put him back down and told him to get the hell out of there. He was a smartass and had been drinking. We were serving nickel beers, and there was a steady stream.")

Mark Hoskins joined the crew at Toby and Moon's as a senior. His parents said it wasn't necessary, but Hoskins had seen so many of his teammates, including Dave Schreiner, working that he decided to work and pay for his own meals.

Tackle George Hekkers worked at the Lawrence Café for his meals. He pre-washed dishes, then loaded them into the revolutionary China Clipper dishwashing machine. Many restaurateurs believed the machine was a needless extravagance that wouldn't last and preferred to stick with human dishwashers.

Halfback Jim McFadzean got two of the prime assignments—counting cars downtown and working at Toby and Moon's—and also worked as a ticket-taker at basketball and boxing matches.

"Bud Seelinger and I worked together," McFadzean says. "I took the tickets, and instead of tearing them in half, I kept the whole tickets, and then Bud would come in. I gave them to him, and he would go out in the parking lot and say, 'Who needs tickets?' We had a sellout every night. At halftime, he and I would go up into the john in the field house, and it would be a dollar for you and a dollar for me. Some nights, we'd get tipped off—'The police are going to be out there tonight, so be careful'—and then Bud wouldn't be so open about it."

The other popular way to collect extra money was to sell the complimentary tickets given to team members. The stars usually had eager buyers; the rest of the players had to cultivate their market. "I was getting six tickets," McFadzean says. "They gave 'em to us, and if somebody wanted to buy them, we could sell 'em. For my Notre Dame tickets, I sold them to one of the sophomore's dads, and I think I got something like twelve dollars a ticket. And that was a lot of money in those days."

Elroy Hirsch, Fred Negus, Paul Hirsbrunner, and Dick Thornally had their all-the-milk-you-can-drink jobs in the dairy. And many of the Badgers worked in their fraternity or dormitory dining halls, but the most curious assignment was Schreiner's continuing work as a waiter in Ann Emery Hall. In a preseason profile box in the *State Journal,* the writer noted that Schreiner "is the object of all eyes each time he carts in a tray."

Yes, an All-American end was taking orders—and not from his coach.

NINE

Camp Grant

Washington, Sept. 16 (AP)—Japan's expected grand-scale drive to recapture the Solomon Islands and again point a dagger at the Australian lifeline appeared developing with do-or-die fury Wednesday.

Battle-tried American forces were fighting back savagely and thus far successfully. The navy reported Tuesday night that "heavy fighting" had been in progress by land, sea and air since Saturday night and that while details were lacking, reports received to date indicate that the Marines are maintaining their positions.

★ ★ ★

As the 1942 fall term began, reminders of the war—raging in Europe as well as on Guadalcanal and other Pacific hotspots—were everywhere in Madison. The university's enrollment was expected to drop from 11,000 to about 8,500, but 1,200 Navy men would be on campus for classes in a hastily organized communications school. Also, 470 WAVES (Women Accepted for Volunteer Emergency Service) would be arriving in early October to be trained as radio operators. The Navy commandeered four dormitories plus the Madison YMCA. Air Forces personnel were in technical school at Truax Field. Housing for students, both on and off campus, was at a premium.

On Thursday, September 17, four days before classes started, the *Daily Cardinal*, the university's student newspaper, put out a huge special edition, and one of the lead items was a message to the students from UW president Clarence Dykstra:

This week you become a member of a university community, which is working overtime for Uncle Sam. You soon will rub elbows with men and with women in Army and Navy uniforms who are liv-

ing and studying on this campus during a period of intense train-
ing. All about you are evidences of training for national service.
We have no time on our campus for those who will not take
our national challenge seriously. You are here to get ready to serve
the nation in the place to which you will be called.

The university dropped many "trivial" classes from its curriculum and
added courses in mathematics and sciences. But there were attempts to
maintain a semblance of the student routine, with a stag night dance in
the Memorial Union, billiards tournaments, cut-rate bowling, and sing-
alongs. The carillon atop Bascom Hall played daily at 1 p.m. for twenty
minutes, and the concerts were a prime meeting spot.

A clothing store ad in the *Cardinal* showed "college men" in suits
and ties and announced: "Students may buy on credit with permission
of their parents." Hart, Shaffner, and Marx suits went for $43.50, and shoe
stores plugged ROTC shoes at $3.50 a pair.

The movies showing in Madison included *The Battle of Midway,*
amazingly out only three and a half months after the Naval fight in the
Pacific; *Fantasia; Call Out the Marines; Gentlemen of West Point;* and
Abbott and Costello in *Pardon My Sarong.*

Noted actor Alfred Lunt was in Madison, along with his wife, actress
Lynn Fontanne, rehearsing the play *The Pirate* before a pre-Broadway run
at the University Theater in the Memorial Union. The famed couple had
a home in Genesee Depot, between Madison and Milwaukee. In an interview with the student paper, Lunt said he selected the lighthearted play
as his latest project "simply to divert people. You see, for two years, we
played *There Shall Be No Night,* trying to arouse the people. Now that
job is done. Our present job is to take people's minds away from the terrible things that are happening."

Lunt added, "Another reason for producing *The Pirate* is that we
wanted to do a play with Negroes. They are wonderful people to work
with, and we feel it is a privilege to perform on the same stage with them.
Where can you get such singing, such musicians? . . . You'll notice that
in our play Negroes aren't given the roles of underlings or villains."

Lunt, Fontanne, and Jack Smart, another leading man from the play,
attended a Badgers' practice with university president Dykstra during the
week of the opening game. The *State Journal's* Henry J. McCormick wryly
reported that the three thespians "made a brief appearance with no cur-
tain calls. No, that's wrong, for the well-upholstered Jack Smart stayed
around until the end. He was the chief attraction for the players with

his luxuriant hair and moustache. He drew envious looks from Stuhldreher and backfield coach Guy Sundt, both of whom are getting somewhat thin on top."

The Badgers lineup crystallized. Ken Currier beat out George Makris at guard, Bob Baumann stayed ahead of his pal Dick Thornally at one tackle position, and Ashley Anderson staved off sophomore Jack Wink at quarterback. But on the same day Lunt's entourage watched practice, Bob Rennebohm, who was winning the race for the first-team end position opposite Schreiner, suffered a severe ankle injury in a tackling drill. That again opened up the starting job for Bob Hanzlik.

Pat Harder's health was also a major concern. His leg and ankle weren't getting better, and although he refused to use the crutches beyond the day he suffered the injuries, he couldn't get back on the practice field. He did some jogging the week of the opener but wasn't able to get back into the heavy practice work.

In the tradition of Knute Rockne, Stuhldreher worked the press, and Henry J. McCormick was a virtual mouthpiece for him. So, McCormick's optimistic game-week assessment of the upcoming Badgers' season was significant: "I think that coach Harry Stuhldreher will frankly admit that the team he now has conceivably could be a great outfit," McCormick wrote.

Stuhldreher appointed a single captain for each game, and the weekly announcement was treated as a headline-worthy disclosure. For the opener against Camp Grant, he chose senior tackle Paul "Indian" Hirsbrunner.

Ads in every publication pushed war bonds and stamps. One stated, "Our boys can take the war to the enemy, if we back them up with ships and tanks and guns. But that takes money." The bonds cost $18.75 and up, and they matured by one-third over a ten-year period. War stamps were ten, twenty-five, and fifty cents.

The stag dances, at which most of the females were local high school students, were under close scrutiny because of controversy the previous spring. Roundy Coughlin, of all people, had railed against the shameful way couples were acting on the lake road and the Union Terrace and demanded that a 9:30 p.m. curfew go into effect for seventeen-year-olds. Roundy didn't report how he knew of this shameful conduct.

* * *

The war affected the Badgers' nonleague scheduling. Two '42 opponents, Camp Grant in the opener and the Great Lakes Naval Training Station in the fifth game, were military teams based in the Chicago area. Most players on those rosters already had played full college careers, and some were National Football League veterans.

Founded during World War I, Camp Grant served as an infantry training site and then was a National Guard center between the wars. The Army took it over again in the spring of 1941, and the camp's reactivated football team had played two games before meeting the Badgers—losing 32–6 to the Chicago Bears and beating a Milwaukee semipro team. The starting lineup included end Sam Goldman of the Washington Redskins and back Reino Nori of the Chicago Bears.

On Saturday, September 19, despite the optimism about the Badgers' season, only about 15,000 fans showed up at the Badgers' Camp Randall Stadium for the opener. Disappointed university officials feared the war would affect attendance all season. The stadium is situated on the west side of campus, on land that had been a Civil War training camp nearly eighty years earlier. Both the training camp and the horseshoe-shaped stadium, built in 1917, were named after Alexander Randall, the state's first Civil War governor. The '42 season came in Camp Randall's twenty-fifth anniversary year, and Badgers' fans entering the stadium that Saturday hoped they were getting in early on a season worthy of celebrating.

The opener was inconclusive. Some fans left grumbling that if the boys couldn't beat those out-of-football-shape soldiers worse than that, it was going to be a long season, and maybe Harry should stop living off his Four Horsemen glory and move on. Others said, well, at least the Badgers won, the sophomores looked promising, and, don't forget, the injured Pat Harder wasn't able to do anything except kick. And a few left the stadium so plastered after enthusiastically downing the contents of bottles and flasks—the same kind of bottles and flasks the freshman Badgers always found, emptied, when they performed the traditional duty of cleaning out the stadium on Sundays to earn more spending money—they couldn't even have told anyone the score.

The score was only 7–0.

The Badgers dominated Camp Grant but couldn't do much on the scoreboard. Wearing blue uniforms with white shoulder patches and dark stripes that made them look a bit like football-playing armadillos, the soldiers managed just six first downs and 130 yards of total offense. Sophomore center Fred Negus, playing linebacker on defense, was a revelation for the Badgers, hitting a soldier so hard on one play that the opponent's helmet went flying.

The Badgers' attack was unimpressive, except for Elroy Hirsch. Though Bud Seelinger got the start at left halfback, Hirsch came in to gain

88 yards on nine carries and had runs of 25 and 50 yards. Mark Hoskins plugged away with 37 yards in 13 carries. Harder's replacement, Bob Ray, scored the Badgers' only touchdown, on a 12-yard run on the first play of the fourth quarter. The play came after end Bob Hanzlik, ensconced as the starter with Rennebohm out, recovered a Camp Grant fumble.

Wisconsin's passers—quarterbacks Ashley Anderson and Jack Wink, plus halfbacks Seelinger, Hirsch, and Regan—combined for only three completions in 13 attempts. In fact, with five interceptions, Camp Grant defenders caught more Wisconsin passes than did the Badgers. The only completions came from Anderson to Hoskins for 7 yards, plus two strikes from Jack Wink—to Dave Schreiner for 28 yards and to Hanzlik for 18.

Anderson made a big defensive play, intercepting a pass and returning it 78 yards to the Camp Grant 2-yard line. He fumbled there when hit by end Sam Goldman, and Camp Grant recovered. "He was cutting in front of me," Anderson says. "I swung inside of him and he threw one arm back. He pulled my arm out and the ball fell out."

The play gave Anderson his first glimpse of Hirsch's impish sense of humor. Later, in the dressing room, Hirsch led his teammates in a musical tribute to Anderson's run, singing:

"Ashley, Ashley, we love you,
"Fumble, fumble on the 2."

Also in the dressing room afterward, with a cigarette in hand, Stuhldreher declared to the scribes: "Now that it's over, I can say it was a fine game for us. . . . We have spent a great deal of time trying to bolster our defense, and I think it has paid off."

Notre Dame coach Frank Leahy was at Camp Randall that day, scouting in advance of the September 26 Irish-Badger showdown in Madison.

"Wisconsin was looking one week ahead and is actually about ten times better than they looked against Camp Grant," Leahy was quoted in the *State Journal.* He smiled and calculatingly added, "I honestly expect Notre Dame to lose here next week. Stuhldreher did a swell job of holding Wisconsin back and will shoot the works next week. I don't believe we'll be ready by then."

In the *State Journal* the next morning, Henry J. McCormick emphasized the Badgers' improved showing on defense. In contrast, Oliver Kuechele of the *Milwaukee Journal* grumbled, "Wisconsin's high hopes this football season were pretty well deflated here Saturday afternoon. The team which many have picked as the darkhorse in the Big Ten barely staggered home in front against a heavy but punchless Camp Grant eleven."

Roundy Coughlin was excited about the two sophomore starting linemen, guard Ken "Roughie" Currier and center Fred Negus. (Sophomore guard Jerry "Toughie" Frei didn't get in the game, and it turned out that he would sit out four of the Badgers' ten games that season.)

"I thought the play of Kenneth Currier a sophomore guard from Rice Lake, Wisconsin, was feature of the game," Roundy wrote (and again, nobody edited). "His play was brilliant. . . . Currier is fast folks he moves around from that guard position like guard should. Is 5:10 tall and goes 190 just ideal for a guard. And this new sophomore center Fred Negus from Ohio, was a standout he played 58 minutes about of the game and was all over the park and looked good on pass defense also."

Roundy also "liked the work of Jack Wink at quarterback folks. He acted fine back there is pretty good passer and is hard tackler and can run with that ball when intercepts any passes. This Wink is going to be all right."

The other sports coverage that Sunday reported that with a little over a week left in the National League season, the first-place St. Louis Cardinals had a two-and-a-half-game lead over the Brooklyn Dodgers. Boston's Ted Williams was going to come up short in his bid to hit .400 for the second straight year, but his .356 average still led the major leagues. His 34 home runs and 134 runs-batted-in weren't bad, either.

TEN

Notre Dame

Moscow, Sept. 21 (AP)—Thwarted in their efforts to take Stalingrad by storm, the Germans began a mighty bombardment with heavy long-range guns that shook the city from end to end Monday, but still the Soviet defenders held and even gained ground at some points in hand-to-hand street fighting, the Russians announced.

★ ★ ★

When Knute Rockne, the former Notre Dame star, was player-coach of professional football's showcase team, the Massillon Tigers, he often escorted a group of local kids through the gate at the stadium on game day.

"They're with me," Rockne always said.

One of the Massillon kids was young Harry Stuhldreher.

In his book *Knute Rockne, Man Builder* (also known as *Knute Rockne, All-American*), Stuhldreher said the great coach "was never too busy to stop to talk to us and give out some pointers on football."

A few years later, Stuhldreher went to Notre Dame to play for Rockne. By 1924, Stuhldreher was Rockne's senior quarterback. The Fighting Irish not only beat Army and inspired Grantland Rice's Four Horsemen salute but also went undefeated, knocking off Stanford 27–10 in the Rose Bowl, and becoming the undisputed national champions. (After that Rose Bowl, Notre Dame officials decided bowl games excessively extended the season and decreed the Irish wouldn't participate in postseason football. The bowl ban lasted forty-five years.) In his book, Stuhldreher didn't even mention the backfield posing on horses for the famous Four Horsemen picture after the Army game, but he did praise the other starters. "I would like to say here and now that the Seven Mules did not get their share of the glory," he declared.

Stuhldreher used Rockne's system at Villanova before moving to Madison. And because Fighting Irish coach Frank Leahy installed the innovative T formation for the '42 season, in some ways the Badgers were more traditional Notre Dame than Notre Dame was as the September 26 game in Camp Randall Stadium loomed.

On Monday, September 21, the day the fall term began, Stuhldreher named Dave Schreiner that week's game captain. With the considerable respect due Paul Hirsbrunner, the tackle who served as captain for the Camp Grant opener, Stuhldreher's waiting until the second week to have the Badgers' All-American end serve as captain was an indication of his fixation with beating his alma mater. "Harry made it a big deal," quarterback John Gallagher says. "He'd blow 'em way up, they were the greatest in the world."

The teams had met only once before in Stuhldreher's tenure, when the Irish won 27–0 in 1936.

★ ★ ★

The same day he was named captain for the upcoming big game, Schreiner wrote a letter to Oz Callan, the head of the Lancaster draft board. He wasn't going to try to hide his switch from pre-med.

> Dear Mr. Callan,
>
> The draft board gave me a 2A classification to be deferred until March 1, 1943. I don't know why they did this unless it was that last year I was a pre-medical student. However, I have been forced to switch my course to economics and would graduate in that this year. This change might make a difference in the deferment and if it does I wish I could be notified immediately. I am planning on entering a reserve soon that will permit me to finish school. I did think, though, that it was only fair that I let you know of my change in courses.

Schreiner also had begged his father not to intervene.

His schedule that semester reflected his change in major. He was taking three economics courses, one history class, and a geography course.

No more medical school.

He was also weighing his military options. Because of his 2A status, he hadn't seen the need to join a reserve branch to start a process of being steered away from the Army. He had all but given up on becoming a pilot because of his color blindness. He was starting to think about the Marines. Unless he was willing to accept being drafted into the Army, he needed to act soon.

★ ★ ★

On Tuesday, the *Daily Cardinal's* "Scene on Campus" column giddily disclosed that Pat Harder, with teammates along for the ride, ran his Model A onto some grass when trying to get a better look at some New Girls on Campus.

Later in the week, the same paper's "Cardinal Troubleshooter" column reported that the campus joke was that the phone number for the Delta Gamma sorority should be "SEX-SEX-1."

During the first week of classes, the *Daily Cardinal* did a story on Ruth Lincoln, a student in the engineering school. The sixteen-year-old freshman was the only woman among 635 enrolled, and the paper noted that, at 5-foot-3 with green eyes and taffy hair, she could pass for a home economics student. "If you like something and you think you're good at it, you ought to make out pretty well," she told the *Cardinal*.

The student paper came back with a more serious story the next day. Jack Geiger's report began with, "A *Daily Cardinal* investigation, searching for the truth behind the stories of Negro, Chinese and Jewish students who cannot find rooms, shows that: Almost 95 percent of the landladies in approved men's rooming houses will not lease rooms to these students because of their race or their religion."

In the same issue, the *Daily Cardinal* editorialized on the matter, addressing the landlords and property managers:

> *The Negro, the Jew, and the Asiatic is being drafted into the Army like everyone else. On many fronts he is already fighting the war. Your war. The war that is being fought to preserve just those liberties and privileges that you have been depriving him of during the past weeks. These men and women wish to come here and train themselves to take the lead in fighting the war and rebuilding the world afterward. It is a sacred right that everyone in America legally possesses. Yet you are refusing him a place to sleep and study.*

The day the story hit the street, Jack Geiger discussed the issue with Wisconsin students and wrote a follow-up story for Thursday's edition. He reported that "more than 90 percent of students contacted in an investigation by the *Daily Cardinal* yesterday see nothing objectionable in living in houses with Negro, Asian or Jewish students."

An anonymous resident at 302 Huntington Court was an exception. "If there were any Negro or Chinese students here we would all move out," the resident told Geiger. "We might tolerate a Jewish student, but we don't believe in carrying things too far. They have their place and we have ours."

Also in the story, a resident at 116 North Orchard said, "I'm charitable but I can't see why the house should have colored people. If one comes in they'll all come in, and then the place will be overrun."

The 1942 Badgers football team had no black players. Other Big Ten schools had integrated their programs on a limited basis, so the Badgers were behind the times in football. (The color line still held fast in conference basketball because of winked understandings.) Also, Wisconsin had black athletes—baseball players Julian Ware and Adelbert Matthews—as far back as 1900, and the track and field and cross-country teams had also been integrated. In fact, in 1939, the campus rallied to support star hurdler Ed Smith when the University of Missouri attempted to ban him from a triangular meet against the Tigers and Notre Dame at Columbia. Faculty and student groups, including fraternities and sororities, denounced the Jim Crow policies, and the *Daily Cardinal* declared that if the UW "allows the 'Southern gentlemen' of Missouri to dictate race discrimination, it will be violating one of its sacred concepts and encouraging racial prejudice."

Yet three years after that principled stand, the UW still didn't have an integrated football team. That had to be laid at the office door of athletic director and football coach Harry Stuhldreher. His defense was that the Badgers did only limited recruiting, under the norms of the time, but Stuhldreher could have joined other Big Ten coaches in integration if he had wanted to do so. So, as the Badgers prepared to meet Stuhldreher's alma mater—which didn't have any black players, either—they remained an all-white program. This wasn't unusual in the national picture, but it was out of character for one of the nation's most progressive public universities. (It wasn't until 1946 that Cal Vernon and Bob Teague became Wisconsin's first black football players.)

In the middle of the first week of classes, Sunny Brown's Orchestra played at a mixer dance at Edwards Park. Admission was thirty cents for women and forty cents for men. The dance was designed to bring together students and the military personnel studying at Truax Field and on campus. The premiere of *Wake Island* at the Capitol Theater was a war bond promotion, with seats on the main floor going for war bond purchases of at least one hundred dollars. The ad for the movie declared it would "put a machine gun in your hand and rage in your heart!"

Preparing to face dynamic quarterback Angelo Bertelli, the Badgers worked against the freshmen players running the T formation. As a halfback in the Box in 1941, Bertelli completed 70 passes in 123 attempts for 1,027 yards. Intriguingly, the Irish's first game since abandoning the Box would come against a team coached by the Four Horsemen quarterback who helped make the offense legendary.

* * *

Moscow, Sept. 24 (AP)—Wendell L. Willkie said Thursday he would take back to Washington from Soviet Russia a story of grow-ing disappointment and dissatisfaction over the failure of the United States and Britain to establish a second front.

"I feel it and you must," said Willkie.

He presented Josef Stalin a large, thick and square envelope containing a personal message from President Roosevelt at a con-ference with the Soviet premier in the Kremlin Wednesday night.

* * *

At the pep rally on the lower campus on Friday night, Roundy Cough-lin was the biggest cheerleader. "Ladies and gentlemen and freshman co-eds who ain't married!" the newspaper columnist hollered. "We'll show the Irish all the damn shamrocks and four-leaf clovers flying around they want." NBC's Bill Stern, the nation's top radio sportscaster, was in town for the national NBC broadcast. He told the fans, "If you win, I'll be back." Stuhldreher said the Badgers were "happy, mighty happy to be in this spot across the scrimmage line from the Fighting Irish, and we're going to give them a fit."

The Badgers stayed at the Maple Bluff Country Club, as they always did on the eve of home games. The Irish traveled to Chicago on Friday and were scheduled to take a train to Madison the next morning and ar-rive all of ninety minutes before the scheduled 2:00 p.m. kickoff.

One Irish star cut it closer than that.

* * *

Washington, Sept. 25 (AP)—Lieut. Gen. Jonathan M. Wainwright and an estimated 6,000 other Americans of Bataan and Corregi-dor were reported Friday to be war captives of the Japanese in a prison camp at Tarlac, north of Manila, in the Philippines.

General Wainwright, commander of the Philippine forces af-ter Gen. Douglas MacArthur was ordered to Australia, was taken

*with the fall of Corregidor on May 6. His fate and that of more than
60,000 others last reported on Bataan and Corregidor has since
been in doubt.*

* * *

On the train ride to Madison on the morning of Saturday, September 26, Frank Leahy was aghast. No, he declared, the managers must be wrong. Bertelli had to be somewhere on the train! Surely he was just wandering around, stretching his legs. That must be it! For heaven's sake, the Notre Dame star couldn't have missed the train, could he?

He had.

Some of Bertelli's teammates told Leahy they saw him walking away from the hotel that morning, but they didn't know where he was. Leahy jumped off the train at Madison and ran to the telegraph office, quickly sending a wire back to the Chicago hotel. Then, when the Irish arrived at Camp Randall at 12:30, Leahy used an athletic department telephone, running up long-distance bills, calling everywhere he could think of—the hotel, the train stations, the police. Finally, it was time to take the field to loosen up. No Bertelli. The Irish went through the short warmup period without him, and Leahy got his substitute quarterback ready to step in.

Bertelli ran out of the visiting dressing room five minutes before kick-off. Sorry, coach, he said, but he had gotten lost in Union Station, and he barely caught another train to Madison and was lucky to make it. Leahy had neither the time nor the inclination scrutinize the story. He just sent Bertelli out on the field.

At midfield, Captains Dave Schreiner of the Badgers and George Murphy of the Fighting Irish greeted each other, shook hands, and said good luck.

They would meet again a few years later, in a very different environment.

* * *

*Washington, Sept. 26 (AP)—Rubber czar William F. Jeffers went the
limit Saturday and ordered nationwide gas rationing to save tires.*
*   "This is a game," he said, "in which we can all win, or all lose."
Jeffers, the Union Pacific railroad president, appealed to drivers
to slow down to the thirty-five-mile-an-hour limit recommended
last week by the committee headed by Bernard M. Baruch, which
went deeply into the whole rubber question.*

* * *

Late in the first quarter, with the game still scoreless, Bertelli threw a pass to Bob Livingstone, who scampered down the sideline for an apparent Irish touchdown.

But wait! The linesman signaled that the Irish end had stepped out of bounds at the Badger 35. The Irish couldn't move, and the game was still scoreless at the half.

Harder returned a Bertelli punt to the Irish 35, giving the Badgers good field position for their first second-half possession. On the next play, Hirsch took the snap, romped around right end, faked a cut inside, played off a block from Harder, and went down the sideline for a touchdown, hurdling a potential tackler and barely beating Bertelli to the goal line. Harder's extra point made it 7–0 with 12:23 left in the third quarter.

Halfback Erv Kissling had a great vantage point from the sideline. "I can remember Elroy jumping over the guy, hurdled right over him," Kissling says. "It actually was illegal according to the rules, but they allowed it."

Bob Ray's interception of a pass that nicked George Murphy's fingers ended the ensuing Irish drive, but the Badgers punted and Notre Dame came right back for the tying touchdown. Bertelli hit passes of 20 and 17 yards to Livingstone in the drive, and Jim Mello scored the touchdown from 2 yards out. Bertelli's kick evened the score.

The rest of the game reverted to offensive frustration. In the final seconds, Stuhldreher sent in sophomore Jim Regan, who had wanted to attend Notre Dame but didn't want to wait a year, to replace a winded Hirsch.

"I wanted so bad to get in to show the coach of Notre Dame he made a mistake," Regan says. With the Badgers on their own 40 in the final minute, Regan got a chance to carry the ball.

"Harry Stuhldreher sent in 'A-41', the left half off tackle," Regan says. "I cut off tackle and I thought I was going to break clear. 'Nobody is around me!' I thought, 'Boy, I'm going to beat Notre Dame! There you are, coach!'"

Irish star Creighton Miller hauled him down for a 4-yard gain.

The final play was a Mark Hoskins run around right end that got the Badgers to the Irish 46.

Statistically the Irish dominated, outgaining the Badgers 292 yards to 152. Wisconsin had only seven first downs to the Irish's 14, but six turnovers killed the Irish hopes.

Wisconsin used only sixteen men: Dave Schreiner, Bob Hanzlik, Paul Hirsbrunner, Ken Currier, Fred Negus, and Mark Hoskins played every second. Schreiner shut down the flank again and caught one pass, a 14-yarder from Hoskins.

Hanzlik, the other end, recalls "looking at the clock and thinking, 'How long is this son of a bitch going to keep going?'"

Negus was so exhausted, he could barely move. "When the game was over, I had cramps in both legs, and Bob Rennebohm was trying to help me up the steps to the dressing room," Negus says.

Bertelli played as if he had left his game on the wrong train, completing four of thirteen passes for only 66 yards. Immediately, second-guessers wondered if Leahy had made a grievous error, tampering with success by changing offenses after the undefeated 1941 season.

In his game story, the *State Journal*'s Henry J. McCormick wrote, "Fighting as gallant a battle against odds as any Wisconsin eleven you've ever seen, the Badgers turned in what amounted to a smashing upset."

Because McCormick was leaving the next day for Norfolk and naval duty, Stuhldreher called for quiet and introduced the sportswriter to the Badgers. McCormick was carrying his portable typewriter case, probably because he was headed back to his office to do the actual writing. He put down his typewriter and told the Badgers congratulations and goodbye.

The Badgers responded with a cheer: "*Sissss, boooooom, baaaaaah. McCormick!*"

Then the Badgers had another visitor—Frank Leahy. He shook hands with his fellow Rockne disciple, Stuhldreher, then asked to be introduced to Schreiner and congratulated the Badgers end.

"Wisconsin played a grand game and well deserved its tie," Leahy told reporters during the visit. "I don't believe we'll meet a better opponent than Wisconsin." Then Leahy joined the Irish for their hurried trip to the train station and the ride back to Chicago.

Bertelli stuck with the rest of the group this time.

The game confirmed the impending stardom for the sophomores in the Badgers lineup—Hirsch, Wink, Negus, and Currier. Hirsch gained 87 yards on only 11 carries and had the one touchdown. "I've never been more thrilled in my life than scoring that touchdown," he was quoted as saying. "What a thrill that was! Gosh, what a thrill!"

The *Capital Times* reported that Negus, usually playing middle linebacker in a 6-3-2 alignment, "was a demon in backing up the line." And the same story said that Wink, the sophomore quarterback, "did grand work."

The result was treated as worthy of toasts and celebration on State Street. At the very least, the Badgers showed themselves to be legitimate Big Ten contenders, before even playing a conference game.

ELEVEN

Marquette

On Sunday, October 27, the *State Journal* ran a guest editorial from Harry Stuhldreher. It's tempting to assume that it came from a publicity department writer, but the tone was more Harry than the typical flowery dispatches from the press agents.

Stuhldreher wrote:

> *We are at war. Our boys are well aware of this. Many of them are in the officers' reserve of the various armed forces. . . . When they join the armed forces in the near future, they will be better able to contribute, will add a little more from their standpoint to that eventual, important victory.*
>
> *There are few relaxing periods left, and of these few, we feel that an athletic contest is one to which all of you may come for a couple hours in the fresh air on a Saturday afternoon and really let yourselves go, forget about your worries for just a little while and get a little of that balance that is so essential.*

Mainly because travel was discouraged, the Notre Dame game had drawn only 32,000 at Camp Randall Stadium. The Dairyland showdown between the Badgers and Marquette, whose fans were only a short drive away, was expected to do better at the gate. The Badgers were out for revenge for the embarrassing 28–7 loss to the Milwaukee Catholic school the previous year.

That loss was so embarrassing, in fact, the usually straight-arrow Mark Hoskins—who hadn't had a very good game—felt compelled to drown his sorrows. He went to a tavern off the State Street drag. He had two, maybe three beers. Assistant coach Frank Jordan cornered him the next Monday and said an offended fan had reported Hoskins to the coaching staff. The coach emphasized that the boys were in a fishbowl, especially if they ventured away from the campus area and were among Madison townspeople. Hoskins vowed never to be seen drinking in public again.

He was in the minority. In fact, some of the Badgers were in the Log Cabin tavern on State Street to witness an event reported by Bob Zigman in the student paper's "Cardinal Troubleshooter" column during the Marquette game week. "Adrian Bates showed the assembled crowd she knew all the words to the 'Strip Polka,' plus gestures," Zigman wrote. The players thought it looked better than the Notre Dame shift. And they were often in on the action on State Street, finding the time among their schedules of practice and games, plus—in most cases—their jobs.

"State Street was the place," says quarterback John Gallagher. "The popular place was the Brathaus, if you could get in there. They had a court-yard in the back, and the crowd would be back there drinking and singing 'On Wisconsin' or 'If You Want to Be a Badger, Come Along with Me.' Honest to God, the other popular place, the Log Cabin, wasn't any bigger than this room," he adds, gesturing around his den. "But did they sell the beer."

★ ★ ★

On Sunday, September 27, many of the Badgers listened to the local radio broadcast of the Chicago Bears' 44–28 romp over the Green Bay Packers in the season opener at Lambeau Field. Chicago coach George Halas knew his days were numbered on the sideline, though. The wheels were in motion for him to reenter the Navy as a commander by midseason.

On Tuesday night, fans of the *Fibber McGee and Molly* radio show crowded around their sets to catch the long-awaited debut of the show's eighth season on Madison's WIBA. The stars, Jim and Marian Jordan, had taken three months off from spinning the adventures of residents of Wistful Vista.

Billed as "famous"—as all orchestras were billed—the Ted Lewis Orchestra was doing four of its "Rhythm Rhapsody Review" stage shows a day at the Orpheum in downtown Madison. The next attraction at the Orpheum was *The Talk of the Town,* starring Cary Grant, Jean Arthur, and Ronald Coleman. Nearby at the Parkway, the timely *Pied Piper,* based on the Nevil Shute novel about an Englishman smuggling children out of occupied France, began its run.

The *Daily Cardinal* offered an intriguing mix of sophomoric humor, salacious gossip, and ahead-of-its-time hard journalism. Its series on housing discrimination was drawing responses. Mayor James R. Law declared in a follow-up story in the student paper that "[we] don't like that sort of thing in our community. We have a broad-minded city here that won't tolerate it. The people of Madison aren't generally prejudiced. Even now they're working to provide recreational facilities for the colored troops and workers that are coming to town."

The Yankees and Cardinals prepared to open the World Series on Wednesday at Sportsman's Park in St. Louis. Billy Southworth's Cards trailed Brooklyn by 10 games on August 5 before going 43–8 down the stretch to win the National League pennant by two games. Centerfielder Enos Slaughter was the catalyst, hitting .318, with 13 home runs and 98 runs-batted-in. Next to him in the Redbird outfield, twenty-one-year-old Stan Musial, checked in at .315, with 10 homers and 72 RBIs. The Yankees got another big season from Joe DiMaggio, who hit .305 with 21 homers, and the largely familiar lineup—also including catcher Bill Dickey, second baseman Joe Gordon, shortstop Phil Rizzuto, and outfielders Tommy Henrich and Charlie Keller—could be recited by millions of American kids.

That week thirty-three Madison men enlisted in the Marines, posing for a newspaper photo before heading to Milwaukee. The newspapers touted them as the "Madison Avengers of Bataan."

★ ★ ★

General MacArthur's Headquarters, Australia, Sept. 30 (AP)— Allied mountain troops, sifting through the difficult jungle and mountain country of the Owen Stanley range, have captured the first objective of the New Guinea offensive, sent the Japanese into a hurried northward retreat and seized quantities of abandoned Japanese equipment, a communique said Wednesday.

★ ★ ★

Marquette was coming off a 14–0 victory over Kansas.

The Badgers got help when senior end Pat Lyons reported for practice, saying he had worked out class conflicts to give him enough time to play football. That gave the Badgers depth at end, where Dave Schreiner and Bob Hanzlik had been ironmen in the first two games. Plus, Stuhldreher kept telling the scribes that he expected sophomore end Bob Rennebohm to be over that "minor" ankle problem any day now. That was a public challenge to Rennebohm, who still was limping severely, and typical of the Stuhldreher outlook on injuries. Looking back, Rennebohm knows he had torn ligaments, not a sprain, but the coach wouldn't stand for that mild diagnosis.

"His saying was, 'Shake it off, shake it off,'" Rennebohm says. "Pat Harder also had a bad ankle, and we'd have to go to the hospital and hold our legs in a tub of melted paraffin for a half hour. You could just barely stand it, but it would build up coats of paraffin on your ankle. It was quite uncomfortable, but supposedly it was the latest thing. It didn't do much for me, but it fixed Harder up. His was just a normal sprain."

Stuhldreher named Mark Hoskins the captain for the Marquette game, and to the southwest of Madison the *Grant County Independent* took note: "It isn't every day a town the size of Lancaster is represented on a state university football team by two boys from the same town, to say nothing of being honored as acting captains. Our hats off to Had and Dave, two fine young men, who have carried the name of Lancaster into every part of the state and nation."

Some of the students had a betting interest in the upcoming game. Football pools were the rage on campus, but mathematical purists railed against them because the pools—actually, multiple-game parlay cards— didn't pay true odds. Most students bet a dollar, and winners were paid five dollars for going three-for-three and ten dollars for hitting a four-game ticket. Stuhldreher was so impressed with a *Daily Cardinal* column portraying anyone who entered the pool as mentally deficient that he wrote a letter to the editor, lauding the exposure of "the racket."

On Friday, Dr. Rheinhold Schairer, a German-born professor at New York University, lectured at the Bascom Hall theater about German youth under Hitler. The *Daily Cardinal* took notes. "When Hitler is defeated on the battlefields and in the air," Schairer declared, "there will come an awakening of the German youth, and this reawakening will come with the greatest task education will ever have."

The Friday night pep rally, with two thousand in attendance, was almost as spirited as the one before the Notre Dame game. Hoskins, who still wasn't comfortable speaking in front of a crowd, managed to say the Badgers would "even the score for last year's defeat."

★　★　★

Moscow, Oct. 2 (AP)—Stalingrad's indomitable will to resist was reported Friday to be producing fresh counterattacks both inside and outside the battered city and the latest German power drive was said to have been limited to 200 or 300 yards in the northern suburbs. Out of the mad maelstrom, on this thirty-ninth day of the siege, there emerged the dominant fact that the Germans, though straining with full reserve power, still were denied even the localized decision sorely needed to salvage their prestige.

★　★　★

Hoskins was right. The Badgers got revenge. On Saturday, October

3, in front of 35,000 at Camp Randall, the Badgers easily beat Marquette 35–7 and improved to 2–0–1 for the season.

It was Dave Schreiner's day. The Badgers scored 28 points in the second quarter, and the star end caught three touchdown passes—two from Jack Wink, for 70 and 22 yards, respectively, and a 13-yarder from Pat Harder. The fourth TD in the period came on Elroy Hirsch's spectacular 20-yard run, when he shrugged off two tackles and carried a Marquette defender across the goal line.

Hirsch threw a 41-yard touchdown pass to Bob Hanzlik in the third quarter for the last touchdown.

"Elroy and I had gone to summer school and rehearsed a play called 44-1," Hanzlik recalls. "It was a down and out, nothing tricky about it. We must have practiced that thing two hundred times. Harry came out and watched a couple of our practices.

"So we got that game with Marquette in Madison, and they called that 44-1, and I went down and made a pretty good move and made a great catch. It was the last time they threw me the ball that year."

Marquette star John Strzykalski ran for 66 yards on 15 carries for the Hilltoppers and threw for 98 yards. The other halfback, Texan Wayne "Rusty" Johnston, managed only 6 yards on five rushes. Schreiner, who would encounter Johnston in another game two years later, brought him down a couple of times.

The big lead enabled Stuhldreher to give reserves their first significant playing time of the season. Among the players who made their first varsity appearances of the year were quarterback Bobby Diercks, halfback Jim McFadzean, halfback Don Pfotenhauer, tackles George Hekkers and Dave Donnellan, guard Jerry Frei, end Hank Olshanski, and fullback Earl Maves.

"They really exploded fast to get those markers, and to me that was most pleasing," Stuhldreher was quoted as saying in the *State Journal*. (Stuhldreher probably never used the word *markers* in his life, unless he was talking about poker debts.) "I was also pleased to be able to play the rest of the fellows on the squad. With game experience under their belt, the reserves will help a lot."

In the dressing room, according to the morning papers, Schreiner teased his Lancaster buddy, Hoskins. "Guess I should have been a halfback, huh, Mark?" asked Schreiner.

"Yes," said Hoskins, who ran for 50 yards on only six carries. "Then maybe somebody else around here would get a chance to score." (One hint that the scribes might have embellished the conversation was that Schreiner never called Hoskins "Mark.")

Hirsch finished with 28 yards on seven carries, and Hank Casserly of the *Capital Times* was still trying to come up with a nickname that might catch on. In his game story, he mentioned "that whirling dervish, Elroy Hirsch, the Wausau free-legged pacer."

Former star catcher and one-time Detroit Tigers manager Mickey Cochrane, a Navy lieutenant, watched in the press box, scouting the Badgers as a coach for their October 17 opponent, the Great Lakes Naval Training Station. "I'd much rather be at the World Series than here," he said in the *State Journal*. "It may seem funny that a baseball man should be scouting football, but I dabbled in the sport in high school and college and have seen numerous games after baseball season."

In the World Series Cochrane was missing, Ernie White's 6-hit shutout led the Cardinals to a 2–0 in Game 3 at New York and gave St. Louis a 2–1 lead in the best-of-seven series.

One of the biggest cheers in Camp Randall came midway through that 28-point Badger second quarter. A flock of geese flew over the stadium, and the fans noticed the flight pattern.

The geese formed a V.

For victory.

TWELVE

Missouri

The WAVES were on their way.

On July 30, 1942, Congress enacted an amendment to the Naval Reserve Act of 1938, establishing a women's branch of the Navy officially called Women Accepted for Volunteer Emergency Service, or WAVES. The bill declared that the goal in creating the branch was "releasing officers and men for duty at sea." There would be only one woman lieutenant commander and thirty-five lieutenants, and WAVES officers would have authority only over other women.

The UW campus's Navy radio training school for the 470 WAVES was scheduled to begin on Monday, October 11, two days after the Badgers played Missouri in their fourth consecutive home game. Most of the WAVES arrived the day before the game. The head of the school was Lieutenant Dorothy Stratton, the former dean of women at Purdue, and the word got around that she could be tougher than Harry Stuhldreher. In other words, none of those WAVES better ask her to fix a speeding ticket.

The WAVES were only part of the military influx to Madison. By early fall, there were several Army Air Forces and Navy training schools and units in town.

Nationally, the Navy was still aggressively seeking male enlistees, and this was the message of the week in ads, including in Madison newspapers: "Let's give the Japs their half of the ocean—the bottom half! Talking won't stop the Japs. These Navy guns will. But they need men to man them—red-blooded Americans from 17 to 50 who aren't going to let any Nazi or Jap tell them where to get off. Read this message and find out what you can do about it—right now!"

Even traditional campus pranks incorporated the war theme. One of the annual rites for fraternity members was to add a coat of paint to the Kiekhofer Wall, erected in 1884 on land then owned by faculty mem-

By October 1942, WAVES were a familiar site on the Madison campus.
WHi (X3) 49901

ber William "Wild Bill" Kiekhofer. Seven members of Theta Delta Chi did the painting over the weekend of the Marquette game and were brought into court Monday to be arraigned for disorderly conduct. Nobody ever got into serious trouble for the ritual painting, but the judge made a point of announcing he was letting the miscreants off because the painted message was a sales pitch for war bonds.

Early in the week, the *Daily Cardinal* ran another piece of investigative journalism, this time in the "Troubleshooter" column. "After long and diligent study your correspondent has discovered the most popular spot on campus, the ski slide hill between 9 p.m. and [midnight]," the column stated. "What ex-campus politico and Sigma Chi inebriate spent last Thursday evening there explaining the finer points of mother nature to what giggling co-ed?"

The answer never ran.

The other major social news this week was that the Amber Inn, one of the many State Street establishments, was awarded a full liquor license, ending a traditional prohibition on hard liquor bars near campus. Now students already twenty-one years of age could get hard liquor by the drink without traveling away from campus. The government was discouraging such trivial travel because of the gasoline and rubber shortages, so the granting of the Amber Inn's liquor license was billed as a patriotic gesture.

The *Daily Cardinal,* however, called for a voluntary student body revival of prohibition on Wednesdays, asking that students use their soft drink, beer, and cigarette money for one day a week to buy war bonds. "Many of us smoke approximately a package of cigarettes a day and buy several Cokes or glasses of beer during the week," the editorial stated.

"Men students may argue that they are giving their blood for the country and therefore should not be asked to give their money. They will do well to remember that by buying stamps now they are literally placing a gun in their hands even before they are in the service."

Most of the students also cut back on calling their parents. Before Pearl Harbor, long-distance calls had been considered extravagant, but now they were unpatriotic. Bell System ads in Madison during the week of the Marquette game tried to *kill* long-distance business. "Unless your message is really urgent, please don't use long distance service," the ad begged. "But if you must, please make your calls as short as you can."

Some of the Badger reserves, many of them sophomores, called their parents that week to tell them about being on the verge of getting some playing time when the B team opened its season Saturday morning against the Milwaukee Extension School. The boys who served as practice fodder would also suit up for the varsity game—and most likely spend all afternoon cheering on their teammates.

Missouri was no soft touch. The Tigers were coming off a 26–13 victory over Colorado and were 3–0 for the season. In fact, Mizzou had only one regular-season defeat in 1941 before losing to Fordham in the Sugar Bowl. Missouri coach Don Faurot was considered a visionary offensive mind, a pioneer of the split-T formation.

Though the Tigers hadn't beaten a Big Ten team in four tries, the game was considered attractive enough to be picked up by KWID, a shortwave station based in San Francisco that sent recorded versions of broadcasts to U.S. armed forces in Alaska and the Pacific. The station would carry the game Saturday night. Football was in the spotlight because the Cardinals had finished off the Yankees with a 4–2 victory in Game 5 of the World Series at New York on Monday. Enos Slaughter and Whitey Kurowski had home runs in the clinching victory, and righthander Johnny Beazley posted his second complete-game win of the Series.

Stuhldreher rewarded backup senior fullback Bob Ray by naming him captain for the Missouri game. Ray had backed up star fullback George Paskevan in 1940 as a sophomore and then was poised to move into the starting lineup when Pat Harder arrived on the varsity in '41. He remained a backup but didn't gripe about it.

Quarterback Jack Wink, entrenched as the sophomore starter ahead of Ashley Anderson, missed a midweek practice. He wasn't injured, but he had a good excuse: he was in Milwaukee, taking his second physical for the Marine Corps Reserves. When he had been conditionally accepted over the summer, Wink had a hand rash that caused doctors to say they wanted to see him again in three months. He passed with flying colors this time, but his teammates had to do without him for a day. When he returned to Madison with the news that the doctors had cleared him, many of his teammates said, "Welcome to the Corps. *Semper Fi.*"

★ ★ ★

On game day, Saturday, October 10, the *State Journal* greeted its readers with a front-page editorial that was a recruiting pitch for the upcoming citywide scrap metal drive, a common occurrence across the country that fall. In a six-paragraph box, the message was that "if you fail to comb your place for scrap metals for this salvage drive, you are as much a deserter as a soldier who throws away his gun and flees from front line warfare. You are a traitor to your own boy, your neighbor's boy, or any others who must face actual combat."

To put the drive in context, war news surrounded the editorial.

★ ★ ★

London, Oct. 10 (AP)—American Flying Fortresses and Liberator bombers—home from the greatest Allied daylight attack yet launched against Hitler's war foundry—again have amazed British air experts, who know from grim experience the hazards of daylight operations.

The return of all but four of the 100 United States bombers which stormed over occupied France with an escort of 500 Allied fighter planes Friday and unloaded tons of bombs on factories and railroad yards apparently erased any lingering doubts concerning the Fortresses.

★ ★ ★

On the Badgers' practice field next to Camp Randall Stadium, the B team had little trouble with the Milwaukee Extension School. John Gallagher and Otto Breitenbach each scored twice, and Bob Omelina got the fifth touchdown in a 33–0 rout. Others who played for the B team that day included George Neperud, Bob Dean, Don Litchfield, Erv Kissling, and Dave Donnellan. After the game, they all returned to the Camp Randall dressing room to get ready for the varsity game.

Before the game, the WAVES marched into the stadium in formation, drawing a huge ovation. Their escorts were band members, plus Navy officers and Navy cadets also involved in communications training. Jarringly, the WAVES—who were drawing fifty dollars a month in salary—still wore civilian clothes. They were going to begin classes on Monday and receive their uniforms later. Their ranks included Edith Kingston Gould, the great-granddaughter of famed tycoon Jay Gould, and Emily

Jack Wink was surprisingly stoic for a signal-caller.
PHOTO COURTESY OF THE UNIVERSITY OF WISCONSIN
SPORTS INFORMATION DEPARTMENT

Saltonstall, whose father was Massachusetts Governor Leverett Saltonstall. The WAVES were settling into two dormitories and were confined to the campus except for Saturday and Sunday nights.

Pat Harder was still far from 100 percent physically, and that showed when he fumbled the opening kickoff and had to fall on the ball at the Badgers' 3. Stuhldreher didn't want to risk handling the ball that deep in Wisconsin territory, so he ordered an immediate punt. But Bob Baumann, the regular punter, couldn't handle the snap and had to pounce on the ball and take a safety, giving the Tigers a 2–0 lead in the first minute.

The Badgers dominated from there. Paul "Indian" Hirsbrunner blocked a punt to set up a Harder 32-yard field goal that put the Badgers ahead 3–2, and the Badgers went on to win 17–9 in front of a crowd estimated at 25,000.

The afternoon was another confirmation that Elroy Hirsch, the pale kid from Wausau, was destined for stardom—if he wasn't there already. He gained 174 yards on 22 carries and threw one of the Badgers' two completions in the game, an 18-yarder to Dave Schreiner. Hirsch's 20-yard touchdown run in the first quarter was a thing of beauty. He stiff-armed Missouri halfback Bob Steuber at the 10, then fought through two more tackles to score. Hirsch added a 7-yard touchdown run later, and the Tigers got a consolation touchdown in the final two minutes to make the final score misleadingly close. A total of thirty-one Badgers got into the game, including tackle Dave Donnellan—the only man doing double duty in both the B and varsity games. The captain of the day, Bob Ray, gained

42 yards in relief of Harder, who suffered yet another injury, a knee strain, late in the first quarter.

Like Frank Leahy, Missouri's Don Faurot visited the Wisconsin dressing room after the game. He shook hands with all the Badgers, which impressed them.

In the paper, Faurot was quoted as saying, "They were too much for us and that boy Hirsch is all that has been said of him, only more so. Our boys played to the best of their ability, but the well-named Badger Iron Men were too tough, too alert and too powerful."

If students wanted to do something other than celebrate in the State Street taverns that weekend, they could go to one of the new movies in town: *Holiday Inn,* starring Bing Crosby and Fred Astaire; and *Pride of the Yankees,* the tear-jerking biography of Yankees great Lou Gehrig, who had died of amyotrophic lateral sclerosis in June 1941. Gary Cooper portrayed Gehrig, and many of Lou's teammates—including Bill Dickey and Babe Ruth—appeared in the film.

The Badgers who saw the movie noticed that NBC sportscaster Bill Stern, who had broadcast their game against Notre Dame, played himself. They remembered that Stern had promised he would be back if they kept winning. They hoped to be able to ask him whether Gary Cooper really could hit a curveball.

THIRTEEN

Great Lakes and Crazy Legs

Washington, Oct. 12 (AP)—President Roosevelt told the American people Monday night he believed it would be necessary to lower the minimum age limit for the military draft from 20 to 18 years.

"We have learned how inevitable that is," he declared in a radio address, "and how important to the speeding up of victory."

The chief executive did not say, however, when he expected action on the drafting of youths 18 and 19 years old, but the tone of his address gave support to the view that he thought Congress should approve the necessary legislation promptly.

★ ★ ★

The long-expected news about the likely lowering of the draft age caught the attention of most college men, of course, and it drove home to the underclassmen what they had already been assuming—that their time on campus was coming to an end. The youngest players on the '42 Badger varsity—Jerry Frei and Otto Breitenbach—wouldn't turn twenty until June 1944, but even they were already eighteen. While most of the Badgers were already in various reserves, the lowering of the draft age meant the acceleration of callups as well. That took nobody by surprise as the first anniversary of Pearl Harbor approached.

During the week of October 12, Congress debated draft-age legislation. The only significant disagreement was over whether teenagers should receive a minimum of one year of training before going into combat.

As that was being played out, the Badgers—appropriately enough—prepared to meet the Great Lakes Naval Training Station's Bluejackets. The game was set for huge Soldier Field, with its majestic columns and façade and more than 100,000 seats, along the Chicago lakefront. The Wisconsin athletic department didn't cut corners on travel, quartering the Badgers at the plush Palmer House in downtown Chicago near the stadium.

At the naval training station north of Chicago, the Bluejackets had a 5:30 a.m. reveille and a 9:30 p.m. lights out and managed to get in practice during the busy day. Many of the men on the football team were instructors in the recruit training division, including a onetime Case Western Reserve player and Detroit Lion Steve Belichick. Most of the Bluejackets were graduated college stars, including Bruce Smith, the Heisman Trophy winner from Minnesota who had run roughshod over the Badgers in the final game of the '41 season. A handful of the Bluejackets had come to the Navy from the NFL, including Cleveland Rams receiver Howard "Red" Hickey, Green Bay Packers end Carl Mulleneaux, Detroit Lions guard Bill Radovich, and Chicago Cardinals halfback Hugh McCullough.

The Bluejackets were 2–1 with victories over Iowa and Pittsburgh and a loss was to Michigan.

Harry Stuhldreher knew how much it meant for his Chicago-area boys to return home, so he named Bob Baumann—the big tackle and left-footed punter from Harvey, Illinois—as the captain for the Great Lakes game. Baumann would be going up against Jim Barber, a former star tackle for the University of San Francisco Dons, who outweighed him by about twenty pounds. The stories in the Chicago papers pointed out that Baumann came from the same high school, Thornton Township, as baseball star and Cleveland Indians manager Lou Boudreau. Also, one of the *Daily Cardinal*'s gossip columns, "Hitting the Badger Beat," reported that Baumann was spotted "recommending the Lathrop Library as the ideal place to study anatomy." His teammates again shook their heads, wondering, *How does he get the girls if he never talks!*

★   ★   ★

The newly arrived WAVES overcrowded the Navy communications school. The men sailors got to sleep in, with a 9:30 a.m. reveille and classes beginning at noon. The WAVES had to be up at 5:45 a.m. and turn the lights out at 9:30 p.m. Before their classes started that week, Commander Charles F. Green delivered a pep talk. "You girls are very important to the Navy," he said. "You have a serious task to perform to relieve the men for the fleet. We hope that you will work toward that end in this most critical period of the national history."

The WAVES' uniforms hadn't arrived from Chicago, so they still wore civilian clothes. The other students learned to spot the Navy women by their shiny white military Oxford shoes.

On campus and around town, tension simmered between the students and military personnel based at Madison. On Wednesday, the *Daily Cardinal* published an anonymous letter to university president Clarence Dykstra. The writer signed it "A Negro Student at the University of Wisconsin" and reported that he had been insulted by a sailor as he studied on the Union Terrace with a female student. A limited number of military personnel living off campus were allowed to use the Union at a given time, but the rule was unenforceable. The Union remained a magnet, sometimes for trouble.

"Two sailors came on the terrace accompanied by two girls," the letter said. "One of the sailors saw me, and said to the other sailor, 'Look at that nigger over there with that white girl. I'm going to go over there and kick his teeth out.'"

The letter said the girls and the sailor's friend had tried to stop him.

"The offensive sailor, whose accent was definitely southern, said, 'I don't give a damn, niggers have no business in this white school anyway.'" The letter writer concluded, "I am serving notice now that it is not my intention to passively submit to physical violence by these Southern men in uniform. . . . It is unwise for the authorities to wait for bloodshed before they take positive steps to adjust this condition."

In the same issue, the *Daily Cardinal* discussed the letter in an editorial, addressing the sailor involved. "The Negro student whom you insulted and evidently attempted to attack is as good as you," the editorial stated. "He has just as much right to the facilities of this university as any white person. You are being trained at the expense of our country to fight exactly this sort of racial and religious discrimination that is going on in the Axis countries. It is painful indeed to see it manifested at the University of Wisconsin."

★ ★ ★

On Wednesday, the Badgers called a team meeting before practice, and Dave Schreiner presented Stuhldreher with a war bond for his forty-first birthday. The card declared, "A gift from all of us to say we think a lot of you and we wish you every happiness today and always, too. From the Squad of '42."

Wisconsin students were implored to travel to Chicago to cheer on the boys, as long as they packed as many fans as possible into every automobile or took the train. With a coupon book, a Wisconsin student could get into the stadium for only eighty cents. Ultimately, the student paper reported that drivers of loaded cars would get free beer at a local tavern before leaving. As it turned out, many of the drivers were as loaded as their cars.

On Thursday, the papers ran short stories saying The Associated Press had ranked the Badgers the seventh-best team in the country. Until then, the papers didn't mention the rankings. The goal was to win the conference championship, and anything beyond that was gravy—or irrelevant.

Many men on campus hadn't made their military choices. As Congress moved toward lowering the draft age, about 1,500 students attended a joint presentation by representatives of the Army, Navy, and Marine Corps at the Memorial Union on Thursday night. The crowd was too large for the Union Theater, so the speeches were piped into other rooms. Then the representatives appeared again at the Union on Friday, answering questions and signing up students. By then, the football players were on their way to Chicago.

The Badgers were limited to a thirty-six-man traveling squad for the varsity game. Everyone on the squad was going to Chicago because the B team had a Friday afternoon game scheduled at Camp Grant. The Badgers won that game 7–0, and a handful of the B team starters were also listed on the varsity traveling squad.

"After the game, they fed us in the mess hall at the camp," says Otto Breitenbach, the B team's star halfback. "Dynie Mansfield was the coach. When we went out to get on the bus, I found I had forgotten my coat in the mess hall, so I said, 'Wait a minute!' and went back to get it. I came back out and they had taken off. I had a hell of a time getting out of Camp Grant as a civilian. But I made it," he adds, laughing, "and got to the Palmer House."

The Badgers who didn't play in the B game gathered excitedly outside the Camp Randall locker rooms after the Friday afternoon light practice and jumped into lined-up taxis. They headed to the Milwaukee Road station, one of two train stations in Madison, and climbed into the last car, a special Badgers-only addition attached to the back of the train. The two-page itinerary given to each player said that the train would leave at 4:50, dinner would be at 5:30, and the Badgers would pull into Chicago's Union Station at 7:40.

After dinner, many of the boys played cards—*Schafkopf,* or "Sheep's Head," the popular German game played with a thirty-six-card deck and brought to Wisconsin and the Midwest by immigrants. The Badgers loved to play the game at the Union after their nightly team dinner, which the team called "training table." (The quarterbacks, though, had to spend that time studying with Harry Stuhldreher.) It was natural to transfer the game to the train.

Jerry "Toughie" Frei, the young guard, kept score of games on the way down and home on the back of his itinerary, and it appears that his pal, fellow sophomore guard Ken "Roughie" Currier, came out of the train rides with some extra spending money. In another game, tackle Dick Thornally whipped Pat Harder, who promptly reminded himself to have the coach's wife, Mary Stuhldreher, rub the cards the next trip—as she had done the year before, when Harder had cleaned up.

At the Palmer House, many of the Badgers—especially the sophomores and the straight-off-the-farm Frei—were stunned when they walked into the ornate lobby. *My God, this is coming up in the world! Football could do this!*

Sophomore halfback Jim Regan, from the nearby suburb of Berwyn, had heard of the Palmer House but hadn't dreamed of staying there. "With ten children in my family," Regan says, "you didn't have much space, so it was quite a thrill to be there." Guard John Roberts remembers, "The Palmer House was pretty fancy for me, an Iowa farmboy." Sophomore John Gallagher remembers it "as the palace of hotels, especially for someone from Eau Claire."

The Badgers took the elevators to the twenty-first floor, where they picked up keys and headed to their rooms. The Lancaster boys, Dave Schreiner and Mark Hoskins, were together. Dick Thornally got to put up with Pat Harder. Bosom pals George Makris and Bob Baumann shared a room. Regan was with end Gunner Johnson, who later became renowned for climbing out of hotel room windows after curfew but this time was intimidated by being twenty-one floors above the ground. Of course, Roughie Currier and Toughie Frei were roomies, as were the two Wausau pals and sophomores Elroy Hirsch and Hank Olshanski. Nobody knew it, but Hirsch's days as "Elroy" were numbered.

★ ★ ★

On Saturday, October 17, the boys left the Palmer House at noon. Harry Stuhldreher had lined up alumni boosters to take the team to the stadium in cars. Mark Hoskins, for example, rode with prominent attorney George Haight.

If Great Lakes' pros and former college stars were in great football condition and mentally attuned to play a strong game, they probably could have won easily against any college team. But in the huge Soldier Field, in front of a crowd of 60,000 (only half had paid, because soldiers in uniform were allowed in free), the Bluejackets struggled to catch their breath.

The Sailors led 7–0 at the half, after Bruce Smith connected with ex-Nebraska star Fred Preston on a 65-yard touchdown pass. In the third quarter, Hirsch raced 61 yards for the Badgers' first touchdown. Ashley Anderson, in at quarterback, threw the block that took out two Sailors and sprung Hirsch.

Willard R. Smith of the *Chicago Tribune* described Hirsch as "twisting and squirming perilously close to the sideline as he ran down the east side of the field, closely followed by an official watching his every step." But he made it, and Pat Harder's extra point—again, he was banged up and was only kicking in the game—tied the score 7–7.

Later in the third quarter, the Sailors seemed on the verge of regaining the lead. Great Lakes reached the Wisconsin 34, and Smith threw a deep pass for Carl Mulleneaux just across the goal line. Jim Regan was covering Mulleneaux and went up to fight for the ball. "I had the eye on the ball and was going to intercept it, and I kind of slipped," Regan recalls. Jack Wink, the sophomore quarterback, cut in front of both of them and made the interception, a yard deep in the end zone. "He reaches up with one hand, intercepts it, and takes off," Regan says.

At the 10, Wink cut to his right. At the 12, Hugh McCullough missed him, and Wink made a beeline for the *left* sideline. Currier and fellow guard Red Vogds made great blocks, and Wink burst out of traffic at the 40 and went on for the 101-yard return for the go-ahead touchdown. Because of Wink's circuitous route and his lack of speed, the Badgers swear it might have been the most time-consuming 101-yard run in the history of football. "Jack wasn't the fastest guy in the world," says a laughing John Roberts, the Badger guard. "He was kind of shifty, though."

Harder's extra point attempt was deflected and went wide, leaving the score 13–7.

That's how it ended.

Carl Mulleneaux, the Packers end, corralled Hirsch coming off the field and took him into the Great Lakes locker room, where Hirsch talked at length with Bruce Smith. Smith told a blushing Hirsch he had a bright future.

Several former Wisconsin players visited Stuhldreher and the Badgers in the locker room. The *Capital Times* reported that Stuhldreher bummed a cigarette from one of them before asking, "Wasn't it a great game and didn't the boys come through?"

Asked about his long touchdown return, the painfully shy Wink said: "I never knew 100 yards could be so long. Boy, I was tired when I got to that goal line."

Stuhldreher asked Schreiner, who again was a stopper defensively, "Want to play in the backfield, Dave? You were in there all day."

The Badgers ate as a team in the Palmer House's elegant Empire Room. "Some of those guys could eat three steaks," says John Gallagher. Then the Badgers walked to the nearby Studebaker Theater for the musical comedy *Best Foot Forward*. George Abbott produced and directed the show, which included music and lyrics by Hugh Martin and Ralph Blane and choreography by Gene Kelly. It had run from October 1941 to July 1942 at the Ethel Barrymore Theatre in New York before going on the road. The Badgers enjoyed the show, from the first song ("Wish I May") to the last ("Buckle Down Winsocki"), but some of them also sneaked over to a burlesque show following their legitimate theatre experience.

On the train ride to Madison the next morning, many of the Badgers played cards. Baumann took a nap, holding the captain's game ball. Others read the Chicago papers, noticing that Francis Powers of the *Chicago Daily News* wrote that Hirsch "ran like a demented duck. His crazy legs were gyrating in six different directions all at the same time."

Hey, Ghost, this says you have crazy legs!

Hey, Crazylegs!

The rest of the season, Hirsch was still primarily referred to as Elroy "Ghost" Hirsch, but Powers's story and the teasing of Hirsch got the Crazylegs name into casual circulation. Eventually, it supplanted Ghost and even Elroy. "Anything's better than 'Elroy,'" Hirsch says, smiling.

The *Tribune*'s Willard Smith wrote that Hirsch "completely eclipsed Bruce Smith, honored as collegiate football's outstanding player in 1941, when he led Minnesota to its second consecutive Western Conference championship. Hirsch, operating behind a lighter line which was just as stout-hearted as that of the seamen, if not more so, scored Wisconsin's first touchdown and outgained Smith throughout the afternoon's play."

The Badgers' train pulled into the Milwaukee Road Station at 12:15 p.m., and a crowd estimated at four thousand greeted the Badgers. Wisconsin was 4–0–1, surpassing the victory total for the entire '41 season.

As the big stars—Schreiner, Harder, and Hirsch—stepped off the train, the cheers were deafening. The Badger fans also hollered for Wink, but before anyone figured out who he was, the shy quarterback was off with friends who gave him a ride home. Midway through his sophomore season, the quarterback's face wasn't yet immediately recognizable in Madison.

Stuhldreher stepped over to a police car and used the police microphone to tell the crowd, "We got off to another poor start in Chicago but we came back with a good finish."

Next up: The Big Ten race.

FOURTEEN

Purdue

Harry Stuhldreher followed coaching convention, always building up even the soft-touch opponents. He poured it on the week of the Purdue game. The boys got the impression he was trying to tell them the Boilermakers, 1–3 so far in '42, would have been in the midst of a 37-game winning streak if they hadn't gotten a few bad breaks. And he spoke of the same perils at the Uptown Coaches Booster meeting that week.

"Wisconsin is ripe for a kick in its collective teeth if the players have any sort of a letdown," he declared, as quoted in the *State Journal*.

At the same meeting, Jack Wink almost fainted when the boosters demanded that he take a bow for the 101-yard interception return against Great Lakes, but Stuhldreher coaxed him to the front of the room for a few moments. Some of the boosters wondered: *This is the guy who calls the signals?*

The Boilermakers had a fine running back, stumpy Henry "Hank" Stram, and at least had managed to surprise Northwestern and star quarterback Otto Graham. Also, the Boilermakers would be at home, in Lafayette, Indiana. Wisconsin had beaten Purdue only once since 1925—and that was a wild 14–13 comeback victory in 1940.

Stuhldreher named senior tackle Paul "Indian" Hirsbrunner captain for the second time.

On campus, the WAVES finally appeared in uniform after trucks arrived from Marshall Field's department store in Chicago. The WAVES bought their own uniforms, with a one-hundred-dollar allowance. They also bought accessories and personal items from the Marshall Field's representatives, and the *Daily Cardinal* said most WAVES chose slippers, bathrobes, makeup, curlers, hangers, gloves, pajamas, nightgowns, and overshoes.

Their instructions told them they didn't have to buy the official WAVE purse, "but you may not carry any other." Guess what? Most bought the official WAVE purse.

When the military women marched to class in formation, they sang, "Oh, How We Hate to Get Up in the Morning."

The Navy didn't follow a conventional academic calendar, so the accelerated-study communications training schools for the men periodically held graduation ceremonies. Another 245 graduated and departed Madison the week of the Purdue game.

The word broke on campus that the Herbie Kay Orchestra—legitimately famous—would play at the Homecoming dance, after the Ohio State game on Halloween. Wisconsin men pondered whether to spring for the $2.50-per-couple ticket.

The week's Treasury Department ads for war bonds spoke of the cost of defeat:

> If the Axis wins, you'll have to find a home in the Japanese rice swamps, in the African desert or in the frozen north. For America, with all its boundless opportunities, will be peopled by the Axis—that's what they're fighting for!
>
> If America wins, you'll be free to live where you want, to go wherever opportunity beckons—and that's what we're fighting for! And the best way to carry on that fight is by investing 10 percent of your income in war bonds.

The *Daily Cardinal's* "Hitting the Badger Beat" told of a student complaining, "That girl I had out Saturday night was as slippery as Elroy Hirsch."

★ ★ ★

Washington, Oct. 21 (AP)—Allied domination of the skies in the vast Pacific battle front appeared growing mightier Wednesday as American bombers slugged Japanese invasion bases in the Aleutians and the Solomons.

The fury of the Allied bombing of enemy troops and supply concentrations in the Solomons seemed thus far to have at least temporarily stalled the full force of a Japanese thrust to retake the American-held Guadalcanal airbase and win control of the southwest Pacific.

★ ★ ★

The varsity traveling squad was reduced to thirty for the Purdue game because the B team had a road game scheduled against the Iowa Pre-Flight School's B squad at Iowa City.

The Badger varsity left on the train on Thursday, stayed at the Palmer House in Chicago Thursday night (Schreiner sent a Palmer House postcard to his parents, saying, "I sure hope we can keep going this week"), then traveled to Indianapolis Friday and worked out at the Indianapolis minor-league baseball stadium.

Back on campus Friday, advanced ROTC student engineers "blew up" a fake Nazi pillbox in a demonstration on campus, to the cheers of their fellow students.

In Lafayette, the Badgers dampened the Boilermakers' Homecoming weekend, winning 13–0 before 19,500 fans at Ross-Ade Stadium. Pat Harder led the way, gaining 99 yards on 25 carries. Elroy Hirsch had 50 yards on 12 carries, and his 26-yard run set up the Harder 4-yard TD run that opened the scoring in the second quarter. A Schreiner fumble recovery and a John Roberts interception blunted the Boilermakers' major threats, and Hank Stram gained only 10 yards on six carries.

The significance? The Badgers demonstrated that they could be subpar and still win. Hank Casserly's game story in the *Capital Times* said, "The score gave little indication of the Badgers' sheer power. . . . Harder, while not in perfect condition, closely approached his old swashbuckling of 1941 as he bowled over the Boilermakers, while Hirsh's elusive running tactics had the Purdue players and fans agape."

It was the Badgers' turn to dress hurriedly and rush to the train station. Eventually they got the word that Otto Breitenbach's touchdown pass to Don Pfotenhauer gave the B team a 6–0 victory at Iowa City over the Iowa Pre-Flight School's B team.

The Badgers' big game was coming up, against undefeated Ohio State and young coach Paul Brown.

FIFTEEN

Ohio State

The Badgers' 1942 schedule was posted on the Camp Randall locker room wall. When the boys arrived back from Purdue, the handwritten addendum in the margin next to the upcoming Ohio State game jumped out at all of them.

It was one word.

MUST.

If the Badgers were going to be bona fide threats to win the league championship for the first time since 1912, they MUST beat the vaunted Buckeyes.

Harry Stuhldreher never spelled it out, but the Badgers understood that he didn't like Paul Brown, and they inferred it involved resentment over how Brown had usurped Stuhldreher's title as the favorite football son of Massillon, Ohio.

When Brown was a kid in Massillon, he had heard of Knute Rockne, but his hero was more of a contemporary—local high school star Harry Stuhldreher. Brown was playing at Massillon High when Stuhldreher was one of the Four Horsemen at Notre Dame. While Stuhldreher was at Villanova and then Wisconsin, Brown coached Massillon for eight seasons, winning six consecutive state championships. He stepped directly into the Ohio State head-coaching position—Stuhldreher's dream job—in 1941. In Brown's inaugural season, Ohio State whipped Wisconsin 46–34.

Publicly, Brown and Stuhldreher were respectful of each other. Actually, the Badgers knew Stuhldreher couldn't stand Brown—and, without knowing, they assumed the feeling was mutual.

Fred Negus, the sophomore center, was the only Badger starter from Ohio, and he told his teammates how much he wanted to beat the team from his home state. His parents were coming to Madison to watch him play at the college level for the first time. He was still trying to convince his mother, who had been raised a Quaker, that football wasn't evil incarnate. "My mother brought up that she didn't want me to hurt anyone," Negus says.

Stuhldreher was late for the Monday practice after making a noon speech to a Chicago organization, the Wailing Wall. The players didn't have the nerve to greet their tardy coach with a "Take Five!" order to run laps.

At the practice, Stuhldreher named Dave Schreiner the game captain for the second time in the season. He also told the Badgers that they would have to get the passing game going to knock off the Buckeyes.

"There's no reason why our pass offense shouldn't be working," Stuhldreher groused to the *Milwaukee Journal.* "Our personnel is the same as last year."

That night, Schreiner received a telegram at the fraternity house from the girls at Ann Emery Hall:

CONGRATULATIONS WITH YOU AS OUR CAPTAIN WE'RE SURE OF OUR GOAL.

Schreiner also gently lectured his parents again in a letter about how he couldn't be expected to line up tickets for everyone in Lancaster who wanted to go to the game.

★   ★   ★

Washington, Oct. 28 (AP)—American and Japanese warships boiled through the southwest Pacific in a titanic slugging match for control of the bomb-scarred Guadalcanal airfield Wednesday while on the island itself land forces were locked in mortal combat.

In the epic land battle on the north shore of Guadalcanal, Japanese forces broke through the American south flank during the night of Oct. 25–26 but were thrown back by army troops who regained their temporarily lost positions. On the west flank, held by Marines against a smashing series of attacks that have been underway since last Friday, the Navy reported the enemy was forced to give ground in "heavy fighting."

★   ★   ★

In the latest Associated Press weekly poll, the Badgers were sixth, behind Ohio State, Georgia, Alabama, Notre Dame, and Georgia Tech. In Columbus, Brown told writers the rankings were "generally classified as a silly type of thing by the men who play the game and know the score."

Indeed, the concept was silly. How could writers from all corners of the country evaluate various teams, some of which—or many of which—they had never seen play? *Caveat emptor.*

The top-rated Buckeyes had a host of stars, including end Dante Lavelli, quarterback George Lynn, halfbacks Paul Sarringhaus and Les Horvath, and fullback Gene Fekete. Bill Stern was returning to do another national NBC broadcast on 184 stations.

To preview the game, which was expected to draw a school-record overflow crowd of about 45,000, Stuhldreher consented to an interview with Lew Bryer of the *Columbus Citizen.* He tried to upstage Paul Brown in Columbus, and Bryer's story was reprinted in the *State Journal.*

"I keep picturing the boys who are playing for me as they may be a year from now, battling a Jap or a Nazi with a bayonet," Stuhldreher said. "We've always wanted our players tough. Now we want them tougher than ever. There's a real parallel between football and modern warfare. And don't think the boys themselves don't realize it. There's a different attitude this fall over anything I've seen either as a player or coach. The boys are preparing themselves not only for the games to come, but for their future in the armed services. Their imaginations are fired by what the Rangers and Commandos are doing to outsmart and outgut the enemy. Eventually the present day football players will go a long way in helping to win this war."

Stuhldreher added, "We coaches don't like to be asked, 'How many boys will you lose to the armed forces?' We don't lose them. We contribute them. . . . Some of my friends feel that it seems brutal to be preparing young men for war. It doesn't seem brutal to me. It seems the opposite. We're in it. They'll be in it soon. All of us may be in it before it's over. I like to think I'm improving my chances of my boys coming through it through what they're getting on the football field. The stamina, teamwork and coordination which goes to make a good football player also goes to make a good soldier."

The campus was in a celebratory mood, with the Homecoming festivities—Friday pep rally, Saturday game and dance—on Halloween weekend. Stuhldreher's remarks were another reminder that this was part of the last hurrah for the men on campus, players and non-players alike.

At the Friday night pep rally on the lower campus, attended by about eight thousand, Roundy Coughlin gave his usual fire-'em-up speech, Mayor James Law said how proud he was to have these boys representing Madison, and Stuhldreher and Dave Schreiner thanked the fans for their support before the team headed off to spend the night at the Maple Bluff Country Club.

The "fun" was just getting started.

The next morning's *Daily Cardinal* (a rare student newspaper with a Saturday edition) reported that a disturbance in downtown Madison was ongoing at press time and had started "within 10 minutes after the close of the pep rally."

The number involved and the extent of the rowdiness would be debated for days. The student paper put the number of those in the mob at four thousand, and the *State Journal's* estimate was five thousand. The *Daily Cardinal* said the event involved "students . . . marching down State Street, blocking traffic, rocking cars and trampling everything in their path." The *State Journal* labeled it a "three-hour near-riot," then erased the "near" over the next few days.

The *Daily Cardinal's* account was more detailed than those in the "regular" newspapers. It reported that the mob went back and forth between campus and the Capitol Square, breaking windows on State Street businesses and rocking—but apparently not turning over—cars. The worst incident took place in front of the Orpheum Theater, where police officers were pelted with water and eggs. The cops responded by spraying tear gas into the crowd. Because of the winds, the tear gas came right back at the policemen, and they scrambled into the theater, giving the impression they were retreating in the face of the mob. Other officers at the epicenter of the action, at State and Johnson Streets, claimed they were targets of thrown glass and debris. They used tear gas and fire hoses to defend themselves. Students later claimed that water broke some of the windows.

The Ohio State Buckeyes, staying at the Park Hotel downtown, were innocent—but apparently affected—bystanders. *Columbus Dispatch* sports editor Russ Needham discussed that night and what team doctors diagnosed as a widespread outbreak of dysentery among the Buckeyes. Wrote Needham:

Ordinarily, the Ohio State squad would have been housed from the time of their arrival until time to go to the field to dress at some other town not too distant from Madison. But that would have meant hiring two buses to transport the squad back and forth. In war time, that's out.

Consequently, they stayed at a Madison hotel, where the corridors inside and the streets outside rang with the din of merrymakers far into the night, Friday, when the Bucks should have been getting a good night's rest. Prior to that they had been in the midst of a riot in which some of them were exposed to the unpleasantness of tear gassing while returning to the hotel from a movie.

Then, too, the squad did not carry its own water, as it had for years. This is believed to have caused the illness that left the Buck-eyes considerably less than at normal strength.

Fekete, the Buckeyes' star fullback, laughs when remembering the weekend.

"We left Columbus Thursday and changed trains in Chicago," Fekete says. "The train took us to Janesville, where we stayed overnight. Then we went into Madison Friday. We were right by the capitol building, and instead of getting a good night's rest, we were kept up all night by people banging on our doors and things like that. The Wisconsin goblins!"

Police made thirty-two arrests that night, and most of the miscreants had headaches as they appeared before Superior Court Judge Roy Proctor the next morning—about when the Ohio State Buckeyes were eating breakfast at the Park Hotel. Bails were set from two to fifteen dollars. Many of the arrests involved students who left taverns carrying beer glasses or bottles and then threw them.

The judge got everyone through his court in time for him to go to the football game.

★ ★ ★

"It was such a bright beautiful October 31, and I can still remember walking across toward the north side of the stadium," recalls Tom Butler, the Madison native who was a freshman student in the fall of 1942. "The atmosphere was so exciting. We hated Ohio State with a passion."

The Buckeyes had an unusual pregame warmup, at least on that day. Part of it seemed borrowed from Angelo Bertelli. The Ohio State party arrived at the stadium about ninety minutes before kickoff, and the Buckeyes walked around the field before going to the locker room. Fekete, giving Pat Harder a run for his money as the league's best at the position, noticed the huge spools of telephone wires on the sideline, near the goal line. According to the next day's *Capital Times*, he pointedly asked a worker if the spools were kept that close to the sideline during the game. "They'd better not," Fekete said. "I'll be down here quite a bit." Fekete doesn't remember the incident, and it seems unlikely to be true, but the story was published and got widespread play after the fact.

The Badgers had been on the field loosening up for nearly a half-hour when some Buckeyes emerged from the locker room. None of them were starters. Fekete and his fellow first-stringers finally took the field at 1:52 p.m., only eight minutes before the scheduled kickoff. The Badgers considered that insulting, but Charles Csuri, the Buckeyes' star tackle, says it wasn't intended to be. Many of the Buckeyes were ill—before, during, and after the game. "Everybody was tired and worn out," Csuri says. "There wasn't any question that dysentery affected our squad." Csuri says he remains curious whether the outbreak was caused by something

For two bits, fans could treat themselves to the game program before the Halloween showdown for the Big Ten lead.

PHOTO COURTESY OF THE UNIVERSITY OF WISCONSIN SPORTS INFORMATION DEPARTMENT

the Buckeyes ate or drank before they left Columbus, during the trip, or after they arrived in Madison.

Fekete isn't sure, either, but he is adamant that many of the Buckeyes were having to make repeated trips to the toilet. "We had dinner on Friday night in Madison, and maybe we're not used to that real rich Wisconsin Dairyland food," he says, laughing. "Whether it was that or the water on the train, that Saturday morning, I would say most of the team had dysentery. You know what dysentery does to your system. It just weakens you."

Early-arriving fans got to see the 150-member marching band parade into the stadium with the Navy men from the radio communications school and the WAVES in formation behind them. Men from the Army Air Forces technical school also sat together in one section. College crowds everywhere were beginning to look like those traditionally at Army-Navy games.

★ ★ ★

London, Oct. 31 (AP)—Fifty German bombers smashed with bombs and machine guns at southeastern England Saturday in the biggest Nazi attack since the 1940 Battle of Britain, concentrating their assault on shopper-crowded streets at Canterbury, where Mrs. Franklin D. Roosevelt was a visitor only Friday. Roaring in at dusk, the raiders dropped bombs in haphazard fashion and machine-gunned a working class area and then a shopping street.

★ ★ ★

The game was still scoreless when the Badgers began their third possession from the Wisconsin 20. On the first play, Elroy Hirsch took the snap and started to his right. Pat Harder escorted him, focusing on Ohio State star George Lynn. Harder leveled Lynn, and Hirsch hurdled them both and was in the open field. Looking at a picture of that play years later, Hirsch laughs. "It's amazing what fear can do," he says.

With the help of other blocks from Bob Hanzlik and Bob Baumann, Hirsch made it to the Ohio State 21 for a 59-yard gain before Buckeye Tommy James pulled him down. The *State Journal's* Willard R. Smith said on that play Hirsch ran "like a scared jackrabbit on the desert with only sagebrush and cactus to hinder him." ("Jackrabbit Hirsch" didn't catch on.)

The scribes noticed that Otto Hirsch, Elroy's father, was sitting in front of the press box, and they watched his reaction to the plays on the field, especially Elroy's runs. They noted that Otto missed the start of the long

Elroy Hirsch (#40) is about to take advantage of a crushing block from Pat Harder (#34) and break into the open field for the long gain that will set up the Badgers' first touchdown.
PHOTO COURTESY OF THE UNIVERSITY OF WISCONSIN SPORTS INFORMATION DEPARTMENT

run because he was retrieving a feather that had blown out of his hat. After the run, he hollered to his son, "You should have gone all the way!"

Hirsch and Harder took turns carrying until the Badgers reached the 1, and Harder made it over on his second try. Hirsch pulled Harder out of that pile and hugged the rugged fullback. If you needed a yard, you gave the ball to Harder, and none of the Badgers begrudged that. Harder's extra point gave the Badgers a 7–0 lead with 13:36 left in the first half.

With Schreiner sealing one side, the Buckeyes couldn't move against the Badgers. Wisconsin threatened to get the lead to two touchdowns, but the Buckeyes managed to bat down a Hirsch pass intended for Schreiner on the goal line, and the Badgers settled for a 37-yard Harder field goal to make it 10–0. That's the way it stood at the half.

Thirty more minutes, the Badgers told themselves, and one another, in the locker room.

On the field, the Homecoming festivities were altered for the times. At one point, part of the band started to spell out OHIO, mimicking the Ohio State band's famous maneuver, and the stunned Wisconsin fans booed. Long before those band members could get to the conclusion, the dotting of the "I," the rest of the band formed a tank, "ran over" the Ohio formation, and "flattened" it. The crowd laughed and cheered.

The halftime was a tribute to former Wisconsin students and residents serving in the military, and representatives of the Marines, Army, and Navy made speeches. After each one, the band played the appropriate song— "The Marine's Hymn," "Anchors Aweigh," or "You're in the Army Now."

The Marine representative was Lieutenant Colonel Chester L. Fordney, chief of the Central Recruiting District. "Wisconsin's men are fighting men," he told the crowd and the international radio audience that included U.S. troops around the world. "They are demonstrating that on the football field today. But Wisconsin men also are serving from the Halls of Montezuma to the shores of Tripoli."

He probably knew that many of the Badgers had signed up for the Marine Reserves.

As the halftime intermission ended, a group of Wisconsin fans turned to the broadcast booth in the press box and taunted NBC's Bill Stern, who on the radio earlier in the week had picked Ohio State to win.

But the game was far from over.

★ ★ ★

On their second possession of the second half, the Buckeyes marched 96 yards for the touchdown that got them within 3 points. Fekete scored the touchdown on a 4-yard plunge, and the Badgers were served notice that the favorites weren't going to fold.

Hirsch took the ensuing kickoff 3 yards deep in the end zone and ran it all the way out to the Badger 34, giving Wisconsin good field position. Several plays later, Hirsch connected with Schreiner for a 12-yard completion that put the Badgers on the 16. Harder made 2 yards on a reverse, and then Hirsch was called on to throw the ball again. Under pressure as he faked a run to the right, he got off a floater for Schreiner, who had a couple of steps on the Buckeye defenders near the goal line.

"Hirsch was such a threat, when he was going around the right side, they had to protect that like crazy," recalls Tom Butler. "He stopped, and Schreiner was wide open!"

Bob Hanzlik, the other end, says, "Hirsch and Schreiner put on a show on that one. We'd been working on this delayed pass, called 82-3. Hirsch takes off around end, then stops and throws back across to Schreiner. Dave bobbled the ball, he was all by himself and almost dropped it, but— and this was typical Schreiner—he overcame it." Drawing in the ball, Schreiner was snowed under. But he was over the goal line.

The Harder conversion kick made it 17–7. Harder was banged up and sore, with swelling on his face that would turn into a black eye. Stuhldreher took him out of the game briefly in the fourth quarter, but

Harder sent himself back in. A Hirsch interception ended the last only major Ohio State threat, and bedlam broke loose at the final gun.

The Badgers' stars shone, with Hirsch gaining 118 yards on only 13 carries. His Ohio State counterpart Paul Sarringhaus had 55 yards on the same number of carries. And Harder won the battle of fullbacks, outgaining Fekete 97–65. Schreiner again was the hero defensively, and the Badger coaches later determined from film study that the Buckeyes had gained only 4 yards around his end. When the Badgers were on defense, he was working against Ohio State sophomore tackle Bill Willis, who went on to be the Buckeyes' first black All-American in 1943 and 1944. Sophomore halfback Erv Kissling, watching from the sideline, marveled at Schreiner's work. "That guy he was going against was an All-American, and Dave put him on his butt," Kissling says.

The Badgers were on top of the world and on track to win their first conference title in thirty years. It was also Wisconsin's first victory over Ohio State since 1918.

Yes, the Badgers had beaten the nation's number-one-rated team, but there was so little emphasis on such imaginary malarkey, most of the fans knew neither of the poll nor the rankings. More important to Wisconsin fans, the Badgers had taken control of the Big Ten Conference race. After that day's games, the Badgers were the only undefeated team in

The Badgers stars celebrate the team's victory over Ohio State with their coach. Mark Hoskins, Dave Schreiner, Pat Harder, and Elroy Hirsch get giddy with Harry Stuhldreher, at center. AP PHOTO

conference play, at 2–0. Ohio State was 3–1, while Illinois, Minnesota, Iowa, and Michigan were 2–1. As long as the Badgers kept winning, they wouldn't have to worry about playing one fewer conference game than the Buckeyes.

In the Wisconsin dressing room, Stuhldreher told the boys how proud he was but that they needed to keep it going. Outside, the scribes couldn't hear anything but his final line: "Let's go all the way!" The boys hollered, and the doors opened.

Otto Hirsch was one of the many fathers in the raucous locker room. Schreiner paraded with the game ball, lifted out of the pile at the final gun. An exhausted Harder couldn't keep his balance and needed help tying his shoes.

Stuhldreher told the scribes it was "the greatest victory any team ever won for me. Boy, am I glad it's over. Ohio State has a great team, haven't they?"

The *State Journal* talked with Schreiner for a sidebar story. "I don't believe we could have won if it hadn't been for coordinated teamwork," Schreiner was quoted as saying. "This was distinctly a team victory, and that's the way games should be won. And, boy, I was nervous on that perfect touchdown pass from Elroy Hirsch."

The sign on the locker room chalkboard, scribbled by manager Eugene Fischer, announced: "Seven down, three to go."

Stuhldreher went to the visiting dressing room, but the door was still closed. He briefly waited outside with reporters. Paul Brown emerged, spotted Stuhldreher, and shook his hand, with the *Columbus Dispatch* writers, among others, watching close enough to reproduce the conversation in print the next morning.

"Congratulations, Harry," Brown said. "You had the best ball team—today at least."

Responded Stuhldreher, "Thanks, Paul. Sorry it had to be this way."

He almost sounded as if he meant it.

At first, as he spoke with reporters, Brown was angry and terse. The *Capital Times* said he greeted reporters with, "I'll give you a statement. Quote: Wisconsin won the ballgame. Congratulations. Unquote." But then he added, "Wisconsin has a good ballclub."

Brown was more philosophical a few minutes later when he talked with Columbus reporters in the dressing room. "You can't take anything away from Wisconsin," he said, according to the *Columbus Dispatch*. "They have a great football team and we have an ordinary one. Today they were better than we were. They were inspired and they had the whole crowd cheering for them."

Brown called Hirsch "a great one. He was the outstanding back on the field today, one of the best I've ever seen. He makes their whole offense move because he's a touchdown threat every time he has the ball."

Brown said a loss removed some of the pressure. "I had no dreams. I kept saying it would come sooner or later. It just wasn't to be. From the time we left home, even in practice things have been funny. Everything has conspired to do us wrong. And this transportation problem and staying in the hotel in the town where the game is being played didn't help us either."

Later, after the word filtered back to Madison that Brown said the Buckeyes were weakened because of dysentery and blamed the "bad" water in Madison, the Badgers scoffed. Years later, they still consider that sour grapes.

"Brown was complaining that there was so much noise they couldn't sleep, but that was a lot of B.S.," says reserve tackle Jack Crabb. "We just beat the shit out of them."

Csuri, the Ohio State tackle (who went on to earn fame as an Ohio State professor and a pioneer of computer art), is decisive when asked if Wisconsin saw the real Buckeyes on the Camp Randall field. "No," Csuri says. "I'm convinced of that."

Fekete says the most graphic example of the Buckeyes' illness that day came on a play on which Les Horvath carried the ball. "I did a spinner play and handed off to Les," Fekete says. "Right in front of our Ohio State bench, about three Wisconsin guys just buried him. He got up real slow and walked over to Coach Brown. He said, 'Coach, I think I just did something in my pants!' Paul Brown's words were, 'Les, you get back in there! Better men than you have done something in their pants!'"

Bottom line: On the only afternoon when two of the nation's best 1942 teams were on the field together, Wisconsin was better.

That day, *Columbus Dispatch* sportswriter Paul Hornung* typed away for his readers. The next morning, his story began: "Madison, Wis. Oct. 31—The honeymoon is over; the ride on the clouds is ended; we're just common folks again, we Buckeyes."

★ ★ ★

After the game, about five hundred fans, most of them students, celebrated in a mob going down State Street—under the watchful eye of Madison police officers, who had replenished their tear gas supply and were wondering if the Halloween atmosphere might add to the trouble.

---

* No relation to 1956 Heisman Trophy winner and Green Bay Packer halfback Paul Hornung.

"We went uptown and partied at the Park Hotel," Tom Butler says. "Some guys were tipping over the sand-filled cigarette deals, and everyone was snake-dancing up State Street. It was just huge."

But the night, including the Homecoming dance, went peacefully. Many of the Badgers didn't bother to make the State Street rounds or attend the dance. Mark Hoskins, who had gained only 13 yards on seven carries but had drawn accolades for his blocking, went straight back to the fraternity house—and stayed there.

SIXTEEN

Iowa

Dave Schreiner's wry sense of humor showed through in a note to his parents early in the week after the Ohio State game.

> Wasn't it great to win Saturday? It's hard to realize that we did actually knock off OSU but I guess we must have according to all reports. Everybody including myself is physically OK and ready to do a good job against Iowa. We've got three tough ones and wouldn't it be great if we could win all of them?

The military had first call on buses, and the train schedule was impractical, so the Badgers learned early in the week that their trip to Iowa City for the game against the Hawkeyes would be a twelve-car caravan. That was quite a change from the relatively plush train rides, dining cars, and nights at the Palmer House.

"Madison businessmen loaned the cars, and the university was able to get extra gas rations," says end Bob Rennebohm, whose ankle had improved enough for him to be on the traveling squad, though not enough for him to play.

With the Badgers on a roll, the mode of travel didn't seem to be a major issue.

On campus that week, the Badgers were feted for their victory over Ohio State, and it was dutifully noted (but not widely celebrated) that they had climbed to second in the Associated Press poll. The Badgers would have gotten more attention if there hadn't been an ongoing debate over the Friday night downtown disturbance the night before the big win. All week, a serve-and-volley debate continued between the mainstream papers, with the *State Journal* and the *Capital Times* on one side and the *Daily Cardinal* on the other.

The Madison papers were adamant that the students had behaved abominably and that the police had shown admirable restraint. The student paper argued that the police had overreacted, primarily with the indiscriminate and hasty use of tear gas, making a mild disturbance seem worse. A Tuesday *Daily Cardinal* editorial declared, "Madison should take a tip from the way in which the Chicago police control the New Year's Eve mobs in the Loop. . . . No one is arrested except when he tries to do actual damage." Later in the week, Rip Perruse, the *Cardinal's* managing editor for sports, wrote an open letter to Madison police chief William H. McCormick. "We at the university are not the least ashamed," Perruse wrote. "Rather, we believe that the Madison police should be ashamed. If you think our attitude is the worst you have ever seen, the feeling is mutual, for we think the attitude of your staff was the worst we have ever seen."

At practice that week, Stuhldreher was concerned about the Iowa passing game, led by quarterback Tom Farmer in the T formation. To make his point, he put ends Bob Hanzlik and Schreiner with the freshman team when it ran the Iowa plays. The freshmen were able to move the ball, with Schreiner and Hanzlik snagging passes, and that worried Stuhldreher even more.

The coach had a guest at both the practice and the booster meeting: U.S. Senator Robert M. La Follette, Jr., the Senate's only Progressive Party member. La Follette had taken over his famous father's seat in the Senate when the trail-blazing politician died in 1925. His brother, Philip La Follette, had served as Wisconsin's governor from 1931 to 1933 and from 1935 to 1939. The family was a Wisconsin dynasty.

★　★　★

Washington, Nov. 3 (AP)—United States destroyers have moved in to bombard enemy positions on Guadalcanal, the Navy reported Tuesday, while aerial attacks continued against the enemy.

Despite the sea and air attacks to the westward of the vital Henderson airfield, however, the Navy said that the Japanese had landed troop reinforcements eastward of the field on the north coast of Guadalcanal.

★　★　★

Stuhldreher wrote a weekly letter to former Wisconsin players in the armed services. But the week of the Iowa game, he delegated that duty to Schreiner, who was formulating plans to join the Marines. The All-

American end might have been coached through the assignment by the athletic publicity department, but Schreiner—who typed or wrote almost daily to his parents—likely contributed much of the sentiment and at the least signed the typed letter. The writer, whether it was Schreiner or someone else, took care to keep the letter relatively timeless, because there was no way of knowing how long it would take to reach the former Badgers. The letter read, in part:

Dear Badgers in Uncle Sam's Armed Forces,

As you probably have deduced from Harry's weekly letters, we have been having a great season. It certainly has been a lot of fun winning, and you can bet that we are going to keep it up as long as we can.

You will remember that last fall we were able to score a lot of touchdowns, but we couldn't do much about keeping the other boys from scoring. In spring practice we did a lot of work with our defense and it has paid off.

In fact, we are having a merry old time evening up for a lot of past scores all over the place. How we are going to come out the rest of the way remains to be seen, but you can bet (don't go hog-wild and lay the whole paycheck) that we will be in there fighting all the way.

Most of us will be in there with you boys in a short while and the season has certainly helped to get us in shape for the days to come.

Since Uncle Sam has decided that he wants some of us to stay in school while we are waiting our call for the services, most of us are taking courses which will be of aid to us when we are called into active service. Aside from that we have a group of sailors here who are very close to the action. Then last month a group of WAVES came in who add quite a bit to the campus. Of course, training rules keep us from seeing too much of them, but the rest of the campus is seeing that they get a real Wisconsin welcome.

Well, we have three mighty tough ball games to prepare for and we have a big job to do in attempting to swing that Badger flag from the top of the Big Ten pole for once. After that, many of us soon will be joining you.

The best of luck and we'll be seeing you all,
Yours in the Badger Bond,
Dave Schreiner
For the 1942 Varsity Football Squad

As the letter went out, the B team again beat the Camp Grant B team on Thursday, this time at Camp Randall.

★ ★ ★

Cairo, Nov. 5 (AP)—Weakened by the loss of thousands of men captured, killed, wounded or isolated in their desert strongpoints, a once-proud Axis Army was in full flight Thursday across western Egypt in a frantic hunt for position to avoid destruction.

Only a rearward moving screen of antitank guns and tanks shielded the bulk of Marshall Rommel's African corps from the pressing advance of the Eighth British Army while a comparatively impotent air force sought to parry the combined blows of American and British imperial airmen.

While 9,000 Axis prisoners streamed dejectedly to the rear, the Allied air forces kept hitting at the foe, and the main coastal line of retreat was described as a veritable graveyard of smoking, twisted tanks, armored cars and trucks.

★ ★ ★

Mark Hoskins, as the captain for the week, drew the assignment of riding to Iowa City with Stuhldreher. The caravan stopped for lunch at a Dubuque hotel, and Hoskins met with friends from his summer job as a lifeguard. The cars made it to Cedar Rapids on Friday, and the Badgers worked out there and stayed overnight before moving on to Iowa City for the game the next morning, November 7.

★ ★ ★

The Badgers sputtered most of the first half and looked as if they had left their game in Dubuque. On his first carry, Elroy Hirsch was held up by a defender who tore Hirsch's jersey—quite an accomplishment considering the uniforms were as thick as sweaters—and then was belted in the face by another Hawkeye, ending up with a bloody nose. He had to change jerseys but came back in the game, periodically wiping away blood.

The proceedings took a comical turn when a dog raced onto the field during the second quarter and displayed open-field elusiveness. After several minutes, the dog ran off the field and presumably up a tunnel. Play resumed, but the mongrel soon reappeared to hold up the game again.

The Hawkeyes took a 6–0 lead with five minutes left in the second quarter on a 23-yard touchdown pass from Tommy Farmer to Bill Burkett. The Badgers blocked the extra point, then seemed on the verge of taking the lead by the intermission.

In the drive, Hirsch hit Hoskins for a 14-yard completion, and Pat Harder connected with Schreiner for 17. In the final minute, Hirsch threw a screen pass to Harder, who was dragged down on the Hawkeyes 2-yard line. Twenty seconds remained in the half, and the Badgers quickly ran a fullback dive. Linesman Perry Graves signaled that Harder had scored, but the referee, Frank Birch, overruled him. Harder was livid, screaming that he was in, and his teammates on the field agreed.

Student manager Robert Angus, watching near the goal line, screamed—both to the officials and to his teammates down the sideline in the bench area—that Harder was in. The players respected the hard-working Angus, a sharp Madison-area native who despite a leg withered by polio had played high school football and understood and loved the game. The Badgers on the sideline took Angus's word for it and joined in the yelling.

Hurriedly, because timeouts were illegal in the final two minutes of a half, the Badgers tried to get off one more play, with Harder carrying again. He was short this time, no question. News accounts the next day varied on the issue of whether that second play got started before time ran out, but the consensus among the Badgers is that the ball wasn't snapped until after the half ended. But the Badgers were shocked to see Schreiner— Gentleman Dave Schreiner!— confront the officials after the half was deemed over, arguing that Harder scored on the first plunge.

Angus animatedly told the coaches and the reserves the same thing, and seeing both the gentlemanly All-American end and the mild-mannered manager so angry convinced even those who didn't have a good angle.

"The officials couldn't see straight," reserve sophomore tackle Dave Donnellan says. "Harder crossed the goal line three times in the first half. If I was coaching, and again, I'm sitting on the sideline, I would have put in the second-team line. The second-team line was almost as good as the first team, they were fresh, and I think if they would have put them in, it would have made a difference."

The rest of the game was a nightmare. Stuhldreher again used only sixteen players. The coach lost his temper with junior end Bob Hanzlik, who had been an ironman all season and generally played well, though most teams attacked his end because of their respect for Schreiner. The way Hanzlik remembers it, he made it clear on the field that he believed one way to beat the Hawkeyes was to throw him the ball, and Stuhldreher considered that unacceptable insubordination. "I went over to the sideline, and Harry put me down," Hanzlik says. "He didn't talk to me." Pat Lyons played the final stages of the game at left end.

The Badgers didn't significantly threaten, and the final possession ended when Bud Seelinger—in for Hirsch to provide a better deep passing threat—threw an interception on a play that began at the Iowa 46.

The Badgers had only 170 yards of total offense. Hirsch could manage just 37 yards on 21 carries.

Later, when talking to the scribes, Stuhldreher was diplomatic. "Iowa deserved to win," he said. "The best team won, and that's that." At least for public consumption, Stuhldreher said Harder probably hadn't crossed the goal line.

In the press box, Roundy Coughlin was apoplectic. "I said all year long that Wisconsin was due for one fall and I figured Iowa City was spot it was coming in," he wrote. "And it did happen here folks. The Wisconsin team will come raring back now you can bet on that. . . . Northwestern and Minnesota will find different Wisconsin team than played at Iowa City Saturday. You can write Grandma letter about that."

Some of the Badgers believe they were so flat and Iowa so pumped that the Hawkeyes would have found a way to win, even if Harder had been ruled to be in the end zone.

Bob Rennebohm doesn't share that opinion. "We clearly won," he says. "Pat Harder was over the goal line. We were so disappointed, we knew that knocked us out of the top ratings in the country." And out of the conference lead.

In Madison, the Badgers' followers were shocked. "I listened back home on Lakeland Avenue," says '42 freshman Tom Butler. "Oh, and this town was as low as you could get after that game. Such a disappointment! You'd understand, though, that after such an emotional high there was no way you could get up, especially at Iowa."

Hank Casserly's game story in the *Capital Times* didn't credit the Badgers with any excuses. "The Hawkeyes were as sharp as a hound's tooth Saturday," he wrote. "The Badgers were far below the form which they displayed in blasting Ohio State a week previous. The Badgers tackled and blocked poorly and save for one spirited march in the second quarter, they never had a chance."

Then they had that long ride home. "Oh, god," quarterback Ashley Anderson says. "There were a lot of tears around. Everybody was very, very unhappy and it was a long ride."

In one car, Stuhldreher made it clear that the diplomacy he showed in his remarks to the reporters was an act. Over and over, he griped about "getting beat down there in that damn cornfield with that dog running around the field!"

In Rennebohm's car, nobody talked. At least not for a while.

★　★　★

Washington, Nov. 7 (AP)—Powerful American expeditionary forces are landing on the Atlantic and Mediterranean coasts of the French colonies in Africa in the first big-scale offensive of the war under the star-spangled banner.

The White House statement said the purpose of the move was two-fold:

1—To forestall an Axis invasion there which "would constitute a direct threat to America across the comparatively narrow sea from western Africa."

2—To provide "an effective second front assistance to our heroic allies in Russia."

★   ★   ★

"The owner of the car turned on the radio, and we got the message that we had invaded North Africa," Rennebohm recalls. "That's when we started talking about the military."

SEVENTEEN

Northwestern

In the rain at practice on the Monday after the Iowa loss, Harry Stuhldreher wept—right in front of his boys. Tearfully, he groused about the defeat and how the Badgers had let control of the Big Ten race slip out of their grasp. Fred Negus, among others, laughs when recalling it. It wasn't funny at the time.

"You let those goddam farmers beat you, what's the matter with you?" Stuhldreher bellowed.

He paced back and forth, tears falling and spit flying as he spoke.

Stuhldreher decided to make the boys pay for ruining his dream of joining Knute Rockne among the ranks of coaches who had guided teams through undefeated seasons.

Negus and the starters ran laps, a normal loosening procedure. Except they kept running. And running. The reserves, going through drills under the supervision of the assistant coaches, kept waiting for the regulars to join them.

Finally, senior backup halfback Jim McFadzean was exasperated. "Tell 'em to stop running!" he said to backfield coach Guy Sundt.

"Can't do that," said a shrugging Sundt. Stuhldreher was the boss.

After a few more minutes, the coach allowed the starters to join the reserves for the beginning of grass drills. Stuhldreher barked, "Front! Up! Front! Up!" The boys—starters and reserves alike—ran in place, dropped to the ground, jumped back up, and ran in place some more. They were so winded, some were dropping to the ground while others were getting up, and all pretense of synchronization disappeared.

They believed their coach—any coach—was the supreme authority. They were raised that way, and they never challenged it. But they were wondering if Stuhldreher had gone nuts.

As the boys dropped one more time, Pat Harder remained standing, one hand on his hip.

Stuhldreher kept barking. "Front! Up!"

The nation's best fullback glared at his coach.

One by one, other Badgers noticed the confrontation and stopped, including Dave Schreiner and Mark Hoskins, usually unconditional Stuhldreher supporters. Harry stopped yelling. The practice field was silent.

"OK, that's enough!" barked Stuhldreher. He sent the Badgers out of the rain, into the fieldhouse, for more light work.

"Harder just defied him," remembers sophomore halfback Erv Kissling. "He just stood right there. Harry couldn't say too much against Pat, ever. Pat Harder would have played with a broken leg or a broken arm."

The next morning, the *State Journal*, undoubtedly spoon-fed by the publicity department or Harry himself, reported that the Badgers had gone through a light drill that was cut short by the rain before they headed inside.

Stuhldreher's anger and Harder's defiance weren't the only dramas unfolding. Bob Hanzlik was starting to pay for what the coach considered his insubordination at Iowa. Hanzlik says that before the weeping and running began at that Monday practice, Stuhldreher ran through the lineup and had starting tackle Paul "Indian" Hirsbrunner in Hanzlik's spot at left end, with Lloyd Wasserbach taking over at tackle.

After the practice, Hanzlik says, Stuhldreher all but challenged him to quit. Of course, Harder's defiance and the virtual mutiny of other players left the coach in a foul mood—and perhaps looking for a scapegoat. Hanzlik says Stuhldreher told him, "I'm going to dress you, and people will be saying you're going to play, but you're not going to play."

Later in the week, the *State Journal* dutifully reported that Lyons was "pushing" Hanzlik for the starting spot.

★ ★ ★

The Badgers had a chance to win the Big Ten outright, but because they were playing fewer conference games than the other contenders, they needed a lot of help. Ohio State, Iowa, and Illinois all were 3–1, the Badgers and Michigan were 2–1. Northwestern, the Badgers' upcoming opponent in Evanston, was 0–5 but had the dangerous Otto Graham throwing passes.

Stuhldreher wasn't the only one continuing to lament the Iowa loss. Roundy Coughlin griped in print all week. "At Iowa City they had dog that was on the field most the time he ran across field all during the game. He near drove the fans nertz," Roundy wrote. "How the dog roamed all over that field for full game with out being removed from stadium is thing I'll never understand."

★ ★ ★

London, Nov. 11 (AP)—Goaded by the American coup in Africa, Adolf Hitler scrapped his armistice with France Wednesday, sent his gray-clad columns racing south toward Toulon and Marseilles and launched parachutists and air-borne infantry into French Tunisia.

The Mediterranean took its grim place as the great new front of the war.

★ ★ ★

Because the Badgers were returning to Greater Chicago, Stuhldreher again named tackle Bob Baumann the captain of the week. There were no further rebellions, but Stuhldreher continued to drive the Badgers harder than usual, and many of the boys—who didn't mind hard work—complained that they wouldn't have much left for Saturday.

Both to the Badgers and the scribes, Stuhldreher built up the Wildcats as the unluckiest outfit in the history of college football, and he praised Graham. Plus, he noted that the Badgers had had only one victory over Northwestern in the previous ten years, and the Wildcats had easily beaten Wisconsin in 1941.

Stuhldreher wasn't punitive enough to cancel the reservations at the Palmer House, so the Badgers got to stay one more time in the opulent downtown Chicago hotel.

★ ★ ★

Washington, Nov. 13 (AP)—The teenage draft bill awaited President Roosevelt's signature Friday. Prompt approval would mean that some 18- and 19-year-old youths may be called to the Army by Christmas.

About 800,000 youngsters out of a total of approximately one and one-half million available 18- and 19-year-olds are expected to be called up this winter, deferring the same number of married men and men with families. Maj. Gen. Lewis B. Hershey has estimated that his selective service organization will "lose" possibly one-half million of the one and one-half million to the Army, Navy, and Marine Corps through voluntary enlistment.

★ ★ ★

With one minute to play, the Badgers were desperate. Trailing 19–14 in Dyche Stadium, where about 10,000 Badger fans had joined the Northwestern faithful, Wisconsin was in danger of becoming the Wildcats' first Big Ten victim of the season.

Deciding that the Badgers needed the passing game, Stuhldreher sent in halfback Bud Seelinger, his best thrower, for Elroy Hirsch. Ashley Anderson was at quarterback because Jack Wink had been knocked out of the game earlier in the fourth quarter with a knee injury.

The Badgers were on the Northwestern 36.

Seelinger, the diminutive Montana cowboy, rolled out on first down, decided to run, and made it all the way to the Wildcats' 15. Two Pat Harder carries got the ball to the 6, but the clock was running, and less than 30 seconds remained. Anderson barked out the play. On third and one, Seelinger took the snap, looked to his right, and spotted Mark Hoskins, who had drifted out from his usual blocking wing position. Seelinger's pass was slightly behind the halfback from Lancaster, but Hoskins reached back, drew the ball toward him with one hand, and cradled it as he fell to the turf in the end zone. The Badgers led 20–19.

"I think the experience of losing to Iowa helped us against Northwestern," Anderson says. "We didn't panic. The play I called had a fake into the line with Harder. They came in and Hoskins just faded out into the flat. Bud just tossed an easy pass."

Seelinger was in the game because of a change of plans. Stuhldreher originally tried to replace Hirsch with sophomore Jim Regan, the boy from the Chicago suburb of Berwyn.

"The coach from my high school brought the entire team to watch the game, so I really wanted to get in," Regan says. "Harry turned to me and said, 'Regan, warm up!' In the olden days, you had to run up and get in the ready position and jog. He said that to me about three or four times. About the fifth or sixth time, he said, 'Go in for Hirsch.' In those days you had to report. I said to the referee, 'Regan for Hirsch,' and Hirsch said, 'I'm not coming out!' I was a green sophomore and he was about to be an All-American, so I said, 'See you,' and ran back to the sideline. I said, 'Coach, he doesn't want to come out.'"

Stuhldreher gave Regan a disgusted look.

"Well, right toward the end of the game, when there were one or two plays left, and we're losing, Harry said, 'Regan, go in for Hirsch and throw the 131 pass!' 'Yes, sir,' I say, and I get up and start running. But as I'm starting in he grabs me by the shirt and yells, 'Seelinger!' He sent Seelinger in instead for that series. The reason he sent Seelinger in is that he led the Big Ten in passing his junior year. So Seelinger goes in and completes a pass for a touchdown to Hoskins."

The time remaining was variously recorded as 18 seconds and 21 seconds. Northwestern blocked the extra point, but the Badgers won 20–19, keeping them in the Big Ten hunt. They whooped and hollered, but deep down they blamed their coach for killing their morale and unnecessarily draining them physically during the week.

"We were lucky to win that one," Negus says.

McFadzean, the senior halfback, says, "We barely beat 'em, and one reason was our first team was worn out and he hadn't substituted anybody. So in the fourth quarter, Otto Graham was throwing that ball, and Harry puts me in."

Indeed, the weary Badgers almost lost the game after taking a 14–0 lead in the second quarter. Harder scored the first two touchdowns for the Badgers, one on a recovery of an Elroy Hirsch fumble in the end zone, the other on a 6-yard screen pass from Hirsch. The Wildcats stormed back on two touchdown passes from Graham to Bob Motl, sandwiched around an Ed Hirsch (no relation) touchdown run. Fortunately for the Badgers, the Wildcats made only one of the conversions.

The Badgers weren't staying overnight this time, so most of them headed back to Madison on the train. A few had gotten permission to stay behind to attend the Packers-Bears game the next day at Soldier Field.

Hanzlik, still in the doghouse, didn't play a second against Northwestern. He says he got in even deeper when he remained in Chicago overnight and didn't let Harry know that he wouldn't be on the train with the team. Stuhldreher chalked up another black mark against the big end from Chippewa Falls.

"I said, 'The hell with you, I'm leaving,'" Hanzlik says. "I left. I didn't accompany the team back, and that was wrong on my account. I'm not making excuses, but I'm eighteen, nineteen years old, and I couldn't stand not playing. I was very selfish, because other guys deserved a chance to play, too, and I've regretted that for a long time."

★ ★ ★

Washington, Nov. 14 (AP)—Dauntless Eddie Rickenbacker has been rescued, in good condition, the Navy announced Saturday, three weeks after his airplane radioed that it was about out of gasoline and then vanished in the Pacific.

Rickenbacker, America's ace of aces in the first World war and the country's embodied proof that you can't keep a good man down, was picked from a raft bobbing in the sea by a Navy Catalina flying boat along with two of his crew. They were 600 miles north of Samoa.

★ ★ ★

Mark Hoskins's girlfriend, Mary Carthew, was attending the National College of Education in Evanston, and she went to the Northwestern game.

For a while.

"I was working at Simmons's Drug Store," Mary says. "I had to be back at work before the game was over. I was down when I walked into the drugstore, but Mr. Simmons had this big smile on his face and said, 'Mark Hoskins won the game!' I hadn't known it."

A small crowd greeted the Badgers at the train station. Much of the attention was paid to Seelinger and Hoskins, the heroes of the game-saving play. Wink, who was limping badly, quickly headed for the infirmary for knee X-rays.

The *Capital Times* reported that Stuhldreher told the crowd, "It was one of those storybook finishes. The boys answered the call and came through in the last minute."

Elsewhere, Ohio State beat Illinois, and Minnesota whipped Iowa. The Badgers were alone in second place, a half-game behind the Buckeyes. Ohio State was 4–1, Wisconsin 3–1, and Michigan, which defeated Notre Dame in a nonleague game, remained at 2–1. The scribes figured out that for Wisconsin to win the Big Ten title, three things had to happen. On November 14, the Badgers had to beat Minnesota in the final game, and Michigan had to knock off Ohio State; then Iowa had to knock off Michigan on November 21. Nowhere in any of the discussions was it questioned that Ohio State would be the undisputed conference champion if the Buckeyes finished 5–1 and the Badgers 4–1, despite Wisconsin's head-to-head victory.

Stuhldreher couldn't even complain to the athletic director about the scheduling that had left the Badgers at a mathematical disadvantage. Or, if he did, he would have to do it while looking in the mirror.

EIGHTEEN

Minnesota

The Badgers hadn't beaten the Minnesota Gophers in the schedule-ending rivalry game since 1932, so nine consecutive Wisconsin seasons had ended on a sour note. The Gophers' highly regarded coach, Bernie Bierman, had left the Minneapolis campus after a second straight Big Ten championship in 1941 to serve in the Marines. His successor was Dr. George Hauser, who received considerable input from young assistant coach Bud Wilkinson.

The Gophers had no chance to take the '42 Big Ten title, but they could end any Wisconsin hopes of succeeding them as champions—and do it in front of a sellout crowd at Camp Randall.

A handful of Badgers watched the Bears whip the Packers 38–7, making their record 8–0, in Soldier Field on Sunday, November 15. Then, mindful that they had promised Harry Stuhldreher to travel back to the campus as soon as possible after the game, the players hurried home. Bob Hanzlik, the AWOL end, returned as well, but he was getting in deeper trouble every day.

On Sunday, manager Eugene Fischer's weekly note on the locker room chalkboard proclaimed: "Nine down and THE ONE to go."

Hanzlik met with Stuhldreher before the Monday practice, and Hanzlik says the coach issued him an ultimatum. Hanzlik says Stuhldreher made it clear that if Hanzlik wanted to return to the team in 1943, he would suit up all week and practice but have no hope of getting in the game. Hanzlik, enlisted in the Marine Reserves, didn't know if he would be in college in the fall of '43, but he knew he would want to play football if he was.

"He said, 'You're not going to get a letter or you're not going to be able to eat meals with us,'" Hanzlik says. "He was really popping it to me, understand? After three years there, never missing a practice in my life . . . well, I'm defending myself now. I think I can go along with him if I look at it from both sides now. But that was the reason I didn't play in the last two games."

Hanzlik swallowed his pride and practiced all week. Curiously, neither of the Madison papers carried an account of why a Badger who had started seven of the first eight games of the season—all but the win over Great Lakes—suddenly was *persona non grata*. Stuhldreher didn't even bother to make up an injury. The *State Journal*'s Marv Rand reported that Hanzlik was working with the third-string unit all week and noted that the onetime starter "apparently has fallen behind." Behind? Paul Hirsbrunner—the tackle-turned-end who had moved into Hanzlik's spot—didn't practice much of the week because he was having problems with his shoulder, which he'd had surgically repaired a couple of years earlier. Still, Stuhldreher wouldn't move Hanzlik above the third unit. If Stuhldreher told the scribes why Hanzlik was in his doghouse, they didn't report it. Nor did anyone ask Hanzlik what was going on.

During the week, quarterback Jack Wink and Hirsbrunner shared a room in the university infirmary. Doctors determined Wink had suffered a strained knee ligament at Northwestern. Though Stuhldreher publicly said Wink would be involved in "at least partial action," the coach knew that was misleading—although it didn't turn out to be a complete lie. As the week went along, the Badger coach pondered his alternatives. He considered having Pat Harder call out the signals from the fullback spot and inserting backup fullback Len Calligaro into the quarterback position. Stuhldreher believed Ashley Anderson could handle the signal calling and other duties at quarterback, but the coach also knew that Calligaro was a much stronger defensive player. Even Anderson acknowledges that was true. The situation was one of the dilemmas involved in limited-substitution, one-platoon football. Ultimately, Stuhldreher settled on a compromise, one that would cost him a five-yard penalty on virtually every change of possession.

Appropriately, Dave Schreiner was named the captain for the Minnesota game. The senior from Lancaster was a shoo-in to be a repeat All-American. Against Minnesota, he would be facing his buddies Dick Wildung and Bill Daley, plus several other Gophers who had also been Camp Kooch-I-Ching counselors. Again, he spent some of his week scrambling to get tickets and telling his parents one more time in a letter: "You were very foolish to let anyone in Lancaster know I had tickets." But he also refused to take anything more than face value for the $2.75 tickets from anyone in Lancaster, though he had to pay $6.50 for some of them because he felt he should pay his buddies at least what they could get on the open market.

The Badgers prepared to honor the fourteen seniors who would be playing their final game for Wisconsin: Schreiner, halfbacks Mark Hoskins and Jim McFadzean; quarterback Bobby Diercks; fullbacks Bob Ray and Calligaro; center Bob McKay; guards John Roberts and George Makris; tackles Lloyd Wasserbach, Hirsbrunner, Baumann, and Thornally; and end Bob Stupka. It was also noted that Fischer, the comanager, was a senior as well.

Stuhldreher again had a guest with him at the Uptown Coaches booster club meeting—Jay Berwanger, the onetime Chicago halfback who in 1937 became the first Heisman Trophy winner. Berwanger was stationed in Madison as a Navy recruiter.

★　★　★

Washington, Nov. 17 (AP)—The United States Navy dominated the battle-quickened waters of the Solomon Islands Tuesday after crushing a mighty Japanese armada in an epic struggle which might well have broken the back of the enemy fleet.

In a savage three-day conflict that sent the foe's naval remnants into hiding, twenty-three Nipponese ships were sunk, seven were damaged and possibly 20,000 to 40,000 Japanese troops were lost in the swirl of sunken transports.

First details of the battle that raged from Nov. 13 to 15 were released by the Navy Monday night.

★　★　★

Roundy Coughlin sensed trouble for the Badgers. "In the last two games 343 yards has been made against Wisconsin by Iowa and Northwestern by scrimmage," he wrote. "You ain't tackling when they do that. You can't tackle that way against Minnesota and beat them they will murder you if you tackle that way."

Stoney McGlynn of the *Milwaukee Sentinel* was also worried, writing:

The Badgers, of late, have not attained the peak reached three weeks ago against Ohio State. That day, in my belief, there wasn't a college team in the country that could have matched the footballers coach Harry Stuhldreher put on the field."

McGlynn concluded he still had faith that the boys "will be at, or right near, the peak reached against the Buckeyes."

The game was sold out for more than two weeks, and the athletic department announced that fifteen FBI agents were going to be sent to Madison to foil ticket scalping. The FBI had far more important concerns, of course, so the much-trumpeted story likely was both a preemptive strike and pure fiction.

★ ★ ★

On game day, November 21, Stuhldreher allowed *State Journal* newsroom columnist Roy L. Matson to watch from the Wisconsin bench area and be in the locker room. Matson provided readers with an inside look the next morning.

On the first play from scrimmage, Anderson barked the signals for a rollout pass by Elroy Hirsch. Hirsch hit Schreiner on the sideline, and Schreiner sprinted the rest of the way for what seemed to be a 69-yard touchdown. However, the linesman signaled that Schreiner had stepped out of bounds at the Minnesota 41, triggering howls from the Badgers, who swore the All-American end had stayed in the field of play. (The film confirmed that they were right.)

The Badgers were unbowed. Pat Harder skirted the left side—the side where Hirsbrunner, in pain, was playing at end—for 24 yards, then gained 6 the other way. Hirsch went for 7, and Harder followed with a 1-yard run that got the Badgers to the 3. Hank Casserly of the *Capital Times* described the sequence this way: "Harder was stopped cold, but like Antaeus of Greek mythology, who became stronger every time he was thrown to Mother Earth, Harder blasted over for a touchdown on the next play, hitting right guard like a huge tank." Only two and a half minutes into the game, the Badgers were ahead 6–0.

Matson told *State Journal* readers that Stuhldreher then turned to Wink. "All right, Wink!" he said. "Come on, Wink!" Amazingly, Wink—torn ligament and all—peeled off his jacket, with the help of Fischer, and hobbled onto the field to hold for Harder's conversion attempt. Wink put his good knee on the ground and stuck the bad one out straight. If a Gopher had wanted to play dirty, he could have "tripped" over the extended leg. Nobody did. In fact, after the game, Stuhldreher told the scribes, "When we first thought of using Wink to hold the ball for points after touchdowns, the players were worried about Minnesota players jumping on Wink's injured knee. I swear I saw several Gophers deliberately veer away from Wink when rushing in on the attempt to block Harder's kick. That thrilled me to think they would do that, when winning meant so much."

After the touchdown, Stuhldreher's strategy came into focus. Anderson left the game when the Gophers took over, and Calligaro, normally a fullback, filled his defensive spot. That wasn't remarkable, but when Anderson came back in when the Badgers regained possession, Wisconsin drew a 5-yard penalty for the illegal substitution—technically, it was called "too many timeouts"—and started out first-and-15. Stuhldreher accepted the same penalty throughout the rest of the game, even when that meant the Gophers began many possessions with a first-and-5. "I think that's the first time that kind of substitution ever was done," Anderson recalls. "He did that the whole game. I just played offense."

While Calligaro was on the field, Anderson donned a parka and stood at Stuhldreher's side, talking about plays the Badgers might use in the next series. Anderson kept one eye on the field, ready to scramble to avoid players piling over the sideline, but also twisting and turning to avoid the smoke from the cigarette always planted between Stuhldreher's fingers or in his mouth. When the coach raised his right hand to make a point or exhaled after taking a puff, he nearly asphyxiated his quarterback.

Matson enjoyed the antics of guard Ken "Roughie" Currier when the sophomore came out of the game for a short break near the end of the first quarter. Currier worked as hard taunting the Gophers from the sideline as he did playing. "Hey, Frickey, you're going to fumble," Currier yelled to halfback Herman Frickey. "Hey, Frickey, you better let it go." To Minnesota quarterback Bill Garnaas, Currier hollered, "Hey, Pee-Wee, you can't pass. Look out, Pee-Wee, they'll run over you."

Matson was awestruck by what he saw on the sideline, as when guard Red Vogds came out for a brief break late in a quarter because he was cut on the face and bleeding from the nose. "That happens every game," an unidentified Badger reserve told Matson. "He likes it." And Matson noted that while Harder seemed to be cut on his face and on every extremity, he didn't seem to mind it, either.

Matson lost track of all the nicknames Calligaro's teammates called him every time he came off the field to give way for Anderson. Among them were Gooper, Batchy, Batchygaloop, and Pooshemup.

Negus, finishing a great sophomore season, recovered a Frickey fumble on the Gopher 32 to set up Wisconsin's second touchdown. Hirsch connected with Schreiner, who broke Gopher Bob Solheim's tackle and dived across the goal line. Later, Minnesota back Bob Sandberg, who like Currier came from Rice Lake, Wisconsin, talked about the play to the *Minneapolis Tribune.* "He caught that pass right over me," Sandberg said. "He can really wheel. I know he was fast because I was at camp with him last summer and we used to run races but I didn't figure he was THAT fast."

The Badgers led 14–0 at halftime.

Anderson suffered a highly personal injury on the second-half kick-off, taking a helmet to the groin area. As Anderson tried to gather himself on the ground, Stuhldreher himself took charge, coming onto the field and giving his prone quarterback the traditional treatment of repeatedly pulling him in the air by his belt and then lowering him to the ground. "Breathe!" barked Stuhldreher.

Anderson was recovering from the original injury, except now he had a bruised tailbone. He stayed in the game.

With the Badgers still leading 14–0 early in the fourth quarter, the Gophers failed on a fourth-down play deep in their own territory. After the 5-yard penalty because of Anderson's return to the game, a Harder-to-Schreiner pass got the Badgers to the 3, and Anderson scored from the 1 on a quarterback sneak out of the T formation.

Hirsbrunner's shoulder hurt so severely that he had to leave the game. The "Indian" was in tears, both because of the pain and because he knew he had just played his final down of college football.

Bill Daley's 1-yard run got the Gophers on the scoreboard late, before Currier and Hirsch made interceptions in the final minutes. Negus played another great game at center and linebacker. Stuhldreher managed to get his stars out of the game, hugging them individually as they came to the sideline, and used twenty-five players that afternoon. As the final seconds counted down, the Badgers hugged and cheered and popped one another's pads.

Final score: Wisconsin 20, Minnesota 6. The Badgers had only eight first downs and were outgained 257–198, but that didn't matter. Anderson did a superb job of field generalship, primarily calling the plays and blocking and leaving the passing to Hirsch and Harder, who each had run for 43 yards. Mark Hoskins, in his final game, blocked well and added 9 yards on seven carries. Schreiner caught all three Wisconsin completions for a total of 82 yards. Daley, the Gophers' star, ran for 89 yards. But seven turnovers—five interceptions and two fumbles—killed Minnesota.

"That game was fun, really was fun," says backup guard John Roberts. "That was such a big rivalry there, and because I was from Iowa, I didn't realize how big it was until I got up to school there. But beating them helped make that season what it was."

★　★　★

The athletic department had declared November 21 Dad's Day, and the players' fathers were allowed in the locker room after the game. Matson recorded the proceedings in the paper the next morning.

Bert Schreiner, the Lancaster scion, called out as he crossed the room. "Davey! Davey!" he exclaimed. "Oh, Davey, what a game!"

Hirsch greeted his father, Otto. "Hi, Pop. How are you, Pop?"

Elroy reached over and pulled his pop's hat down, scrunching it on his head. Otto responded with a warm hug. "Aw, Pop," Elroy said, embarrassed. Then he noticed that a photographer wanted to take their picture. "Hey, Pop," he said, "you better fix your hat."

Seconds later, they faced the camera.

Outside, the Wisconsin band was playing its post-game show. The strains of "Praise the Lord and Pass the Ammunition" were audible in the dressing room. The sting from the Iowa loss was diluted, though the Badgers realized it had cost them the Big Ten title. Ohio State beat Michigan 21–7 that day to clinch the championship by a half-game over the Badgers.

"I've never been more proud of a bunch of fellows in my whole life than I am this afternoon," Stuhldreher said.

In the press box, Roundy Coughlin wrote for his Sunday readers: "Boy, I'll bet the Wisconsin boys in service celebrated last night when that score went out Wisconsin 20, Minnesota 6. I'll bet the closest tap room got an awful work out. Did Schreiner ever play a game. Did you see him ride those blockers. That's prettiest football picture I ever saw. All the printer has to do is get the type set up for Dave Schreiner as the All-American right end." He also had kind words for Schreiner's Lancaster buddy. "The blocking and tackling by Hoskins was really a thing of beauty and he had that winning spirit in his body."

Dick Wildung complimented the Badgers. "That's a powerful outfit you have here at Wisconsin," he said. "I can't understand how they ever lost to Iowa. You know, we've played some tough clubs this year and these Badgers rate with the best."

Bill Daley added, "It was a tough way to bow out, but I'm sure glad it was Wisconsin and Dave Schreiner who finished it up for me. Isn't that Dave a man, though? I'm sure proud I became friends with him last summer. He's a corker."

Hauser, the Gophers' coach, told the *Minneapolis Tribune* that his young assistant, Wilkinson, remarked to him that the Gophers "had those pet plays of theirs well scouted. We had worked on them all week, especially those plays with Harder carrying the ball and the passes to Dave Schreiner. There is a fine football player. Harder, too. I do not mean to take anything away from the Badgers. I think Harder is a better back than Hirsch and Schreiner is an outstanding end."

Minnesota lineman Paul Mitchell was shaking his head about trying to tackle Hirsch. "Yes, he's got crazy legs all right," Mitchell said. "You've got to hit him high, you can't stop him low. We were told that and I guess we caught on."

Anderson's fraternity brothers, who had downed a few beers by the time the quarterback arrived back at the house, remembered Hirsch's friendly teasing in song after Anderson's fumble in the Camp Grant opener. This time they serenaded Anderson as he came in the door:

"Ashley, Ashley, we love you,
"Touchdown, touchdown from the 2."

Downtown, the bars and taverns were doing ring-it-up business. A bellman told the *State Journal* that it was the busiest single night in Madison since the celebration following the repeal of Prohibition.

"I think we sensed it at the time, that it was never going to be the same, that it was the last hurrah of carefree college kids," says Tom Butler, who celebrated the victory that night as a UW freshman. "Our age of innocence was over. I always said we were born in the middle of the roaring '20s, we grew up during the Great Depression, and graduated from high school and went into World War II."

The Badgers were about to be called to serve Uncle Sam. But they had a while longer to savor Wisconsin's best football season in thirty years.

NINETEEN

So Close

The Tuesday after the Minnesota game, the Badgers met in the Camp Randall dressing room and elected captains-of-record for the season. Dave Schreiner and Mark Hoskins, the Lancaster boys, won in a landslide. Stuhldreher took them to the Uptown Coaches booster meeting and broke the news. The *Wisconsin State Journal* reported the speeches the next morning.

"Mark and Dave don't like either the way I pronounce Lancaster or the fact that I label it a small town," Stuhldreher told the boosters. "But the fact remains that there is quite a story behind this pair." (Like most people, Stuhldreher pronounced it "LAN-cass-ter." Natives preferred "Lan-cus-ter," with no real accent on any syllable.)

The coach told the boosters about the boys' long friendship and then added, "They started out their first game in a blaze of glory, with Hoskins rifling a touchdown pass to Dave. They finished three years of outstanding work with an even more brilliant game against Minnesota last Saturday."

The boosters demanded speeches, and Schreiner and Hoskins reluctantly obliged.

"Your backing meant an awful lot to us all, and we appreciate it," Schreiner said. "The team couldn't have gone half as far this year if you hadn't been behind us."

Hoskins joked, "I resent all the cracks about our hometown, but can only echo Dave's words. We had a swell time playing ball in every game."

Stuhldreher also reported that the Badgers awarded twenty-seven players "major" W letters, while twenty-two others received "minor" letters. Stuhldreher unilaterally made the calls. In theory, major letters went to Badgers who got significant playing time and were on the first or second team at some point. Minor letters went to other squad members, but only if Stuhldreher wanted to reward them. (In later years, the major-minor distinction was eliminated.) Stuhldreher had carried through on his threat: Bob Hanzlik wasn't awarded a letter of any kind.

★   ★   ★

Washington, Nov. 25 (AP)—Details of a campaign which Dr. Stephen S. Wise said was planned to exterminate all Jews in Nazi-occupied Europe by the end of the year are to be laid before a committee of leading Jewish organizations Wednesday in New York. The story—which Dr. Wise said was confirmed by the state department and a personal representative of President Roosevelt—deals with how more than 2 million Jews already have been slaughtered in accordance with a race extermination order by Adolf Hitler.

★   ★   ★

After all teams finished their seasons, Schreiner was third in national receiving yardage, with 16 catches for 350 yards. Hirsch was the number 6 rusher in the country, with 766 yards in 10 games. Rudolph "Little Doc" Mobley of Hardin-Simmons was the leader, with 1,173. There was no mention of a possible bowl berth for the Badgers, and the Rose Bowl invited Georgia and UCLA. (That game would be returning to Pasadena in January 1943; a year earlier Duke and Oregon State played in a Rose Bowl game that was relocated to Durham, North Carolina, due to security concerns regarding a large gathering of people on the West Coast less than a month after the attack on Pearl Harbor.)

On the Friday after the end of the season, the day after Thanksgiving, Stuhldreher made his second appearance in five years at the Lancaster postseason football banquet. The program honored both the local high school team, still coached by Fausto Rubini, and the "Touchdown Twins," the Badger cocaptains from Lancaster. Both Madison papers sent writers to cover the banquet. The printed program for the event included this line for one part of the proceedings: "Comments . . . Had and Dave." No further identification was necessary.

The *State Journal*'s Roy L. Matson reported, "The little kids down here are about evenly divided: Half of them play Dave Schreiner and the other half Mark Hoskins . . . and then they shift around."

Master of Ceremonies O. F. Christenson said that Lancaster was proud "mostly because they're still the same good clean-cut straightforward boys they were on the corner lot. They're All-Americans to all the rest of the world. They're All-Lancaster to us. Because of all we can say about them, they never got too big for Lancaster."

Hoskins still wasn't comfortable talking to crowds, and he was overcome in his hometown. "I-I-I- can't say a word," he said. "This is the best thing that ever happened to Dave and to me. I-I-I- . . . all I can say is thanks."

Schreiner labeled the banquet "the greatest thing Had and I have ever been given."

Stuhldreher said he turned down an invitation to speak at a Philadelphia banquet with sportswriter Grantland Rice to come to Lancaster. "Communities are judged by the products they turn out," the Badger coach said. "You'll never forget these boys. I'll never forget them either. Never."

The next Tuesday, December 1, back at Madison, the team held its annual banquet in the Memorial Union. By then the Badgers had worked up anger over how Ohio State was considered the league champion, even though Wisconsin had beaten the Buckeyes and both teams had one conference loss. The banquet program included excerpts of local columns on the matter, and, as usual, Roundy Coughlin was the most vocal.

"They say Ohio State is champion but that don't go with me," he wrote. "I say Wisconsin is tied with Buckeyes. You can use a pencil a mile long with eraser half mile long and you can't show that we ain't tied for the championship. They can bang these Phi Beta Kappa keys around, they're supposed to be the smart keys and I still wouldn't give in. I think we tied for the championship, Ohio [State] lost one game and we lost one and we beat Ohio State. I'm dumb but does this paragraph still make me dumb?"

Shortly after the season, Mary and Harry Stuhldreher invited the seniors and their dates to their home. The coach's wife later wrote in her book *Many a Saturday Afternoon* that "[a]fter a buffet supper, there were dancing and games. Then, one by one, the couples made their excuses and left. We didn't mind that they left, but Mark [Hoskins] and Dave [Schreiner] thought we did, so they stayed until midnight and helped Harry and me clean up."

By then, Schreiner was certain of his decision about the military. He wasn't going to medical school, and it seems a safe bet that even if he had remained on that academic track, he wouldn't have accepted the deferment. He didn't want to watch others serve. His partial color blindness ruled out trying to become a pilot and joining Hoskins in the AAF reserves, so he decided the best course was to follow many of his teammates and sign up for the Marine Reserves.

At some point in late 1942, most likely wedged into the busy two-week period following the November 21 Minnesota game, but possibly earlier, Schreiner and two senior teammates who had signed up earlier in the year—tackles Bob Baumann and Dick Thornally—drove to Milwaukee to visit the Marine recruiting station. Thornally believes they were probably taking their physicals and that Schreiner was attempting to finalize his enlistment, but he is more certain about another aspect of the trip.

The speeding ticket.

The three Badgers had borrowed Stuhldreher's big green Mercury. Thornally, Baumann, and Schreiner were close to Milwaukee, in the small city of Waukesha, when a police officer pulled them over and cited Thornally for speeding. In the small-town fashion of the time, the officer took the boys straight to a town building to face a judge. The judge recognized them and made convivial small talk, telling the three Badger football players—including the All-American Schreiner—that his grandson was on the Wisconsin baseball team. The boys exclaimed at the mention of the name. Sure, they knew him!

"Tell you what, boys," the judge said, "you go to Milwaukee and do your business with the Marines and stop back here on the way home, and we'll take care of this!"

The Badgers inferred that if they brought back their Marine paperwork and showed it to the judge, he would throw out the ticket. On their way back they stopped in Waukesha and again appeared before the judge. They expected congratulations and a pardon.

"He fined me twenty-five bucks!" Thornally says, his anger undiminished. "Twenty-five bucks was a lot! What we had done didn't seem to have any effect on him."

Back on the road, when they weren't lamenting the judge's stupidity, Thornally, Schreiner, and Baumann discussed their future as leathernecks.

But Schreiner had one more hurdle to clear. While not as stringent about the ability to distinguish colors as the Army Air Forces, the Marines were concerned about Schreiner's partial color blindness. Schreiner went to the Great Lakes Naval Training Station in early December, apparently to take another vision test. He passed and wrote to his parents:

> I now have until Dec. 15 to complete my enlistment and I don't think that I will have any difficulty. This test I took in Chicago was simple. In the corner of the dark room there was a lamp. It could be adjusted to throw out different colors of red and green. All I had to do was call out which color it was.

About that same time, the final Associated Press poll placed Ohio State number 1, Georgia number 2, and Wisconsin number 3. The Helms Athletic Foundation, formed in 1936 by Los Angeles philanthropist Paul H. Helms to support sports, had begun naming its own national champion in 1941, when it chose Minnesota. For 1942, the foundation named Wisconsin the champion, but that announcement was largely overlooked and of little consolation. The Badgers and their fans were still distressed that Ohio State was considered the conference champion.

Wire services and magazines were in a rush to get their honors out first, so it wasn't long after that final game that Schreiner was named a first-team All-American by virtually every outlet that named a mythical squad. He and Notre Dame's Bob Dove were the consensus All-American ends. Schreiner, Harder, Negus, and Hirsch were named to the all-conference first team, selected by the coaches for The Associated Press. Hirsbrunner made the second team, and Wink and Hoskins were on the honorable mention list.

In late December, Schreiner was named the winner of the *Chicago Tribune*'s Silver Football award as the Big Ten's most valuable player. He met up with members of the East All-Star team in Chicago, and the team traveled to San Francisco for the January 1 East-West Shrine Game, a fundraiser for the San Francisco unit of the Shriners' Hospital for crippled children. After receiving the award in a ceremony carried on another

With Harry Stuhldreher watching at left, Dave Schreiner accepts the Silver Football in Chicago as the Big Ten's most valuable player.
PHOTO COURTESY OF JUDY CORFIELD

radio station, he appeared on Chicago's WGN radio with sportscaster Jack Brickhouse to talk about the award.

"I still don't know why they singled me out for the most valuable award, but I certainly appreciate their respect, and I'm deeply indebted to the coaches and officials who awarded me the Tribune silver football," he said.

In the East-West game, played in San Francisco's Kezar Stadium, Schreiner recovered a West fumble and then caught a 34-yard touchdown pass on the next play from Columbia's Paul Governali. East won the game 13–12. Years later, Governali told the *State Journal*'s Henry J. McCormick that at one of the practices leading up to the game, Schreiner had chided his teammates. When they told him to take it easy, he said, "You kiddin'? Gotta get in shape for those kids."

Mark Hoskins was invited to play in the Blue-Gray All-Star Game in Montgomery, Alabama, but he passed. The Badgers in the Army Air Forces Reserves were getting the impression they would be called up soon—sooner than their buddies in the Marines—and Hoskins wanted to spend as much time as possible during the Christmas break with his family and Mary Carthew.

After the break, Hoskins and the Badgers went back to school, but for the most part their hearts weren't in it. Most of the underclassmen stopped attending class and studying altogether. "We should have all flunked out of school," says Jim Regan, the '42 sophomore halfback. "When football season ended, I got all Fs. Most of us did. Very few of us went to class."

In Madison, Stuhldreher pulled strings to prevent the underclassmen from being flunked out immediately. That was especially important for the younger Badgers in the Marine Reserves, because if they flunked out of school they wouldn't be accepted into the V-12 study program. But most of the Badgers in the Army Air Forces, including Jerry Frei, were indeed called in to the service before the end of the second semester, in early 1943. Hoskins even tried to speed up the process. The Badgers' potential flyers were so eager, they delegated their team cocaptain to go to Chicago. Hoskins brashly made an appointment to see a general in the Fifth Army headquarters. When he was called into the office, Hoskins asked, "Sir, when are we going to be called in?"

The general told Hoskins to pass along a message to his teammates and fellow prospective pilots: "Don't worry, boys, we'll take care of you!"

By March, several of the Badgers were already in the AAF uniform and in training.

On April 8, a few of the Badgers were drafted—by the National Football League. The Detroit Lions claimed Schreiner, the Green Bay Packers took Hoskins, and the Chicago Bears took their hometown tackle Bob Baumann. The football draft was usually a low-profile event, even more so in a year when most of the college seniors were expected to be in the military soon.

"I was on the track team that spring, too," says Ashley Anderson, one of the team's best students. "So I competed in a few track meets, but I was never in very good condition because it was party time, all the time. We knew we were going into the service, and as far as going to class, who cared about that? Even me."

Reserve quarterback John Gallagher was one of the young Marine reservists. "After the season, the talk was, 'Well, where are you going?' Everybody was going different directions, Army, Navy, Marine Corps," Gallagher says.

With the draft age lowered to eighteen, America was beginning to look askance at any men who appeared to be over eighteen but weren't in military garb, and the feeling was no different among the Badgers. One by one or in small groups, they left Madison and civilian student life. Stuhldreher, the coach who had talked of preparing his players to face enemy soldiers within a year of that '42 season, bid the Badgers farewell. He asked them to stay in touch and began what would become a steady routine of letter-writing to them, whether they were in training around the country or fighting around the globe. Stuhldreher had his weaknesses, but many soldiers who served with Badgers over the next few years were impressed that the coach wrote periodic and personal letters to most of his boys.

"I think every one of us—and this was true across America—felt we might not come back," says halfback Jim Regan, who ended up in the Army. "I know I thought that."

TWENTY

Off to Serve

The Badger seniors who had signed up for the Marines—including Dick Thornally, Bob Baumann, Dave Schreiner, Bud Seelinger, Paul Hirsbrunner, and George Makris—eagerly finished up their studies in the spring of 1943. "We were called up in May, and they graduated us early because we were pushing for it," Thornally says. "We wanted to get going."

Schreiner discussed the possibility of early graduation in a letter to his parents:

> It is possible that I may be able to graduate by April 29 and go into the Marines the first week in May. I am hoping that this will be possible as I am very anxious to get in. If they don't take me then it won't be until sometime in the summer and I have no desire to stay around awaiting my call when the rest of my friends are in there really accomplishing something. This training which one receives in the service is the best possible type of training which can be had. In later life I'm sure this training will show to good advantage. I'll let you know any more developments as soon as I hear and please don't try and change my mind as it won't do any good and I know I'm right.

Schreiner was by then deeply in love, and it happened fast. He didn't even mention the Delta Gamma sorority girl until a February 10 letter, then merely saying, "I have a date with a girl by the name of Odette Hendrickson who is really a fine girl." They were engaged that spring, although the official announcement didn't appear in newspapers until June. As his graduation approached, Schreiner wrote to his "Aunt Em," thanking her for a generous graduation check he used to buy the engagement ring.

David Nathan Schreiner, USMC.
PHOTO COURTESY OF JUDY CORFIELD

Schreiner was at the Marines boot camp at Parris Island, South Carolina, by May. In a May 21 letter he told his parents, "Right now I'm doing what I want to do because it has to be done."

Schreiner, Baumann, and Thornally stayed together through Parris Island and Officer Candidates School at Quantico, Virginia. At their OCS graduation in September 1943, Vice Admiral John S. McCain, the deputy chief of naval air operations, gave the commencement address in the Quantico recreation building. The Badgers were second lieutenants.

"Baumann and Schreiner wanted to be paratroopers, and I wanted to be an officer of a weapons platoon, with mortars and machine guns," Thornally says. "They both shipped to the West Coast immediately to train for the paratroopers." Thornally regretted the separation—then and later.

"I should have been with those guys," he says. "Dave never told me he was going to enlist in the paratroopers until they had done it. I was an expert rifleman in the range, even won an award. I was a nut about machine guns and rifles and stuff like that. So I wrote down that I wanted to be a weapons platoon lieutenant. When the assignments came through, they got shipped off to California. I missed those guys."

Schreiner and Baumann went to Camp Elliott in San Diego, but Marines junked their paratrooper program because it was deemed inappropriate for jungle and island fighting. They returned to mainstream training, and Schreiner was briefly back at Quantico.

Walter "Bus" Bergman, the senior captain and star halfback at Colorado A&M in 1941, met Schreiner at Quantico. Schreiner was a veteran of pulling officer-of-the-day duty on graduation night, and he counseled

Bergman on how to handle the assignment: *Look the other way, Bus.* "That was a mess," Bergman says. "I had parents and girlfriends falling all over the place. But Dave was real cool about it. He said, 'This happens, don't worry about it, forget it.' I thought that was neat."

Meanwhile, Dick Thornally didn't get his preferred assignment in a weapons platoon. "They decided I evidently knew how to tune a radio or something," Thornally says, "so they sent me up to Connecticut with the Navy to learn communications and the codes. From there I went to Fort Benning, Georgia, with the army to train in field communications—ground wire and field telephones and those things." He assumed he was heading for the Pacific.

George Makris, the Greek tackle and champion boxer, shared Thornally's frustration with the apparent capriciousness of Marine assignments. Like Schreiner and Baumann, he lamented the termination of the paratrooper program.

"My first choice was to be a rifle platoon leader, and my second choice was to be a paratrooper," Makris says. "They told me they were sending me to transport quartermaster school. I asked, 'What's that?' They said it

Marine Pat Harder on the firing range.
PHOTO COURTESY OF THE UNIVERSITY OF WISCONSIN SPORTS INFORMATION DEPARTMENT

was combat-loading of ships, and I said I didn't want any part of that. They said I couldn't do anything about it because that's where I was going."

Pat Harder, a junior, also left school and went through Marine basic training. He was so banged up, some of his teammates were surprised he passed his physical. Some of the Badgers heard rumors—never confirmed—that Harder exercised the time-honored yet highly informal option of challenging his drill instructor to a fight behind the barracks.

They also heard he won.

And what about the Badgers' undergraduate V-12 Marines, who were ticketed to start their duty on campus? They would study military-oriented subjects, primarily engineering, preparing to become lieutenants.

The problem for Harry Stuhldreher was that the V-12 program wasn't based at the University of Wisconsin, after all.

"We got a note telling us to report to the University of Michigan, and that all we could take was one change of clothes and a toothbrush, and that we would have our uniforms issued to us there," John Gallagher says. "At first, I didn't know if anyone else was going. We got to talking, and we'd say, 'Where you going?' 'Michigan.' 'Me, too!'"

The Badgers who went to Ann Arbor included four 1942 starters: Fred Negus, Elroy Hirsch, Jack Wink, and Bob Hanzlik. The others were Gallagher, Bob Rennebohm, Hank Olshanski, Earl Maves, and Farnham "Gunner" Johnson. They reported for duty in July 1943.

"We got on the train and went over there and walked around on Sunday morning to the fieldhouse and the stadium," Hanzlik says. "We had never played at Michigan. Jesus. I looked down at that stadium . . . I had never seen anything like that." The cavernous bowl, which could seat more than 85,000, left the Badgers awestruck.

That month, Stuhldreher wrote to John Roberts, the '42 senior guard who was then in the early stages of pilot training in the Army Air Forces. By then, Stuhldreher knew he would have only one player—Len Calligaro—from the '42 Badgers on his '43 roster. Calligaro, an agriculture major, was going to be allowed to finish up work for his degree before entering the service in December 1943. In the loosened athletic eligibility standards of wartime—essentially, if you were enrolled in school, you could play—it didn't matter that he had been listed as a senior the year before. "We are planning to play him at quarterback in order for him to direct and steady the younger fellows," Stuhldreher said in the letter to Roberts. Freshmen were declared eligible for play that season, and the '43 Badgers were going to be drawn mostly from among the first-year students and Navy men posted on the campus for specialized communications studies, including some who had played a season or two for other schools.

Michigan coach Fritz Crisler got the better deal in the campus shuffling. Early during the former Badgers' stint in Ann Arbor, one of Crisler's assistants watched the V-12 Marines doing their morning exercises and invited them to play for Michigan.

They were dubbed the Lend-Lease Badgers. Most of the Wolverines' players that season were in the Marine V-12 program or in the similar Navy V-5 program on the UM campus. The Navy men included Minnesota star halfback Bill Daley, Schreiner's pal. The players didn't get into perfect game condition that fall, because they had limited time to practice. However, Crisler worked the practice schedule around the military men, and the Badgers came to respect him as a coach, generally more so than they did Stuhldreher. "He was a hell of a coach," Gallagher says. "He just had a personality about him, he could handle people. He never got too excited."

During fall practice, the Allies invaded mainland Italy, and the Italians surrendered five days later, on September 8, 1943.

The 1943 Michigan Wolverines used several starting lineups. This one featured four "Lend-Lease Badgers." Elroy Hirsch is at right in the backfield and behind the other three Badgers in Marine uniforms: Fred Negus at center, John Gallagher at guard, and Bob Hanzlik at tackle. Gallagher had been converted from quarterback, Hanzlik from end.
Photo courtesy of John Gallagher

During the ensuing season at Michigan, Crisler used several lineups, but the Wolverine starters included Hirsch, Wink, Negus, Hanzlik, Rennebohm, and Gallagher. In fact, Hanzlik moved from end to left tackle, and Gallagher, who decided he couldn't beat out Wink and wanted to play, was a starter at guard.

The 1943 Wolverines went 8–1, losing 35–12 to Notre Dame on October 9 in Ann Arbor before an overflow crowd of about 90,000. Gallagher recalls, "The thing I can remember about that game, besides it being intense, was when you walked down to that field and it was a warm day, you could just smell the booze. Honest to god, it just permeated that damn stadium."

Negus recalls, "Hirsch got hurt, Daley got hurt, and the third quarter ran a quarter and a half. Somehow the officials got screwed up, and we said, 'When's the quarter going to end?' The ref said, 'We're giving you guys a chance to catch up.' Well, we were getting our asses beat."

Under the wartime schedule, Michigan was on a condensed three-semester system, and the semester ended just before the Wolverines routed

Elroy Hirsch (40) was as elusive for Michigan in 1943 as he had been for the Badgers the year before.
PHOTO COURTESY OF JOHN GALLAGHER

Minnesota 49–6 on October 23. Classes wouldn't resume for a week.

"Minnesota didn't really have [much talent] because of the way things worked out," Bob Rennebohm says. "They were much like Wisconsin. We had built up a comfortable lead, and Fritz Crisler knew we wanted to go back to Madison for the weekend.

"So he took us Wisconsin kids out of the game and he told us to go to the shower. It looked like the dickens, that you think you're so good you can send half your team away. But we went in, and he had arranged a police escort to take us to the Central Station in Ann Arbor. We switched at Chicago and got into Madison at midnight on Saturday night. And of course everybody was all excited, and we spent Sunday and Monday. We went out and practiced with the Badgers in sweatsuits and spent an hour on the practice field with them, getting acquainted."

On November 13, the Wolverines played Wisconsin at Ann Arbor. In his interview with the University of Wisconsin Oral History project, Hirsch recalled, "Crisler called us all together and said, 'You do not have to play in this game if you don't want to. It's your old school and I can understand your feelings and there will be no hard feelings if you choose not to play.' We were all chomping at the bit, of course, we wanted to get at them."

The Wolverines, with many members of the '42 Badgers in the lineup, beat Wisconsin and their one former teammate, Calligaro. The final score: 27–0.

"It was a weird feeling," Rennebohm says, "but we had to play to win."

The Badgers went 1–9 in the 1943 season, beating only—oh, the irony—Iowa. The Wolverines and Purdue both finished 6–0 in the Big Ten and were declared cochampions. Notre Dame was the consensus national champion.

"Because nobody thought we would be back, we were treated as seniors," Rennebohm says. "They gave us the Michigan uniforms, gold footballs, and beautiful rings."

Evan "Red" Vogds, the '42 senior guard from Fond du Lac, also played *against* the Badgers in '43. He entered the Navy in the spring of '43 and was stationed at the Great Lakes Naval Station as a physical instructor of recruits, and he played football for the Sailors—the Badgers' opponents in the "Crazylegs" game the previous season. The other Great Lakes guards were Bert Bertagnoli of the Chicago Cardinals and Russ Letlow of the Green Bay Packers.

★   ★   ★

In a 1992 interview for the Wisconsin Historical Society's Wisconsin

They hadn't been dating long, but anyone who saw them during their Thanksgiving visit to Lancaster could tell that Dave Schreiner and Odette Hendrickson were crazy about each other.

PHOTO COURTESY OF JUDY CORFIELD

Women During World War II Oral History Project, Dave Schreiner's sister, Betty Schreiner Johnson, recalled Dave's two-week leave following Officer Candidates School. He returned to Lancaster for Thanksgiving 1943, bringing fiancée Odette Hendrickson with him. The family didn't stop with that holiday; the Schreiners also conducted an Easter egg hunt and sat around a decorated Christmas tree, exchanging gifts.

During that visit, Schreiner took Odette to meet and visit with his childhood and campus friend Connie Sherman. Sherman had, by then, left school, gotten married, and had an infant son and was staying with her parents, which was common for many married women during the war years. It was indicative of Schreiner's whirlwind romance that Connie hadn't yet met Odette, and Schreiner was both showing her off and seeking his friend's approval. "I was so touched that he took that time to come and see me and my little boy," says Connie, now Constance Sherman Smyth. "I was *so* impressed with her."

Schreiner shipped out to the Pacific in January 1944 and arrived at the island of New Caledonia in February. On March 20, he wrote to his sister, Betty: "As yet we have not done one thing for the good of the old U.S.A. Not one damn thing! We've been out of the states approx. 2 months now and they have been entirely wasted as far as the war effort is concerned."

★ ★ ★

Mark Hoskins had gotten his wings in the Army Air Forces. His training took him to several stops in Texas, where he was in the same classes with guard Ken "Roughie" Currier. Currier's girlfriend, Eileen, came down to Texas to marry the former Badger, and Currier asked Hoskins to be the best man. Much to Hoskins's chagrin, though, he was walking off a punishment for a minor infraction when the wedding was held and wasn't allowed to be part of the ceremony.

Eventually, Hoskins and Currier were separated, with Hoskins going to Salt Lake City for training in the four-engine B-24 Liberator bomber. During the training period, he and Mary Carthew were married at her parents' home in Lancaster on January 17, 1944. Charles Hoskins, Mark's younger brother, was the best man.

The brass told Hoskins he would be a replacement pilot in a group heading overseas. Much to his disappointment, Hoskins received B-24 specialized training for only about a month before he and his pilot buddy were sent to Italy. The unit didn't need any more pilots, so Hoskins was sent to another unit, this one flying B-17 Flying Fortresses out of Foccia, Italy. Hoskins had never seen a B-17 before, and in the spring of 1944, after a month of training, he flew his first mission as copilot.

★ ★ ★

At Michigan, Hirsch's credentials as an all-around athlete were strengthened. He went out for basketball because he wanted to get to Madison to see Ruth Stahmer, who had let it be known she was going to date others if Elroy didn't demonstrate a commitment. After checking the basketball schedule, he at first volunteered to be a student manager. That job wasn't open, so he went out for the team . . . and started. In a track meet on May 15, 1944, he leaped 24 feet, 2 $\frac{1}{4}$ inches to win the broad jump and defeat, among others, Illinois star Buddy Young. On the same day, he threw a one-hit shutout for the Wolverine baseball team, which won the Big Ten championship. During the 1943–1944 school year, Hirsch won four Wolverine letters.

Negus, the Badger center, also ran track at Michigan on a standout mile relay team.

A center on a mile-relay team? It could happen in those days.

TWENTY-ONE

The Last Mission

After flying thirty-three missions, Mark Hoskins was told that after one more trip over enemy territory, he would move up from copilot to pilot. On his final mission as a copilot, to Budapest, he was with a pilot and crew he hadn't flown with before. Hoskins's B-17 was the second in formation.

It was June 27, 1944, three weeks after the D-Day landings at Normandy.

The weather was cloudy and terrible, and the planes broke formation. That was ominous for Flying Fortresses, which depended on formation flying for protection from enemy fighters. Some of the B-17s turned back, but the pilot to Hoskins's left decided to press on. He didn't talk much with Hoskins, and they never discussed alternatives.

The German fighter pilots, excited to encounter a lone bomber, pounced and fired. Suddenly, Hoskins's right engine was on fire.

Hoskins could see the flames, smell the cordite, and sense the crew's time running out.

The captain yelled to abandon the plane.

Hoskins scrambled down to the nose, joining the navigator and bombardier, expecting to follow them out the opened hatch.

But they were struggling with the little door. They yanked and shoved and twisted but couldn't get it open. The flames burned and the smell grew stronger. If they didn't get out soon, they wouldn't get out at all, and their frenzy showed they knew it.

Hoskins pulled them away from the door.

He told himself he was a blocker again, leading a sweep for Elroy Hirsch or Pat Harder in Camp Randall Stadium. Against Notre Dame or Ohio State, it didn't matter. He backed up, charged at the little door, and crashed into it with his shoulder.

Not only did the hatch open, but Hoskins flew through it and found himself in the skies over Hungary. Stunned, he managed to pull his parachute ripcord and begin to drift to the ground, where he would take his chances.

Then he saw the German fighter plane, presumably the one that had nailed the B-17.

The pilot, his guns at the ready, was flying toward Hoskins, a floating and defenseless target.

"Uh, oh," thought Hoskins. "Here it is."

The pilot took a picture to verify that he had shot down the B-17.

He left Hoskins alone.

Hoskins drifted down and landed in a tree. He was in Hungary, near the Danube River and the German border. "I came down at an angle," Hoskins recalls. "Those parachutes had those big canvas straps that came around under your butt. As I came down, I sheared off one of the limbs. It pierced right through the twin strands of that canvas strap and it made a little rip in my pants leg, but it never cut skin. That's how close I came to getting ripped open. Really ripped open. I didn't get hurt."

He shed the parachute and climbed down from the tree. Gathering and burying the parachute would have taken quite a while, so Hoskins decided to ignore that training lesson and get moving. He walked until he encountered an ancient farmer in a field, riding a plow pulled by a team of horses.

"I tried to make a motion that I wanted to ride, and he gave me a ride to this little settlement, a very small village nearby," Hoskins says. "They knew I was American."

In a small home in the Hungarian town, Hoskins spotted a telephone. He signaled to the occupants of the home that they shouldn't call anyone, then pantomimed that he was tired and wanted to lie down on a bed.

"I don't know if they misunderstood me or disregarded me, but they called somebody," Hoskins says. "These were just country people, old folks. Anybody who had any youth to them at all was in the service, no matter what country. I don't know whether the men who came for me were police or militia, but they had guns, and they were more excited than I was."

The men with guns marched Hoskins to a local schoolhouse, and within moments he was standing in front of a German officer. After being placed under guard, Hoskins and several other captured Americans— including other members of his B-17 crew on that final mission—were driven to a Frankfurt prison, Dulag Luft.

★   ★   ★

LANCASTER—Lieut. Mark Hadley Hoskins, star right halfback on the 1942 Wisconsin football team, is missing in action over Hungary, the war department today notified his parents, Mr. and Mrs. Mark Hoskins, Lancaster.

Lieut. Hoskins, pilot of a Flying Fortress, had been based in Italy. The message said he had been missing since June 27.

Lieut. Hoskins and a fellow townsman, Dave Schreiner, now in the South Pacific with the Marines, made grid history at the university and were known as the "Touchdown Twins" after they made good as sophomores. —WISCONSIN STATE JOURNAL, JULY 1944

★ ★ ★

Mary Carthew Hoskins had lined up a job teaching kindergarten in the upcoming school year, and she was staying with her parents for the summer.

"We were eating lunch, and someone came to the front door," Mary recalls. "My father wasn't home yet, and my mother went and answered it. She came back to the table and looked kind of funny, but didn't say a word about it."

The man from the local depot was delivering the telegram, and in the male-oriented world of the time, he thought it best to make the delivery to Mary's father—the prominent attorney—and let him break the news to his daughter. "Pretty soon, Dad came in the front door with the Hoskinses," Mary says. They shared the news.

Mark was MIA.

★ ★ ★

Hoskins spent sixteen days in solitary confinement. Locked up. Alone. Looking at walls. Thinking. Waiting. "They tried to soften you up," he says. "But there was no mistreatment. They didn't put their hands on you or anything."

Finally, he was led out of the cell and taken before a German intelligence officer. The German kept referring to a thick book.

"Is the clock in your ready room still 15 minutes fast?"

"I see you graduated from Lancaster High School and went to the University of Wisconsin."

Then, the officer got around to what he really wanted to know.

"Tell me about the new bomb. We know you can control the direction through the tailfin by radio. Tell me about it."

Hoskins didn't have to bluff. "I said I didn't know anything about that, and that I'd never even seen one," Hoskins says. "And I hadn't."

Hoskins says even after he made it clear he couldn't provide any intelligence, he wasn't physically abused. He has heard the stories about others who were, but he wasn't. He also knows that he wouldn't have been as fortunate if he had been shot down in the Pacific, where his best friend was about to join the island fighting.

Dave Schreiner was sent to Guam and went into combat against the Japanese defenders early in the battle as a replacement second lieutenant with a weapons company. Bob Baumann, also a second lieutenant, was there, too.

At the start of the battle, Schreiner's platoon had two half-tracks—essentially half-truck and half-tank—each with a 75-mm gun and a light machine gun. Schreiner was brought in as a gun captain for one of them, but the men had already abandoned it and moved on. "We were on a half-track at the start, but we used all our ammunition, so from then on we were infantry," says James Singley, a private first class under Schreiner. "I don't think we ever had the half-track after Dave was there."

Singley says that when Schreiner arrived, he "called us all together, introduced himself, and asked every man his name. He said, 'Some of you men have been through three campaigns. I've been to OCS. I want you to help me and guide me.' We did, and he turned out to be one of the best lieutenants we ever had."

At first, Singley had no idea Schreiner was an All-American football player. The lieutenant hadn't seen any need to mention that in the introductions. "I wasn't a football fan, and I knew nothing about football," says Singley, who joined the Marines after attending Northeast Missouri State Teachers College. He vividly remembers one patrol and an incident with a Browning automatic rifle.

"We were out on patrol, and we got some fire from a cave," Singley says. "I was laying there, giving support fire into the cave, and Dave was firing beside me. We had guys coming from each side going into the cave. I broke a firing pin on my BAR. I told Dave I'd done that and he'd have to cover. I changed the firing pin in less than five minutes."

Singley says that after the skirmish was over, Schreiner confronted him.

"You didn't break a firing pin!"

"Yeah, I did."

"They taught us in OCS that you had to detail strip the BAR to change the firing pin."

Singley explained to Schreiner that when he was part of a Raider unit (disbanded units modeled after the British commandos), experienced veterans taught him how to change the firing pins without completely breaking it down.

"That's why I want you boys to help me," Schreiner said. "You know what's going on." He added that he already had learned more from his men than he had at Quantico.

Singley says that when the platoon reached the north end of Guam, the men came to a steep vertical bluff with a path leading down it. The Marines could see caves at the bottom of the drop-off, and about fifty yards of jungle separated the cliff and the ocean. They also saw Japanese soldiers near the mouths of the caves.

"Dave asked for volunteers to go down and clear out the caves," Singley says. "Everyone volunteered."

Schreiner picked a small squad for the duty, and after they left, he turned to Singley. "I can't believe that," he said. "I thought you Marines learned not to volunteer a long time ago."

Singley shrugged. "Wait'll they come back. You'll see why."

Later, the patrol returned with its spoils. Each Marine carried a sake bottle. Two also hauled a wild pig on a pole they carried on their shoulders.

Schreiner said, "*Now* I see why they volunteered."

It turned out that after the platoon had reached the cliff, a few of the Marines had spotted the Japanese with sake bottles and also noticed wild pigs on the fringe of the shore jungle. The word had gotten around to virtually everyone but the lieutenant.

On July 27, Schreiner suffered a slight head wound. Some reports said it came from shrapnel. John McLaughry, a former Brown University and New York Giants football player also with the weapons company in an antitank platoon, remembered with great clarity in an August 1944 letter home that Schreiner was "creased by a bullet down the back of his head." In writing out his recollections of his service with Schreiner in 1993, McLaughry stated that "the bullet pierced his helmet, but . . . was deflected from doing serious, possibly fatal damage."

Schreiner wrote to his parents that it was "no worse than a scratch."

By August 10, Guam was under U.S. control and secured as a crucial bomber base for future battles. That month, after hearing that Mark Hoskins was missing in action in Europe, Dave Schreiner wrote to his parents that Hoskins was "my best friend and the greatest guy I ever knew." At the time, the past tense seemed appropriate.

Schreiner also knew that another former Badger teammate, tackle Paul "Indian" Hirsbrunner, was recovering from wounds he suffered while fighting with the First Marine Division on Saipan. Shrapnel lodged in Hirsbrunner's shoulder and upper arm and tore a finger off his right hand. He was shipped to the West Coast for recuperation. "When he came into San Francisco, I was an instructor," says Arlie Mucks, Jr., who had been Hirsbrunner's teammate with the 1941 Badgers and had entered the Army Air Forces after that season. "I took my airplane, a T6, and I flew it over to Oakland and went to see him in the hospital. He had a big hole in his arm. I picked him up at the hospital and flew him around, then took him back."

Hirsbrunner was moved to another hospital, in Chicago, where his girl-friend and future wife, Patricia, was able to visit him. He was done as a fighting Marine. Some of his teammates weren't.

In part because he wanted to be with a rifle platoon, Schreiner re-quested, and eventually was granted, a transfer to the 4th Regiment's 1st Battalion, where he would join Baumann.

★ ★ ★

The V-12 Marines went to Parris Island for basic training in the sum-mer of 1944. One group—Fred Negus, Elroy Hirsch, Hank Olshanski, and Bob Rennebohm—stuck together as long as they could get away with it.

"A year to the day after we went to Michigan, we were on a train for

Paul Hirsbrunner pretends to fire a rifle—something he knew he'd never have to do again in combat, due to serious shrapnel wounds he suffered on Saipan. (Note the bandages and missing finger on his right hand.)

Parris Island," Rennebohm says. "We had been Marines for a year in uniform and everything else, but we hadn't had that tasty experience of going to boot camp."

The drill instructors were tough on everyone, of course, but they positively salivated when they got to go after college boys. The barking drill instructors, often spitting as they screamed in the Badgers' faces, called the V-12 boys "coeds."

And how are the coeds today?

You coeds make me sick!

We'll make Marines out of you coeds yet!

"We fixed it so we got the same Quonset hut," Negus says. "We'd get a wrinkle on a bed or something, and we would have a good day of scrubbing the floor with sand and water. Then they found out we were all together and mixed us up. Hirsch was devastated. He said, 'If it wasn't for you guys, I never would have made it!' We laughed at each other. It looked to us like they had a habit of trying to force you out of the V-12 program, out of the officer program. They'd start calling you all kinds of names, hoping you'd fight back, and if you did, you were out."

Bob Hanzlik came down with a serious infection in his hand during boot camp. "I ended up in the naval hospital in San Diego," he says. "I had what they called osteomyelitis. It's a bone infection, but they didn't know what it was."

During a leave to Madison, he says, his arm was swelling. "That identification bracelet on my right wrist was getting so tight, I had to take it off," he says. "I went to the naval hospital in Madison. They gave me sulfa. Sulfa in those days was what did things, but it did not take effect. My whole hand and my arm got like a rotten apple, like a brown apple. They tried everything, they went in there and operated and cleaned it out, so I was going to lose my right arm. Harry Stuhldreher"—yes, the same Harry Stuhldreher who had denied Hanzlik his letter—"came to visit me twice in the hospital.

"There were all these young Navy doctors, thirty-one or thirty-two years old. One of them said, 'The Brooklyn Navy Yard has this new product called penicillin, and we've asked them to fly some out. We don't know how to give it, how much to give, but we'll give it to you.'"

Hanzlik got an injection, and his hand got better, although doctors had to remove a knuckle in surgery.

Eventually, in January 1945, Hanzlik was discharged "with a 10 percent disability, which I still have today."

★ ★ ★

Mark Hoskins is "missing in action over Hungary."

That's one of the heartaches of this war. Everyone will sympathize with his parents in Lancaster, and everyone will hope that "Had" will still turn up alive and well...

It's tragic that boys like these, like your own son, or the boy you knew next door have to lose their lives when the future seemed to hold so much for them.

But war always has reaped its toll of a nation's finest.

While there is still room for hope, however, we will pray that "Had" Hoskins turns up alive and well. The nation is going to need men of his character when this mess is over.
—HENRY J. MCCORMICK, *WISCONSIN STATE JOURNAL*, JULY 1944

★ ★ ★

In mid-July the Germans transported Hoskins and other captured Americans via train to Stalag Luft III, near Sagan, Germany, about ninety miles southeast of Berlin. The camp had five compounds. Hoskins was in the South Compound, which was used for American officers and populated largely by airplane crews. Opened in September 1943, it was the last part of the camp constructed and was the most secure. Each barracks, with the floor raised off the ground to discourage tunneling, had fifteen rooms. When Hoskins arrived, about eight Americans were bunking in each room. Later, the number was as high as fifteen. Hoskins says he believes all members of his crew survived the mission but says that he saw only a couple of them at Stalag Luft III, because the camp was for officers only.

The Germans told Hoskins and other new arrivals that they would treat escape attempts harshly, and it wasn't bluster. After a mass escape by seventy-six British, Dutch, and Norwegian prisoners from the North Compound on March 27, 1944, most had been recaptured—and fifty had been executed by firing squad. Five hundred prisoners had pitched in to dig three tunnels, which they named Tom, Dick, and Harry, and Harry was the one used for the flight. (Later the event would be the basis of the film *The Great Escape*.) After that attempt the Americans in the South Compound had to put up with extra roll calls for a while, but, as Hoskins quickly discovered, the others continued their attempts to construct an escape tunnel of their own.

★ ★ ★

Jim Regan, the sophomore reserve halfback from Berwyn, Illinois, was in the Army in the China-Burma-India Theater, fighting off repeated cases of malaria. He was sent there in 1943 from Camp Grant, where he had been planning to play for the football team that fall.

"Then they said they needed a group of men to learn how to drive jeeps and tanks," Regan says. "They'd go over to the CBI to fight the Japanese and teach the Chinese how to drive these things."

It was right up his alley.

In India, the Burmese jungles, and then China, Regan's job was to help ferry the jeeps and tanks to foreign troops and teach the soldiers how to use them.

In July 1944, he took written tests and was told he would be sent to the United States Military Academy at West Point. But the Army soon discovered he was ten days too old for the program. "I would have become a second lieutenant," Regan says. "In those days, they did a lot of strange things."

He stayed in the CBI.

★　★　★

Jim McFadzean, the '42 senior halfback, helped unload tanks at various landing points for American troops in Europe and North Africa. He had gotten his degree in May 1943 and within days was in Navy midshipmen's school at Columbia University. He was one of three former college players in the school who received letters from Harry Stuhldreher inviting them to play for the college all-stars against the NFL champions in the *Chicago Tribune*–sponsored all-star game.

"They were having trouble getting players," McFadzean says. "We went over to one of our instructors and asked if he thought we should ask to be allowed to go. He said, 'You can ask for that, but let me tell you, they'll say OK, but when you come back you won't come back to midshipmen's school, you'll go to basic. You'll end up being a sailor or something.' So we dropped it."

He became an ensign and was assigned to landing craft tanks, or LCTs. "It was an open deck. We had Mark Sixes, the new ones. There were living quarters and a galley and usually fifteen enlisted men and two officers."

He eventually helped land tanks off North Africa, Italy, and France. Enemy fire was especially threatening during the landings of the tanks in southern France. "There was a lot of stuff going on," McFadzean says softly. "After we unloaded our initial load, our other job was to go out to Liberty ships and get more stuff like gasoline and food and take it into the beach. That was usually an all-day affair.

"My roommate in midshipmen's school went to Normandy, and he wrote me a letter one day and said, 'Don't be afraid to duck.' I never was afraid to duck."

TWENTY-TWO

Flyers

When Mark Hoskins was shot down, a handful of his teammates took the news especially hard.

By the summer of '44, Jerry Frei and several other members of the '42 Badgers had passed muster and become Army Air Forces pilots. A couple more were in ground roles in the AAF.

Jerry Frei got his wings and became a full-fledged AAF pilot at age nineteen.

PHOTO FROM THE AUTHOR'S COLLECTION

George Hekkers, the '42 sophomore tackle from Milwaukee, was learning to fly the twin-engine B-26 bomber and had survived a training accident at Del Rio, Texas.

"I was lucky to make it out," Hekkers says. "I was scarred for a long time. Four aircraft took off. I was the fourth one. I remember hearing and seeing that another plane was having a problem, and then all of a sudden my plane burst. The right engine exploded.

"I don't know if you've flown over Texas, but they have a lot of old streams, old washes. I landed on one of those. When I pulled the wheel back I busted the face of my

156

copilot. I had to help him. He was the smallest man in the squadron, and I was the biggest.

"I was burned on my arms, legs, and around the bottom of my neck. They put some yellow sulfur power on it, and had me in and out of a tub."

Hekkers was allowed to make a choice. He could give up flying and serve elsewhere. Or he could go back up on a training mission as a copilot. After that, if he still wanted to fly—and his superiors felt he still was up to it—he could go back to pilot status.

Soon he was a pilot again.

"I wanted to fly very much," Hekkers says. "I was dedicated to being a pilot and flying. I always thought it was remarkable that they could take someone who was a knucklehead like me in college and then within a short period of time have you flying a bomber. That B-26 was notorious for crashing. It was called the Flying Prostitute; it had no visible wings of support. They put that thing into service without giving it much preflight. That's the one where they used to say, 'A marauder a day in Tampa Bay.'"

After those B-26 adventures, Hekkers was assigned to fly an A-26, a low-level attack bomber. He flew his missions off an island in the South Atlantic and then from North Africa. "It was just the pilot and a midship gunner in that plane," Hekkers says. "He had two guns on top and two guns on the bottom, and he could fire 360 degrees in any direction. We would be low-level, maybe five hundred feet off the ground. Most of the time unless you were flying out of problem areas, you flew higher to get in. We fired on stuff, and we were so low I don't know what we were hitting. We also did a lot of going over the ocean and trying to pick out submarine patrols."

★ ★ ★

Don Litchfield, the '42 sophomore reserve quarterback from Eau Claire, had taken flying lessons, so he was fast-tracked. He trained in California, New Mexico, and Florida and was ticketed to step directly into the left-hand seat as a B-17 bomber pilot—the job Hoskins was on the verge of filling when he was shot down.

★ ★ ★

Before leaving school, '42 sophomore halfback Bob Omelina, from Cudahy, Wisconsin, often ran around with the young guards Roughie Currier and Toughie Frei. All three became pilots for the Army Air Forces. Omelina did his aptitude work at Butler University in Indianapolis. After a series of training stops in California, he ended up at Williams Field

Ken Currier taught others to fly.
PHOTO COURTESY OF CHARLES CURRIER

in Chandler, Arizona, for twin-engine fighter school. Like Frei, Omelina ended up in the envied position in the cockpit of a one-man, twin-engine P-38 fighter.

Roughie Currier went through much of his early training with Hoskins and guard John Roberts, the wrestling star, and then became a flight instructor at training facilities in Texas, Kansas, and Nebraska. Usually Currier taught pilots how to fly the huge B-29 bombers, which didn't go into service until 1944.

"He enjoyed teaching and thought it was certainly as critical a contribution as dropping bombs," says his son, Charles Currier. "I don't think he ever regretted that he didn't go into combat, or felt it was lost glory. It was something he enjoyed doing."

* * *

Reserve quarterback Otto Breitenbach and Roberts were also AAF flight instructors.

"My notice was to report to Miami Beach for basic training," Breitenbach says. "I'll never forget the train ride. I think everyone on the troop train had diarrhea from whatever we ate."

His group studied math and navigation at Middle Georgia College. After pilot training in twin-engine B-26 bombers, Breitenbach was selected to be an instructor. Sometimes it seemed almost as if the AAF decision-makers simply closed their eyes and pointed to a name on a roster of each training class, selecting that pilot to remain behind to teach. Of course, it was far from being that simple, and teaching aptitude and flying ability were both prized. All three Badgers who became flight instructors were hoping to become educators and coaches, and that couldn't have been a coincidence. But despite the usually extensive training process, Americans emerging with their wings in the final years of the war—including those who remained stateside to instruct—often were amazingly quick studies.

"Like everyone else, I was disappointed at the assignment," Breitenbach says. "I thought I should be going overseas and doing what had to be done. But you do what you're told, and there was never any explanation for it. I guess you always looked at it like a job and didn't let the emotions get too involved in it. You knew that others were going into an experience you probably should be going into, so there was a little guilt feeling in some ways."

Breitenbach was stationed at Dodge City, Kansas, for most of his two-year teaching stint before the Army Air Forces moved the B-26 teaching operation to Del Rio, Texas—the town where George Hekkers was training when he was almost killed. "Part of the time I taught Free French pilots," Breitenbach says. "The French would send them over here for training, then take them back for combat. There were some real characters there."

Roberts was also called into the Air Forces in 1943, and all of his training was in Texas. He was sent to single-engine training. Typically, his first ride in an airplane was his first training trip. "I remember the pilot spinning me down," Roberts says. "I think it was a BT19. After my eighth hour, we were doing takeoffs and landings, and he jumped out of the plane and said, 'OK, John, all yours.' I was never more scared in my life."

Yet, he was an instructor soon after that, teaching others and saying, "All yours."

"All of our instruction was in the air, in two-seaters," Roberts says. "You had the student up in the front, you were in the back seat. I was surprised to see that I was kept there. I think the fact that I was in school, in education, had something to do with it. But maybe I was a good pilot, too. I never did know. I just expected to go, but after I was made an in-

Madison native Otto Breitenbach was a pilot and instructor.

PHOTO COURTESY OF OTTO BREITENBACH

structor, I thought, OK, they aren't going to send me. I took my job pretty seriously as an instructor at that point."

★　★　★

Other Badgers in the AAF served on the ground. Ashley Anderson, the cerebral quarterback, wound up at the First Strategic Air Depot in a small English town. "I was an enlisted man in the big hangar, supplying parts for all these planes," he says.

Reserve guard Bob Dean, from Tomahawk, went to the AAF's version of radio school. In Costa Rica, he worked at a communications station involved in the around-the-world radio chain. The station was deep in the jungle, and he carried a machete with him, both to cut through the foliage when necessary and to attack snakes. When the men came out of the jungle, they would sometimes be invited to the Costa Rican president's home for dinners and parties, and Dean later said that when he flirted with the president's daughter, he was taken aside by presidential guards and told to back off—or else. He backed off.

TWENTY-THREE

Stalag Luft III

At Stalag Luft III, Mark Hoskins discovered the South Compound was a society unto itself, with the American officers governing it. The Germans held roll call twice a day, and other than that the prisoners were largely on their own. The American officers ordained that no escape could be attempted without approval from the escape committee. After the failed escape attempt by the British, Dutch, and Norwegian prisoners, the American officers ruled that German-speaking soldiers would be at the front of the line for any American escape attempts, because they would have the most chance of surviving on the run.

"When I was there the escape officer was Colonel Clark, who later ended up as one of the officers at the Air Force Academy," Hoskins says.

In addition to the barracks, the American compound had a separate theater building where the prisoners could gather, put on shows, or stage other activities to pass the time. The Germans had allowed the prisoners to build it themselves, and the construction took from October 1943 until February 1944. They made the building's four hundred seats from Red Cross boxes.

By the time Hoskins arrived at the camp, five months after the theater was completed, the Americans had started an attempt to tunnel from the building and under the nearby fence. The escape committee, also called the X Committee, supervised the digging. With 1,500 men in the compound, many weren't directly involved, including Hoskins. The tunneling, undertaken in shifts, was painstaking, perilous work, and everyone was painfully aware of the British escape attempt and the retribution they faced.

"The soil there was quite sandy," Hoskins says. "As they would dig, they would protect the integrity of the tunnel by putting boards along the roof and the sides. You had bunkboards in your bunk, and each month or so they'd come along with a requisition of so many boards from this one room. We were sleeping with fewer and fewer boards all the time. Our mattresses were filled with wood shavings and sawdust, so it was more uncomfortable all the time."

One tricky part of the process was getting rid of sand and dirt from the tunnels. Prisoners often started "projects" above ground just to create an excuse for having loose soil exposed so they could mix in dirt from the tunnel.

The ostensible goal, of course, was to eventually provide a means for escape, but more realistically—given the slow progress under the conditions—the project was a way for the prisoners to preserve their own sense of collective defiance and hope. The Germans were handing out literature emphasizing that they followed the rules of war set forth by the Hague Convention but insinuating that dastardly Allied tactics were making the Germans doubt the wisdom of their civility. The implication: the executions of the British prisoners after their recapture would be the order of the day if other prisoners tried to follow their lead. One flyer, reprinted later in *Clipped Wings,* an amazing Stalag Luft III commemorative "yearbook" published by former prisoners, declared, "Stay in the camp where you will be safe! Breaking out of it now is a damned dangerous act. The chances of preserving your life are almost nil! All police and military guards have been given the most strict orders to shoot on sight all suspected persons. Escaping from prison camps has ceased to be a sport!"

The prisoners continued to use the theater virtually every night, which helped camouflage the tunneling. The events included plays, musicals, and reviews. The prisoners wrote a few of the shows and staged others after painstaking copying of scripts from anthologies. Participants dressed in women's clothes for the female roles. Their productions, both before and after Hoskins's arrival, included *The Invisible Duke; Bishop's Candlesticks; Veni, Vidi, Vici; Amazing Doctor Clitterhouse; You Can't Take It with You; The Front Page;* and *Room Service.* Hoskins played a role in the musical *Kiss and Tell,* which included a band on stage. He also sang in the camp Glee Club, which practiced and performed in the theater.

★ ★ ★

In late August, when Hoskins was two months into the camp routine and learning the ropes, the news got around Stalag Luft III that Paris had been liberated.

A little over a week later, the news got *out* of camp that Mark Hoskins was alive.

```
9:23 P.M. SEP. 4, 1944
WUX WASHINGTON, D.C.
```

MRS. MARY C. HOSKINS
LANCASTER, WIS.

REPORT JUST RECEIVED THROUGH THE INTERNATIONAL RED
CROSS STATES THAT YOUR HUSBAND SECOND LIEUTENANT MARK
H HOSKINS IS A PRISONER OF WAR OF THE GERMAN GOVERN-
MENT LETTER FOLLOWS FROM PROVOST MARSHALL GENERAL.

J.A. ULIO

THE XXXXXX ADJUTANT GENERAL

WUX WASHINGTON, D.C.
SEP. 13, 1944
MRS. MARK M [sic] HOSKINS
453 SOUTH MONROE

LANCASTER, WIS.

FOLLOWING UNOFFICIAL SHORT WAVE BROADCAST FROM GERMANY
HAS BEEN INTERCEPTED QUOTE DEAREST MARY AM PRISONER OF
WAR PERFECTLY WELL YOU MAY SEND PACKAGES AND LETTERS TO
GIVEN ADDRESS TELL EVERYONE LOVE MARK M HOSKINS AND LT
STALAG LUFT 3 GERMANY UNQUOTE THIS BROADCAST SUPPLE-
MENTS PREVIOUS OFFICIAL REPORTS RECEIVED FROM INTERNA-
TIONAL RED CROSS STOP.

LECH PROVOST MARSHAL
GENERAL

All along, Mary Hoskins had been hopeful that her young husband was still alive. She even had a dream in which Mark bailed out of the bomber and his parachute opened. But she couldn't be certain he had survived. "That was a bad summer," she says. "All the girls had their fellows away, so we did things [together]. But it was a bad summer."

Then the telegrams came. This time, they contained good news. The uncertainty, the fear, and the hope were transformed into a single emotion: joy.

"Oh, it was terrific," Mary says.

She wasn't a widow. Mark was alive! But then the sobering reality set in. He was a prisoner of war, and there was no guarantee of his survival under those conditions, either. Immediately, Mary, her parents, and her in-laws began writing Mark letters and sending him parcels. "They told us exactly what we could send, and we sent the parcels often," Mary says. "Some he got, some he didn't."

★ ★ ★

For Mark, day-to-day life in camp was a fight against boredom and malnutrition. Men in each room drew cook duty for a week at a time, and they were assigned "stooges,"or helpers, in one- or two-day stints. The cooks for all fifteen rooms in a barracks had to take turns using the single tiny stove, primarily working with food from the International Red Cross. The prisoners learned to make cakes from ground-up crackers, and the Germans contributed bread—horrible bread, and each prisoner received one loaf per week—and a soup that wasn't much more than gruel. Occasionally, the Germans would taunt the prisoners by presenting them with the soup with a cow's head still in the pot. The weekly Red Cross parcels to each prisoner included one can apiece of powdered milk, Spam, corned beef, liver paste, salmon, cheese, margarine, biscuits, instant coffee, jam, and prunes or raisins, plus one small box of sugar, two chocolate bars, two bars of soap, and five packs of cigarettes. The diet added up to stubborn cases of dysentery, severe weight loss, and other problems.

Barter and bribery fueled the camp's underground economy. Prisoners took unwanted portions of parcels from the Red Cross or from home to the compound's trading post, where they bartered mainly for clothes, food, cigarettes, and reading material.

The Americans followed BBC war news on a homemade radio. "They got the radio by working on the guards," Hoskins says. "As soon as you could get something on a guard, you'd have them by the balls. You'd give them a cigarette, and they weren't supposed to take cigarettes. You'd get them to take one, then another the next day. You could always hold that over them, tell their superiors. So they were able to get things like parts of radios. This was a vast group of guys with different skills. We had radio people who could make their own radios if they got the works."

The other way to assemble a radio, Hoskins says, was to have a prisoner get one part in a Red Cross parcel, and another prisoner receive another part in a different parcel. Slowly the men would accumulate enough parts.

"The bread the Germans issued was unlike any bread that you ever saw," Hoskins says. "There was a lot of sawdust in it. Well, the prisoners with the radio would hollow out this bread and keep their radio in there. Every noon this one guy would turn on the BBC for news. . . . There would be eight or ten runners who would take that news by word of mouth to the different barracks. So we could follow it quite well. We knew what was going on."

In the camp's camouflaged language, the men called the radio the "canary" and called war news "soup."

* * *

Betty Cass wrote the "Madison Day by Day" column in the *Wisconsin State Journal.* There she passed along the news that Roundy Coughlin had been offended when he mailed a letter to Hoskins at Stalag Luft III in Germany and the post office returned it because the stamp carried the message "Win the War." Roundy wanted everyone to know that when he complained, he was told letters to POWs didn't need postage at all and that the post office had returned the letter because the Germans wouldn't deliver any letters carrying war slogans. So, Roundy said the recommendation was that citizens hand their letters to Hoskins directly to a postal clerk, so the letters would be set aside and not canceled with any pro-victory message.

* * *

As the months passed, the American prisoners continued to find creative ways to pass the time. In addition to staging plays and shows, they threw themselves into providing programming for their camp "radio station" KRGY. They billed it as an "overseas division of the American Broadcasting System," but it actually only went out over the compound's public-address system. Most of the men working for it had been in the radio business before the war. Programming, airing mostly during the day, included roundtable discussions, news commentaries, and music, most of which came from records sent to prisoners by their families.

The South Compound's library, which had started with contributions from the older British compound and books sent from home, was popular and heavily stocked. The prisoners also created "shops" in which they made goods that could improve prison life—utensils, tools, dishes— and produced handicrafts and artwork. The autonomy the Germans granted the prisoners remains stunning.

Inside the compound, the men had a recreation field where they played football and softball. "There was an exercise path that ran around the interior of the wire, too," Hoskins says. "If you threw a ball and it landed between the barbed wire and the path, which was about ten yards, you had to ask the guard's permission to go in there and get it. If you didn't, they'd shoot you or shoot at you."

Most of the games were informal pickup games. But in late October 1944, when Hoskins had been in the compound for three months, the South Compound's *Circuit* newspaper—a one-page, five-column, typewritten sheet posted on the cookhouse wall—reported that Hoskins had starred in the Bombers' 19–0 victory over the Fighters in the "Kriegie Bowl grid classic." (*Kriegie* was the prisoners' shortened version of *Kriegsge-*

fangener, the German term for "war prisoner." It was also the inspiration for the radio station's call letters, KRGY.) The newspaper story reported, "The Bombers, led by Mark Hoskins, had too much speed and deception." The former Badger halfback played quarterback, and halfback Jess Tunstill threw for one touchdown and ran 30 yards for another.

The "soup" got around that U.S. troops had invaded the Philippines in late October. As the end of 1944 approached, the prisoners knew the Allies were tightening the noose on Germany, and they wondered what the Germans would do.

On Christmas, Hoskins sang in the prisoners' production of Handel's *Messiah*. Thousands of miles away, his pal Dave Schreiner was recuperating from a football game played the day before.

TWENTY-FOUR

Guadalcanal

In late 1944, Badger Marine Dick Thornally ended up in the Pacific, stationed in the Marshall Islands as a communications watch officer. The important duty involved monitoring and coordinating the communication between the Marine headquarters on the West Coast and the officers in the Pacific. "They were getting us ready for moving up the line to Iwo Jima and Okinawa," Thornally says.

At a conference in San Francisco in September, the Joint Chiefs of Staff had decided to invade Luzon, Iwo Jima, and Okinawa. The Joint Chiefs chose that strategy over Admiral Ernest J. King's recommendation to invade Formosa as the final stopping-off point before Japan.

Meanwhile, Dave Schreiner, Bob Baumann, and Bud Seelinger were on Guadalcanal with the Sixth Marine Division. The Sixth, comprising the 4th, 22nd, and 29th Regiments, was formed on Guadalcanal on September 7 but wasn't completely green. Most of its infantry battalions—including Schreiner's—had been in combat. The 4th Regiment, mostly wiped out or captured on Corregidor in 1942, had been re-formed earlier in 1944 from four former Raider units after Marines deemed the commando model obsolete. (Woe to anyone who calls the Sixth Marine Division the "Sixth Marines." In Marine terminology, that type of designation was used for regiments. Thus, the 4th Marines and the 29th Marines were regiments, part of the Sixth Marine Division.)

Schreiner had gotten his wish and was leading a rifle platoon. "My job is to organize and train this platoon—to hold school on weapons, tactics and other relevant things," he wrote to his parents from Guadalcanal. "It's a hard job pleasing everyone—I don't try to. All I do is play fair and square with them all and call 'em as I see 'em. After all I'm not running a popularity contest but want a good hard-hitting platoon."

Schreiner and Baumann were working under Captain Clint Eastment, commander of A Company in the 4th Regiment's 1st Battalion. At full strength, each company had 240 members. Eastment, a first lieutenant at the outset of the fighting on Guam, had moved up under the field promotion system and become a respected commander. He remembers meeting both Badgers and noticing how modest Schreiner was, especially considering he was a two-time All-American football player.

"Well, he didn't hide it, but he didn't blab it all over, either," Eastment says.

Others blabbed it all over for him, including young Vic Anderson of Milwaukee, a private first class and Eastment's runner (a job that required being at the beck and call of the company commander, primarily to deliver and receive messages). "Dave never said, 'Well, I made All-American two years in a row,'" Anderson says. "So I told everyone I could." Anderson entered the Marines straight from a standout high school athletic career. "I used to go to Madison for games with my coach, so I watched Dave play in college," Anderson says. "Oh, he was so humble."

Dave Schreiner in the Pacific.
PHOTO COURTESY OF JUDY CORFIELD

As he would with others, Schreiner encouraged Anderson to enroll at Wisconsin after the war and go out for football.

Frank Kemp, a captain in the 4th Marines, was also on Guam as a first lieutenant. On Guadalcanal, he got to know Schreiner and Baumann. "We used to talk about their football careers, of course," Kemp recalls. "They were both extremely well known. I had played football at Yale, so I certainly knew a lot about them and read about them and was extremely proud that they came into the 4th Regiment. You wouldn't have known they were both great football players. They didn't brag. They were just interested in being very, very good Marines."

In December, Schreiner received a Purple Heart for the wound he had received on Guam, but he belittled it in a letter home, calling it "a lot of baloney. You get it for just a scratch nowadays."

During training, Schreiner and the other Marines played games to pass the time, including volleyball and touch football. The men organized several games, and the most notable was a matchup between the 29th Marines and Schreiner's 4th Marines on Christmas Eve, 1944. The game, which the Marines labeled the Football Classic, was designed to settle the beer-fueled debates over which regiment had the best players. Organizers mimeographed rosters and lined up a public address system and announcers.

As kickoff approached, the frenetic wagering continued among the thousands of Marines ringing the so-called field. Money was thrown out and matched, which could involve a day's pay, a week's pay, a month's pay, all risked as if the thrill of the wager and the bluster behind it were the attractions. The game was touch football—officially, anyway—because the brass had ordained it, reminding the boys that they had best save their most ardent aggression for the upcoming island fighting. They knew it would be fierce and ugly and—well, they didn't talk much about the rest.

The gridiron was the 29th's parade ground on Guadalcanal, an open space with as much coral and gravel fragments as dirt, and no grass at all. The men had dubbed it Pritchard Field, after Corporal Thomas Pritchard, a member of a demolition squad who had been killed on Guadalcanal that fall. "It was a training accident," recalls Walter "Bus" Bergman, the former Colorado A&M star, who played that day in the 29th's backfield. "All the companies sent their demolition squads to this training camp for exercises and schooling. They were putting on an exhibition at the end of the class, and they got in the wrong place, I guess, and were blown up. So, when they leveled the field off, they named it after Pritchard."

Wearing a green T-shirt, khaki pants, and field boots, Schreiner surveyed the field. He saw many familiar faces—ones he had seen under leather helmets during his playing days at Wisconsin. He could argue again with George Murphy, the former Notre Dame captain he had greeted at midfield at Camp Randall Stadium less than three years earlier, about which team really got the best of the other in the 1942 tie. He could tease Rusty Johnston, the fine back from Marquette, about the way the Badgers had routed the Hilltoppers that season.

Baumann again would be on Schreiner's side, but Seelinger was set to play for the 29th, partly because he had caught such hell when he played on the same side with his Badger buddies from the 4th in previous pickup games.

Schreiner shook hands with the opposing team's coach and captain, Chuck Behan, who had come to the Marines straight from the Detroit Lions. After this mess was over, they said, they might be Lions teammates.

Major General Lemuel C. Shepherd, the commanding general of the Sixth Marine Division, diplomatically watched the first half on one side of the field and moved to the other side for the second half. Both the 29th and 4th Marines had bands, and both performed, along with the 29th's drum and bugle corps.

The game was spirited, violent, and inconclusive.

Nobody scored.

"They put on quite an exhibition," recalls Jim Harwood, a private first class in the 4th Regiment. "Hell, they were all All-Americans! Dave was playing end and they sent three guys out to block him, and by god they couldn't knock him down."

"It certainly was rough," Frank Kemp says. "They were so well coordinated, I guess, the defense was better than the offense."

John McLaughry, the former New York Giant in the 4th Marines, served as the playing assistant coach and drew up most of the plays, borrowing them from his Brown University days. "It didn't get out of hand," McLaughry says. "But it came pretty close."

McLaughry, in fact, described the game in depth in a December 26 letter to his parents:

It was really a lu-lu, and as rough hitting and hard playing as I've ever seen. It ended in a 0–0 tie, but the game was a wild see-saw affair, up and down the field, with many almost T.D.'s and field goals, both teams getting on the 5-yard line several times. . . . As you may guess, our knees and elbows took an awful beating due to the rough field with coral stones here and there, even tho the 29th did its best to clean them all up. My dungarees were torn to hell in no time, and by the game's end my knees and elbows were a bloody mess. Since then I've had a hard time navigating as in spite of prompt first aid they became infected. You have no idea how germs propagate out here until you see a little scratch go into a sore in no time.

In the letter, McLaughry said the game's standouts were Schreiner and

Bob Herwig, an All-American lineman at the University of California in 1936. "They can easily be picked out as All-Americans," McLaughry wrote.

Herwig had been recruited to officiate, but he couldn't resist playing for the 4th Marines. The men also knew him as the husband of Katherine Windsor, the author of the best-selling, banned-in-Boston historical novel *Forever Amber,* which had been published in mid-October and was an international sensation.

Behind Schreiner and Baumann on the line, the 4th Regiment's backfield included quarterback Bob Spicer, a sergeant from Leavenworth, Kansas, who had played guard for the University of Colorado in 1942. Spicer intercepted a pass on the final play of the game to preserve the tie, which provided a "push" for all the wagers and left the brass happy that fights wouldn't break out over payment.

"It was two hands above the waist," Spicer recalls of the rules of play, "but it could be a two-handed jab to the shoulder, guts, or knees. It was fun!"

Bus Bergman lined up next to Bud Seelinger, who played fullback for the 29th.

"I know it was real hard-hitting," Bergman says with a chuckle. "But in a nothing-nothing game, there isn't much going on. And we didn't have much practice with each other, either."

The United Press issued a dispatch written by Sergeant Harold T. Boian, a Marine Corps combat correspondent. The *State Journal* printed an excerpt of Boian's report:

SOMEWHERE IN THE SOUTH PACIFIC—(Delayed)—(UP)— Tropical heat and the lack of equipment failed to stop the leathernecks of the Sixth Marine division when they decided it was football time back home.

They arranged the Mosquito Bowl football classic. One team was captained and coached by All-American Dave Schreiner, a Wisconsin star in 1941 and 1942, now a Navy lieutenant.

To beat the heat, the game started at 8:30 a.m. Paraphernalia consisted of a football and nothing else.

The result was a scoreless tie.

Despite the prohibition on tackles, Marines made the most of body blocks.

Other participants were not exactly unknown in the football world. Schreiner's opponents were captained by Lieut. Charles E. Behan, 26, former star with De Kalb University and the professional Detroit Lions.

Other well-known players were Tony Butkovich, 23, of St.

David, Ill., All-American fullback at Purdue in 1943; Lieut. George Murphy, 24, of Indianapolis, Ind., Notre Dame captain and end in 1942; Corp. Saxon Judd of Tulsa, Okla., who caught seven consecutive forward passes from Glenn Dobbs for Tulsa University in the 1943 Sugar Bowl game; Corp. Jack Castignola, 24, of New Philadelphia, [Ohio,] formerly of the University of Dayton and Penn State, and Pfc. Frank Callen, 24, of Bingham, Utah, a star with St. Mary's (Cal.) in 1942.

Surviving participants don't remember the game being called the Mosquito Bowl at the time. The Football Classic game program, which had been printed a week ahead, had the kickoff scheduled for 2:15 p.m., so if Boian's story was right, the kickoff was moved up. Plus, Schreiner wasn't listed as a coach; the program listed the 4th Regiment's coach as Lieutenant Bill Lazetich, formerly of the Cleveland Rams, with John McLaughry as his assistant.

Boian had no reason to mention Hank Bauer, who came to the Marines from East St. Louis High School and started as one of the 4th Regiment's halfbacks. Bauer went on to earn fame as a major-league baseball player (mostly with the New York Yankees) and manager. Boian also didn't mention that when the 29th lined up for its first offensive play, the ex-Badgers on the other side had a hard time not laughing through the snap. The 29th had a team the year before at Camp Lejeune in North Carolina. Their coach was Jack Chevigny, who had been on Knute Rockne's staff when Rockne died. He served as head coach of the Chicago Cardinals from 1932 to 1934 and at the University of Texas from 1934 to 1937.

Thanks to Chevigny's influence, the 29th was running the familiar—and disdained—Notre Dame Box.*

---

* Chevigny was killed in action on Iwo Jima in 1945.

TWENTY-FIVE

On to Germany

In late 1944 and early 1945, the Badgers were well represented by Dave Donnellan, Erv "Booby" Kissling, and Jack Crabb in the Battle of the Bulge, the Germans' desperate gambit to defeat the Allies and buy enough time to stop the Russians' assault to the east.

Donnellan, the '42 reserve sophomore tackle from Eau Claire, had originally flunked his Army physical, and he blames John Gallagher. "I got a hernia from carrying Gallagher around on my back at college," Donnellan jokes.

The Eau Claire buddies were separated, with Gallagher as the V-12 Marine, Don Litchfield as the AAF pilot, and Donnellan as the outsider. Others considered hernias and rejection to be good fortune, but Donnellan kept writing to his draft board. "Everybody was gone," he says. "Ol' Dave was down there by myself. So I wrote the draft board and said I was ready, and finally, they were ready, too."

After spending time at Camp McCoy in Wisconsin, Donnellan went to Camp Polk, Louisiana, to train with the 8th Armored Division's 7th Armored Infantry Battalion. There he volunteered for the 7th Armored Infantry Battalion's boxing team. "I wasn't very good, but I was better than nothing," he says. "They had to have somebody. We went over to an airfield in Louisiana, and we got to sleep between sheets! It had been many months since we had done anything like that. And, then we had all this delicious fruit." Donnellan smiles wryly, targeting his teasing at his Eau Claire buddy, Litchfield. "The Air Force had it pretty good. There's no question where I'm going the next time."

Donnellan also played for the 7th Armored Infantry Battalion's football team against the Randolph Field all-stars in Dallas's Cotton Bowl. The Air Forces team rolled to a 64–0 victory in front of what Donnellan recalls was a crowd of about 40,000. He laughs when remembering pro star Rudy

Macha blocking a short field-goal attempt late in the game to preserve Randolph's shutout. "I swear, he got there before the ball did," Donnellan says.

Donnellan was sent to England in October 1944. His teammates later joked that Donnellan's deployment showed that the Army wasn't perfect—he had horrible eyesight and yet was a forward observer at the Battle of the Bulge.

Donnellan says that isn't true. He only *started out* as a forward observer before becoming a platoon sergeant.

The Battle of the Bulge part they got right.

Germany was losing the war, with the Allies retaking France and taking Italy and Russia finally repelling the Germans in the east. Adolf Hitler believed an ambitious offensive in the west could reverse the Germans' fortunes and discourage the British. Generals tried to convince Hitler to scale down the plan—a desperate, extremely risky, and all-or-nothing push through the Ardennes in an attempt to reach Antwerp.

The Germans attacked five U.S. Army divisions near the Ardennes on December 16, 1944. Donnellan's armored unit—the 7th Armored Infantry Battalion's 81st Mortar Platoon—joined the fighting, which lasted six weeks. One reason the Germans dared to hope for success was that many of the U.S. troops in the region, including Donnellan's platoon, were untested in battle. General Dwight Eisenhower quickly rushed in reinforcements.

"There was a lot of confusion," Donnellan says. "We went in at night, and you could see all the tracer bullets flying around. I had a driver in my half-track, Charlie Kelly, and he said, 'Dave, you better duck down, them's real bullets they're

Dave Donnellan talked the Army into taking him; then he set up mortar firing during the Battle of the Bulge.

PHOTO COURTESY OF DAVE DONNELLAN

shooting at us.' Things settled down after a couple of days. I would say probably the best thing about it was that once we learned how to shoot back and so forth, I think the Germans ran out of good manpower. I won't say it was routine, but it wasn't like the D-Day invasion or anything like that."

Donnellan's job was to direct the artillery firing after an infantry company called for support. The mortar unit would stop, set up, and fire. "I would try to get it on the target," he says. "Sometimes we did it and sometimes we didn't."

That brought return fire, and there were other hazards as well. "It's kind of silly to talk about it," he says, shrugging. "Chance played such an important part in it. But once when we were moving, I was going down one side of a brick wall, and the guy with me was going down the other side. He got a leg blown off by a land mine. If we would have been moving the other way around, I would have gotten it."

Eventually Donnellan's unit was moved to Germany. Donnellan was struck by the Germans' preference to surrender to U.S. or British troops rather than to the Russians.

"We crossed the Rhine and went to Essen and some of the industrial cities in the Ruhr Pocket," Donnellan says. "We went right down a superhighway with our lights on. We hadn't had our lights on for two years. We could do that because [the Germans] guaranteed our safety. They were so afraid that the Russians were going to come across the Elbe River. The Germans gave up by the company and the battalion, and we had piles of guns so high, you couldn't believe it. We had to stop at the Elbe River." He smiles. "That was OK with me."

★ ★ ★

Like Donnellan, Booby Kissling, the Schwyzerdeutsch-speaking halfback from the Swiss immigrant community of Monticello, joined the Army. He and his Camp Grant buddies indulged in a betting pool after they boarded a train and were told only that they were headed for basic training. Forty-eight men put up a dollar apiece, and each drew a slip of paper with the name of a state written on it. When they arrived at the camp for basic, the holder of the corresponding state got the forty-eight dollars. "I drew New York," Kissling says. He lost. They ended up at Fort Jackson, South Carolina.

While he was waiting for an opening at officers training school at Fort Benning, Kissling took aptitude tests. Instead of officers training school in 1943, he was assigned to the Army Specialized Training Program, or ASTP, the equivalent of the Marines' V-12 program. He spent three semesters studying first at Clemson University and then at Yale. A Kissling buddy from basic training, Jim Clark, was assigned to the same program and was sent to the University of Wisconsin. The two men tried to work a trade, but the Army refused, so Kissling spent weekends with Clark's family in Bridgeport, Connecticut, and Clark often went to Monticello to stay with Kissling's family. (Situation normal, all . . .) "My dad let him use our car," Kissling says. "His parents treated me just like a son."

The ASTP suddenly ended, which Kissling attributes to a campaign led by *Chicago Tribune* publisher Robert McCormick, who had served in the First Division in World War I. "Colonel McCormick says, 'Why draft married people who have children while we have 40,000 individuals going to schools in the [ASTP]?' That guy had enough power with that *Chicago Tribune*, so the program stopped just like that."

Kissling ended up at Camp Pickett, Virginia, and joined the 78th Infantry division, which landed in France from England in November 1944. He also fought in the Battle of the Bulge.

"The Germans came around behind us," Kissling says. "They had Army uniforms, just like us. We always had a password with a baseball team involved. They didn't know anything about baseball. 'Who goes there?' 'Chicago Cubs?' Then we had Afghans with us, too. They'd sit like this all day long," he says, pantomiming tranquil immobility. "They never cut their hair, either. Then they'd go out at night. They'd sharpen their knives, and then they'd go out at night and if there was anyone in a foxhole, they'd get 'em and just wipe the blood off the knives. The Germans were afraid of them.

"Nobody knew what the hell was going on. One of the things that really gave away the Germans, though, was that their uniforms were clean and, of course, the passwords. If they couldn't answer the question, you'd shoot 'em."

Kissling's unit helped take a key dam. In March 1945, after the Battle of the Bulge, the unit came to Remagen, Germany, the site of a critical railroad bridge over the Rhine. The Germans' attempts to blow up the bridge had failed, and it remained passable.

"Right after the bridge there was a hill, and they were firing artillery," Kissling says. "We probably had half a squad of men left, that's all. It was scary. Anybody who says he ain't scared, they weren't in combat. It's survival of the fittest. You don't know what the hell to do, actually, because it was artillery, 88-millimeter, and 88s usually are on tanks. That was the best offensive weapon the Germans had. The 88 was just a killer. They would actually aim for trees, and the shells would hit the trees and just shatter into a million pieces."

Kissling made it across the bridge, but once on the other side he felt a burning pain in his left knee.

"One of the guys said, 'Hey, sergeant, you're bleeding!' I looked at it. 'Uh, yeah, I am,' and I could hear it, like slush. The first sergeant told me to go back, but I wanted to wait until night. We dug into the foothills. You know how you dig in? You just take a hand grenade, pull the pin and lay it on the ground, and roll away from it. A grenade always explodes downward, and it just pulverizes the dirt. You roll over and you take your hands and that little shovel you have and you dig in. If you can just get below the ground that far, you can save yourself.

"The Germans were getting to the point where they knew they were done, and they were retreating. And what was left were some tanks with the damn 88s. They didn't fire at night. Tanks always pulled away at night. Even ours." Kissling pauses. "If they would have had another division there, that battle still would be going on, I think."

Kissling went to the evacuation hospital. "When I left, I was the only guy left in our company, along with the first sergeant. The others were replacements. We had quite a few killed."

He was sent to an Air Forces base hospital, where his leg eventually healed. "The thing I remember is that I was there for one of the last bombing excursions they had to Germany," he says. "I remember the planes taking off and coming back and refueling as they put more bombs on. They took right off again."

★ ★ ★

Jack Crabb, another reserve sophomore tackle on the '42 team and Pat Harder's former roommate, had joined the Army—after the Marines rejected him because of his eyesight. He was hit near Bastogne, Belgium, in the Battle of the Bulge. Though he can laugh about it now, it was a near miss. "I was with a weapons squad, with machine guns and mortars," Crabb says. "One of my friends from another company came struggling back, and he had been shot in both legs. He said the sergeant was down. I went nuts! I said, 'Anybody want to come with me, we're going to go get him out!' Nobody wanted to go with me, so I took off. When I got up there, I helped the medic with him, but I got shot by a sniper. He hit me, and he hit me right across the chest. I had two holes in my T-shirt, and the armpit torn out, and all I had was a scratch on my chest. I started bitching like a stuck dog because it was no million-dollar wound!"

A million-dollar wound was one that got the combatant sent home.

A little later, Crabb says, "We were under an artillery barrage, and there was snow on the ground. This stuff all started to come in, and we wanted to run for cover. I was smart enough to know that if you dived in the snow, all you're going to do is get wet and cold. I slipped, and I was under a tree. The tree got hit by a shell, and the tree came down on my back. It broke my helmet, and it took eight guys to get it off me. It could have been worse. I was just lucky. The government doesn't believe me, but I ruined my right shoulder and part of my back. I've had a spinal fusion since, but that's all right. I'm not complaining. I made it through it. A lot of guys didn't."

Including Badgers.

TWENTY-SIX

V-E

By 1945, B-17 pilot Don Litchfield, the '42 Badger sophomore from Eau Claire, was flying missions over German targets. He was following the lead of his team cocaptain Mark Hoskins, while knowing that Hoskins was languishing in the prison camp. The world can be small, even in wartime. Another of the Stalag Luft III prisoners was airman Tommy Litchfield, Don's brother. And one of Don Litchfield's roommates during his freshman year at Wisconsin, Dick Rist, was a B-17 pilot killed in action in August 1944. "He washed up on the shore of Belgium," Litchfield says.

"We got a new plane and flew it over from St. John's, Newfoundland, to Wales," Don Litchfield says. "We were assigned to the 401st Bomb Group, 613th Squadron, and we ended up at Deenethorpe, England. A bomb group consisted of around one thousand men, and they had to put thirty-six aircraft over a target, so there were probably fifty airplanes on the base."

Because Germany was weakened, the military raised the number of missions needed for a bomber pilot's tour from twenty-five to thirty-five. Litchfield's bombing missions targeted war plants, marshaling yards, oil refineries, military installations, and troop positions. He flew three missions over Berlin and at least one to Munich.

"A trip to Berlin in a straight line was probably eight hundred miles, but you never flew in a straight line," Litchfield says. "You pretended to go down to Munich and fake them out. They would send all their airplanes up, and just before you get there, you make another turn. You might make two or three of these fake turns through this whole deal with thirty-six aircraft. It was a pretty long procedure. Some of those trips were ten hours in the air."

Litchfield found himself in major trouble on a mission to Berlin in early 1945.

"We were close to Berlin, and we got a pretty direct hit underneath the pilot's seat on the left side. It was a hole perhaps as big as this table," he says, gesturing to a restaurant table. "I didn't know that at the time because my oxygen was knocked out. At 22,000 feet, you can't maintain your senses, so I fainted in less than a minute.

"I came to, and my turret gunner right behind me gave me an emergency bottle. My copilot, Freddie Burton, was a little nervous about whether the engines were going to make it. We dropped our bombs and got out of there and had to fly home all alone. When we got home it was quite exciting. We had to shoot the red flares and all the good stuff and crank down the flaps with no electricity and no anything."

They made it.

★ ★ ★

George Neperud, the reserve lineman from Chippewa Falls, went into the Navy's V-5 program. He got his wings as a Navy flyer in December 1944, and by early '45 he was preparing to join the combat in the Pacific with Air Group 5. The training experience seemed to accelerate his physical development, too. While attending the preflight school at St. Mary's College in Oakland, he played football for a Navy team that also included former Minnesota and Great Lakes star Bruce Smith. When Neperud joined Group 5, the survivors had stories to tell him. They had been on the carrier *Franklin*, which suffered nearly two thousand casualties when it was bombed off the coast of Japan. The group returned to the United States to re-form and pick up replacements. Assigned to fly F4U Corsair fighter-bombers, Neperud met the group at Klamath Falls, Oregon.

★ ★ ★

That spring, George Makris, the boxer, was worried about his buddy Bob Baumann. Baumann was with the Marines on land; Makris's job was to help get the leathernecks to the islands. As a combat quartermaster, Makris combat-loaded ships for invasions in the Pacific, including Iwo Jima and Okinawa. Makris didn't come across Baumann, his partner in that wager-winning run around Lake Mendota, or Schreiner, "but I kept in contact with them," he says. "They were good friends of mine. Believe it or not, they were all looking forward to it. When you're young, you think you can do anything. You don't look at the danger side of it."

★ ★ ★

Like Jerry Frei, '42 sophomore halfback Bob Omelina flew P-38 fighter planes in the Pacific. Omelina was in the armed version of the aircraft, with the 49th Fighter Group.

"We were flying cover for bombers, and we were doing attack bombing," Omelina says. "We also flew cover when they were picking up downed pilots. Some of the missions we had were ten hours long, and in P-38s, that's pretty unusual."

The worst part, he said, was "the anxiety, all the time. When you go on the long missions, at least the P-38 had two engines, and that made you feel pretty good. But it seemed like every time you went off on one of those things, the engines weren't synchronized, they didn't sound right, you sensed this wrong and that wrong. So, that could make you anxious."

His closest call? Omelina was dropping napalm bombs on Japanese forces in northern Luzon. "We were trying to get the Japanese out of the hills," Omelina says. "Those are fire bombs, and one hung up under my wing and I tried to shake it off and it ruptured. It just scattered all over the wing and the motor and set the plane on fire. I headed out to the ocean and bailed out. A Navy PT boat picked me up."

He was lucky the Japanese didn't get to him first.

★ ★ ★

As deaths mounted in the island fighting, the Badgers' V-12 Marines came to the gruesome realization that they were ticketed to be part of an invasion of Japan.

"It was a pool, and you were expendable as lieutenants," says John Gallagher, the '42 reserve quarterback and '43 Michigan guard. "You'd look at the roster at Quantico, and you'd say, 'Look at all the lieutenants who got killed!' You'd see these guys who just got out of Quantico two or three months ago, and already they're dead. The obituaries would come through on the Teletype. The sergeants would pass them around and say, 'Well, we lost such and such number of officers from the class of so and so.'"

The worst battles were yet to come. The V-12 Badger Marines knew that, too, as they scattered to units at Camp Lejeune and other posts.

"You knew something was going to happen, but you had your duties and your assignments to do and you had to get them done," Gallagher says. "If the world comes to an end, it comes to an end."

★ ★ ★

At Stalag Luft III, the prisoners could flood the athletic field in the winter and use it as a hockey rink for pickup games. On January 23, 1945, the South Compound beat the Center Compound 3–1 in an organized hockey contest. But the whole camp, including the Germans, seemed distracted.

"The Russians were coming, and we could tell they were coming because of the air traffic and the German planes over our camp all the time," Mark Hoskins says.

On January 27, four days after the hockey game, Hoskins was in the audience in the South Compound's theater, watching a prisoner production of *You Can't Take It with You.* Suddenly the South Compound's senior Allied officer, Colonel Charles G. Goodrich, stepped onto the stage. He announced the Germans were evacuating Stalag Luft III and said the prisoners had to be ready to march out in an hour.

Russian forces under Marshall G. K. Zhukov were only about twenty miles away. The Germans didn't want the British and American officers freed to rejoin the fighting, even though most of the men were emaciated.

The evacuation of ten thousand prisoners, including two thousand Americans, began at 11 p.m. The prisoners marched in the bitter cold through the night. Many collapsed and had to be left behind to freeze to death. After dawn, the prisoners were finally allowed to rest. "We were at a place with some barns, and we slept in the hay," Hoskins says. "They got us out the next day, and we traveled a good ways until we came to a town called Maskau. They put us in a glass factory. The workers were all gone, but it was heated because of the fires from the glass machines. A friend of mine from my room slept that night on the floor of a glass furnace."

They resumed the march the next day and made it to Spremberg, a small German town that served as headquarters for a German tank unit. The prisoners were gathered in a square and encircled by tanks. "I thought, 'Jesus Christ, this is it,'" Hoskins says. "I thought they were going to use those tanks on us. But they just used them to keep us from doing anything."

The prisoners jumped and moved to keep from freezing. Then, they were loaded onto trains. The cars were packed, and the stench was choking.

"Those cars were called 'forty and eight,'" Hoskins says. "They were freight cars made to carry forty men or eight horses. They had a lot more than that in each car. They must have marked 'Red Cross' on the top, or something like that, because they had notified the bombers we were on this train so they wouldn't attack us. And they didn't.

"There were a certain number of guards on the train, not one per car. The train would have to stop every three or four hours to let the men out to go to the bathroom. The trouble was there weren't enough guards to open all the cars simultaneously. They'd start at one end of the train, and by the time they got to the other end, everybody was ready to go again. Here you'd be crapping in the snow and have to finish and have to hustle back in the car."

On the night of February 1, the train arrived at Moosburg, twenty-two miles northeast of Munich. The prisoners had to stay in the boxcars until the next morning, when they were moved to Stalag VII-A.

Stalag VII-A made Stalag Luft III seem like the Waldorf-Astoria. It had been built to house 10,000. Eventually, the camp held 110,000 prisoners, including 30,000 Americans. Tents were wedged between barracks, and most of the prisoners didn't have beds and slept wherever they could find space. But news of Allied successes filtered into the camp, and the prisoners were hopeful they would be liberated—unless the Germans violated all rules of war by staging mass executions.

Soon Allied air traffic in the area was heavy, mostly involving P-47 and P-51 fighters attacking German targets and B-17s heading to Munich. Artillery thundered in the distance. Red Cross parcels were delayed, so for a time the German gruel was the prisoners' only sustenance. The Germans became more lackadaisical in their control of the prisoners, who could wander from compound to compound. In late April, the artillery barrages began flying over the camp, toward Moosburg. "I had never heard artillery close up before," Hoskins says. "It was scary as hell, kind of a shriek or like a sheet being ripped." During the second night of overhead artillery, the prisoners heard German trucks leaving the camp. In the morning, most of the guards were gone.

On Sunday, April 29, some prisoners climbed onto the roofs of the buildings and watched American tanks closing in. They took cover during the ensuing one-hour battle outside the camp between the Americans and the remaining Germans. In midafternoon, tanks from the Army's 47th Tank Battalion rolled into camp.

Ten months after his mission to Budapest, Hoskins was liberated.

Hitler committed suicide in his Berlin bunker the next day. And the day after that, General George S. Patton, Jr., visited the Americans at Stalag VII-A.

"There was no place for us to go," Hoskins says. So, after several more days at the camp, he and many of the prisoners were taken to Englestadt, about fifty miles away. "It took about three or four days for the planes to come and get us," he says. "[At Englestadt] we went into a factory that manufactured alpine equipment for the German army. There were hundreds of thousands of skis there. We discovered that if you put the skis between two abutments, that would give you a place to sleep. So, we slept on the skis for a couple of nights. Finally, the planes came."

The planes took the men to Rheims, France, where they received much-needed medical attention. Hoskins weighed 135 pounds, down 55 from his playing (and flying) weight. "We were given shots, and they started filling us with food."

The war was over in Europe.

* * *

Don Litchfield had flown twenty missions when the Germans surrendered on May 7. After that he ferried French and English prisoners of war back to their home nations. When the plane crossed over the Rhine River and was over France, his French passengers variously shouted "Vive le France!" and sang "La Marseillaise" and cried.

The pilot got a little misty, too.

* * *

George Hekkers, the sophomore '42 tackle and the veteran of low-level A-26 bombing, was brought from Europe back to the United States. He was told he would be sent to join the fight against Japan.

Also stateside, pilot instructors Otto Breitenbach and John Roberts got the impression they soon would be flying in the Pacific. Roberts, in fact, was assigned to learn to fly the new P-40 fighter, expected to be a major force in the invasion of Japan. "Most of my P-40 work was formation and planning," he says. "That was really kind of fun, because formation flying was the fun part of flying, and we didn't get to do that when we were teaching."

* * *

After the German bombing of England stopped, quarterback Ashley Anderson, working in the First Strategic Air Depot, played for an Army Air Forces football team that played exhibition games, including one against a Navy team that drew 60,000 fans in London. "It was exciting because Jimmy Doolittle [the daredevil aviator and Medal of Honor winner] came down between halves and shook hands with all of us," Anderson says.

Anderson was named the most valuable player on the AAF team and was sent to Paris to be on a radio program that would be transmitted back to the United States. While he was in France, Germany surrendered. The next day, May 8, was V-E Day.

"It was wild," he says. "Everybody bought drinks for us. When victory was declared, they canceled the broadcast. But they said, 'Well, since you're here, stay a few days. You'll probably never see it again.' I stayed five days. I stayed a couple of nights at the Red Cross and then I found a cheap hotel, just off Place du Havre, and all you do is wander around and see the sites. I went to the Eiffel Tower, Arc de Triomphe, the Louvre. I saw quite a bit.

"And they were right. I've never been back."

Anderson never ran into Erv "Booby" Kissling, the Army man wounded near Remagen. After getting out of the hospital, Kissling was in Paris, too.

"I was in the office of the chief quartermaster as mail clerk," Kissling says. "The mail came in at 10 in the morning, and it took me about five minutes to deliver it. I had the rest of the day off. On the bulletin board one day I saw, 'Would anyone like to go out for the Seine football team?' So, I went down there and got signed up with the Seine section and played football. We went down to Nice, France, and we played Teddy Scallisi from Madison Central High and Ripon College and the pros. He was with the 87th Division. Each division had a football team. . . . [W]hen we were there, Teddy took me down an alley one night, an unauthorized area for military personnel. We come to a peephole, and the guy opens it up, and Teddy talks to him. Teddy can speak German and French, and he got us in there. The women! We had a steak dinner! Lettuce! I had a glass of milk, the only milk I had when I was overseas. Teddy says, 'How did you like the steak?' 'Good,' I said. He said, 'You're eating one of the German Army's cavalry horses.' We went back the next night, and I had another one, and it didn't bother me one bit. I played with that football team, and we stayed down there about three weeks. Then we got called back to Paris because they had a ship ready to take us home."

★ ★ ★

Jim McFadzean, the '42 senior halfback who helped unload tanks as a Navy man, was brought back to Pearl Harbor after V-E Day. As soon as the Navy rounded up enough landing craft tanks, he was going to go head for Japan and the likely invasion. By this time, the United States already had paid a fearsome price on other Pacific islands.

TWENTY-SEVEN

Okinawa

Dave Schreiner, Bob Baumann, Bud Seelinger, and the rest of the Sixth Marine Division left Guadalcanal—the site of the Football Classic—on ships in late March 1945. Their destination was Okinawa, about four hundred miles south of the Japanese home islands. The narrow island in the Ryukyu chain was roughly sixty-five miles long from north to south, and it would be the staging ground for an invasion of Japan.

On the ship, as he realized he was about to be in another fierce island battle, Schreiner read Jesus' Sermon on the Mount. In a letter to his family dated March 31, he wrote, "The Bible certainly gives one faith in everything—knowing that with faith everything is bound to come out alright."

At 4:06 a.m. on April 1, Easter Sunday, Admiral Kelly Turner issued the order: "Land the landing force." Ultimately, Schreiner was among more than 60,000 troops landing uncontested over a nine-mile stretch on the Hagushi beaches on the west side of the island. The Japanese strategy was to wait and fight elsewhere, not on or near the beaches where U.S. forces invaded.

The Northern Attack Force, under Rear Admiral Lawrence F. Reifsnider, included screening destroyers, twenty transports, sixty-seven LSTs with equipment, and the First and Sixth Marine Divisions. Baumann and Schreiner were in A Company, 4th Regiment of the Sixth Division, leading separate platoons under the company commander Captain Clint Eastment.

On the first day of the Okinawa invasion, the Sixth Division overran and secured Yomitan Airfield, near the west coast. Most of the 4th Regiment kept going, advancing about another half-mile.

A planning pattern developed. Platoon leaders—including Schreiner and Baumann—met in the morning with other regimental officers to discuss strategy for the day. Captain Frank Kemp remembers those meetings with Baumann and Schreiner and all the officers.

Kemp says that Schreiner and Baumann "just knew what was right to do. You didn't want to have any problem about deciding where to go, who to put in front, who to have behind with the mortars, and so on. You never had to worry about that with them. They listened and learned quickly. They were just fantastic."

The 4th Regiment's commanding officers, Kemp says, were "great men. Alan Shapley, who had played football at Navy, was our regimental commander, and there wasn't any finer man I had served under. Barney Green, a Penn man, was a major and was head of our battalion. He was a very fine man."

Bernard Green, though, was around for the meetings on Okinawa for less than two weeks.

★ ★ ★

The men were easy and light-hearted on the ride to Okinawa. Even before we landed, I found this cheerful condition was chronic. The outfit never expects to get more trouble than it can handle.

The commanding officer is quite a guy. He is still able to out-hike most of the men in the regiment. He has a football players' outfit. In it, or closely affiliated with it, are Baumann and Schreiner of Wisconsin, Laufer of Notre Dame, Osmanski of the Bears, Farrant of the Eagles, and Topping of Stanford.

One thing which exhilarated the men on the transport journey here was radio news from Germany. "If we get our job rolling the same way," said the colonel, "this can be the biggest week of the whole war."

It rolled at the start and is still rolling as I write this.
—JOHN LARDNER, *SAN FRANCISCO CHRONICLE,* APRIL 1945

★ ★ ★

The 4th Regiment, moving east, encountered Japanese on the second day. Schreiner's platoon came under fire in a valley below Yomitan Airfield. "A couple of their snipers were really kind of playing havoc," recalls Private Vic Anderson, Captain Eastment's runner in A Company. "Dave motioned to me and said, 'Come on, follow me.' So, we circled around behind where these snipers were located, and there they were—two of 'em—in the heavy grass. I raised my rifle to kill them and Dave said, 'No, I want them to know we're here.' He pointed to the one he wanted to take, and to the one he wanted me to take. He said, 'Hey, Japs!' and the Japs turned around, and we shot 'em."

The Japanese resistance on the third day was minimal, and the Sixth Division was almost across the thin Ishikawa Isthmus.

"Dave complained to me that he wasn't getting his share of action," Eastment recalls. "He wanted to get more action. I said, 'Just wait a while. It's a long campaign.'"

Much of the division turned north to secure the lightly defended part of the island. By April 7, much of the Sixth was at Nago, a coastal town about halfway to the northern tip of the island.

★ ★ ★

On April 13, shocking news spread among American forces.

President Franklin Roosevelt, a voice of reassurance and authority throughout the Great Depression and the fight against the Germans and Japanese, was dead, having suffered a stroke the previous afternoon in Warm Springs, Georgia. He had been president since Schreiner was eleven years old. In locations and conditions that permitted it, many U.S. forces on Okinawa held memorial services.

Few Americans knew much about FDR's successor, Harry S Truman. U.S. forces on Okinawa had neither the time nor the inclination to study up on the new commander-in-chief. They mourned the fallen president, however briefly, and went on with the tasks at hand.

The Japanese fiercely defended the Motobu Peninsula northwest of Nago because they had guns on the peninsula that they could use to fire on nearby Ie Shima Island and its landing zone. Otherwise, the northern half of the island was of dubious military value because of its mountainous terrain.

On the peninsula on April 14, the 4th Regiment's 1st Battalion, including Schreiner and Baumann, joined an attack on the Yae Take Mountain stronghold of Colonel Takehido Udo. On the first day, 1st Battalion commander Barney Green was killed by machine gun fire from snipers. With Captain Eastment leading and Baumann and Schreiner among the officers, A Company and C Company scaled the side of the mountain. The Marines fought grenade battles, took control of the summit on April 16, and held it in heavy fighting. Baumann was wounded that day. Marine records—which show his named spelled "Bauman"—don't specify the nature of the wound. Corporal Richard Bush of Company C, who pulled a Japanese grenade under himself to save others, survived and later received the Congressional Medal of Honor for his heroism.

By April 20, U.S. forces controlled the peninsula. Eastment believes Baumann went off the lines only briefly after his injury. After Baumann returned, Eastment named him his executive officer. The division's muster rolls confirm that Baumann was wounded, but they don't specify when he returned to his unit.

Now that the United States had control of the Motobu Peninsula and there was a lull in the fighting, Schreiner had time for socializing, both to talk about the news that the Germans had surrendered and to talk football. Young Larry Parmelee of Milwaukee was a corpsman, officially a Navy pharmacist's mate attached to the Marines, meaning he was trained in emergency medical techniques but he was also an armed combatant. He had enlisted directly from high school and was with the 4th Regiment, 2nd Battalion, E Company. One corpsman in Schreiner's A Company asked Parmelee if he would like to meet the Wisconsin All-American football player. Parmelee, who had played high school ball, jumped at the offer, saying he had listened to Schreiner and the Badgers on the radio and dreamed of playing in Camp Randall, too.

"They were bivouacked about a half-mile from us, and my friend came over and got me and introduced me to Dave," Parmelee says. "We just sat around, cross-legged on the ground, and we talked. We talked a lot about Wisconsin, the hunting and fishing, and about some of his football exploits. He asked me if I was interested in football, and I said, 'Boy, do I want to go to Wisconsin in the worst way.' He said, 'Well, if we get out of this thing OK, you look me up and I'll be available for you.'" Schreiner said he would introduce Parmelee to the coaching staff.

Parmelee returned to his unit and excitedly told his buddies about meeting one of his heroes. And he fantasized what it would be like to have a two-time All-American introduce him to Harry Stuhldreher and say, "Give this kid a chance!"

Schreiner also discussed football with John McLaughry, the former New York Giant now serving in a tank unit. McLaughry expected to return to the NFL; Schreiner was still deciding whether to sign after the war with the Detroit Lions. "He was quite a guy," McLaughry says. "He was a good leader. He wasn't a show-off in any way. He just had a way about him. He got people to follow him."

In a letter to his family on May 1, Schreiner wrote:

You do get a hardened outlook on life but not an unpleasant or mean perspective. Things that used to shock you are more or less taken for granted. But I am quite sure you won't find me greatly changed.

(Schreiner's fellow Marines were accustomed to Dave receiving letters from Odette Hendrickson, in addition to those from his family. The letters from Odette were easy to spot. "They'd have big old kisses on the back," says Gus Forbus, a sergeant and one of Schreiner's closest friends in the battalion.)

The southern part of the island was far more problematic than the north. The Japanese 32nd Army dug into caves and tunnels. They were determined to fight to the death and inflict maximum damage. Monsoon rains, mud, and floods plagued the advancing Marines as they sought out the Japanese. Some defenders were buried alive. Other dead Japanese were left behind to decay, and the island became an ecological disaster, with maggots thriving in the mud.

After the Marines left the Motobu Peninsula and moved south, three companies of the 4th Regiment were involved in the May 13–19 battle for Sugar Loaf Hill, north of the port of Naha. Company A, not involved in that battle, was part of a shore-to-shore landing just as the 4th and 29th Regiments moved from the Naha area to south of the city, on the harbor. The goal was to secure the Oruku Peninsula south of Naha.

On the third day of the assault, June 6, the Schreiner-led platoon was pinned down and under heavy fire. Captain Eastment says that he was directed to move ahead with scouts and that he left Baumann in charge of the company.

Years later John McLaughry wrote his memories of what happened next. He said Baumann's platoon "was blind-sided by heavy enemy fire from the reverse slope to his left flank . . . All this time I was in radio contact with Bob who was only some 50 yards away on the reverse side of the ridge and . . . he was hit and died as we were discussing how to extricate his platoon."

Sergeant Gus Forbus was with Schreiner. "We were getting the shit kicked out of us, to be honest," Forbus recalls. "It was really hot, with snipers firing and mortars, you name it. We were in trouble, and we were trying to get out of there. So, Dave and I were evacuating our dead and wounded. We were running; there's no walking when you're under fire like that."

Bodies littered the trail. Schreiner was used to that, but something clicked in his mind as he and Forbus ran by one of the many corpses.

Schreiner didn't stop.

"That looked like Bob!" he hollered to Forbus.

"Now, don't you go back there!" Forbus responded.

With eyes misting, Schreiner kept running. "We got the ones out we were carrying," Forbus recalls. "He didn't go back. I wouldn't let him go back."

Later, Schreiner's fears were confirmed.

The body was Bob Baumann's.

Eastment recalls, "When I came back, they told me Bob had been hit. He got a bullet right through his head."

Private First Class Jim Harwood says Baumann's death angered some of the former Badger tackle's men. "I should remember his runner's name, but I'm sorry, I don't," Harwood says. "It's been too many years ago. When Baumann got killed, they sent his runner back to get some civilians. Hell, this is a terrible story to have to tell, but it's true. They sent him back to get a bunch of civilians, and he took them behind a hill and killed every god damn one of them because Baumann had been killed."

Two days later, on June 8, according to a later dispatch by Marine Corps correspondent Don Petit, Schreiner was heroic in grenade battles for two hills near Naha. Petit wrote that Schreiner twice charged up the hill and tossed grenades into Japanese positions, and the one hundred enemy soldiers withdrew. (Japanese forces on Okinawa generally pulled back, not out of cowardice but rather to reorganize their efforts toward inflicting maximum damage before dying.)

Eastment was severely wounded that day. "Dave Schreiner pulled me out of the line of fire," Eastment says. "He looked at the holes. He said I had four of 'em, so we thought that I'd been hit by four bullets. But I found later, there were only two bullets that made the holes. He went ahead and found the people who got me out of there, too. That was the last time I saw him."

Eastment's fighting was over, and he hated leaving his men behind. Schreiner became company commander.

On June 11, Gus Forbus was shot in the knee. As he was being evacuated, heading for two years of hospitalization, he made a symbolic presentation to his lieutenant, Schreiner. "I gave him the .45 I used for personal protection," Forbus says. He hoped it would help.

The Marines secured the harbor by June 13.

When Schreiner told the story of Baumann's death to Bud Seelinger, the third Badger in the Sixth Marine Division, Schreiner broke down after describing how he had seen the body.

"That's all Dave told me," Seelinger wrote in a June 16 letter to Harry Stuhldreher.

Stuhldreher passed along news of the letter from Seelinger to Madison reporters, but the printed versions varied. Stuhldreher either read it aloud and the reporters took haphazard notes, or he paraphrased it in different conversations. One Madison paper quoted the letter from Seelinger to Stuhldreher as saying, "Your famous tackle of Harvey, Ill., will fight no more. The shock of that news really put a lump in my throat." Stuhldreher also reported that Seelinger's letter said Baumann was trying to get to a pinned-down Schreiner to tell him that tanks were on the way.

Another of Baumann's 1942 teammates, Marine Lieutenant Bob Rennebohm, was in San Diego, preparing to ship out to the Pacific for the likely invasion of Japan.

"You won't believe this," Rennebohm says. "I was standing at a bridge and a camp newspaper came floating down this little stream. I could read the headline at the bottom."

The headline: "Bob Bauman, Wisconsin tackle, killed"

Stunned, Rennebohm went and found another copy of the Marine newspaper. It wasn't a bad dream. As in the initial reports in the Madison papers, Baumann's name was spelled wrong because of the mistake in the Marine records. That fact didn't change anything.

★ ★ ★

As the Okinawa campaign continued, the men of A Company grew even fonder of Schreiner.

"We were not foxhole buddies or anything like that," recalls Private First Class Ed Liguori. "He was my lieutenant. He knew me as Eddie. They all called me Eddie. One day, we had gone two, two and a half days without food or water. There were a few cans of cheese, but we didn't have much water. He disappeared. An hour later, he comes back up the hill where we were in our foxholes, and he had a box on his shoulder. In it were extra large cans of grapefruit juice. I still remember the color. They were tannish and greenish cans, with no name on them or anything. I don't know where he stole it from or where he got it. But here he comes up this hill, and we all took three slugs of that grapefruit juice. I can't have grapefruit juice now because of medication, but when I could, every time I drank grapefruit juice, I thought of Dave Schreiner."

"We had some officers who were, very frankly, assholes," says PFC Jim Harwood. "Most of the officers we had were good guys. They weren't going to run you up for some little infraction that didn't make any difference anyway. Dave was one of those types of guys who was lenient. He wasn't going to give you a lot of hell for nothing."

On June 18, Schreiner wrote his parents on American Red Cross stationery.

> Dear Mother and Dad—
> Rec'd letter of June 6 from you. Enclosed was a clipping about

Johnny Walsh. No I didn't get any bronze star on Guam. I've still got my medal. I can feel it when I put my hands behind me.

We've been eating very well of late. Fresh meat, good canned food etc. And I've been sleeping a lot. Boy it's good to rest.

Will write next chance I get. Don't forget a company commander is a pretty safe spot.
Much love,
Dave

On the night of June 19, Seelinger, with the 29th Regiment, tracked down Schreiner and gave him several cans of fruit. The two Badgers again spoke of Baumann, and they were hoping the fighting was coming to an end. Japanese had died by the thousands, and the organized resistance was lessening. But there was one more major pocket of resistance on the southern end of the island, near a gap in the American lines. By then, runner Vic Anderson had been wounded and evacuated, but he later heard from his buddies that Schreiner was sent out on what Anderson and others view as a needlessly dangerous mission near the west coast of Oruku Peninsula on June 20. Anderson says the mandate came from a "new silly-ass major who didn't know that we didn't go out after dark or after 4 or 5 o'clock, when the Japs would set up a lot of traps. He said, 'Dave, you take that squad down there and see if there are any Japs in that gully and valley.'"

Gus Forbus, who by then was in a hospital at Tinian in the Mariana Islands, says he also heard that an officer who joined the unit late in the battle ordered Schreiner to check on the lines. "The report I got on it was that they were putting in the lines for the night on the 20th, and he wasn't satisfied," Forbus says. "He wanted Dave to check it out. He was an Annapolis man, but he couldn't pour water out of a boot."

In 1993 John McLaughry wrote his memories of that day:

My platoon of M-7's was assigned to provide fire support for the 1st Battalion in an attack on the last enemy stronghold at the extreme southern point of Okinawa. The immediate objective was some very rugged terrain, an escarpment of boulders, sheer rock and caves . . . rising to nearly 300 feet. Prior to the attack Dave was moving his company into the line adjacent to the company our M-7's were to support and I talked very briefly with him. He then, with a couple of his men, disappeared into the rocky area leading toward the Kiyama Gusuku hill mass.

Petit's later dispatch said Schreiner had walked ahead to scout.

According to the dispatch, gunfire from a cave suddenly ripped into his left side. Vic Anderson said he heard it happened this way: "A Jap with a Nambu machine gun stepped out of a cave and shot him." Petit's dispatch said a grenade exploded and fragments tore into both of his legs.

McLaughry's written recollections made it clear he was skeptical of Petit's version. McLaughry's account:

> The attack had not yet jumped off when word came that Dave had been hit, shot by a sniper. There was no word on his condition. Because of my platoon's connections with Dave, over the next few hours we tried to get as much information as possible and did hear on good authority that a bullet had hit him in the chest area, lodging in his spine.

Schreiner was shot in the upper torso. Despite the myths that spread both immediately and over later years, that's indisputable. The medics treating him and those who saw him remember the upper torso trauma but aren't sure if there were other wounds. That said, even those interviewed acknowledge that they saw so many deaths, involving both friends and those they didn't know, that circumstances sometimes run together in their minds. Plus, they admit the passage of nearly sixty years can make memories—even of very jarring incidents—become foggy. So, Schreiner might or might not also have been hit by grenade fragments.

Regardless of the nature of his wounds, men from the patrol rushed up and got Schreiner back to the unit's lines. William Ramey, a corpsman and pharmacist's mate, recalls working on Schreiner. He says he heard that Schreiner had gone out on that advance patrol with a first sergeant. "We were trying to get plasma started," Ramey says. "He told me, 'Doc, they pulled a sneaky trick on us!'"

Some of the men, including Ramey, who also knew who Schreiner was and respected him immensely, took that to mean that Schreiner had been ambushed while accepting a surrender from Japanese. Word from the command post later trickled in to support that inference. (Depending upon one's definition of *sniper*, that could jibe with the story McLaughry heard.) Ramey says he believed Schreiner meant "they tricked him into coming down and shot him." He is candid that he doesn't remember Schreiner mentioning a white flag and that he drew inferences and then heard others talk of a faked surrender later. "I'm eighty years old," Ramey says. "It's been a long time. But somebody's last words like that, they stick with you pretty good." Ramey's high regard for Schreiner and his familiarity with him virtually guarantee he didn't mix up the circumstances of Schreiner's injuries with anyone else's.

Contrary to myth, many Japanese and conscripted Okinawans—about 10,000—surrendered on Okinawa. In *Typhoon of Steel*, the brother-author team of James and William Belote noted that surrenders increased from an average of about 50 per day from June 12 to 18, to 343 on June 19, and then 977 on June 20—the day Schreiner was wounded. Japanese soldiers indeed were allowing themselves to be taken prisoner on the day Schreiner was on his final patrol. Still, the Belotes wrote, the Japanese soldiers who surrendered were exceptional, because most members of the 32nd Army still fought to the death. U.S. estimates of the Japanese battle deaths on June 19 and 20 totaled 5,000.

Charles Pulford, a private first class posted to the headquarters company, served as a runner for Barney Green before Green's death. He says he was at the command post the day Schreiner suffered his wounds. He didn't hear direct discussions between Schreiner and officers at the command post. Yet he is adamant that word of those discussions spread through the command post—along with the news that Schreiner was shot during a faked surrender.

He says he isn't sure which officers came up with the plan, but that planes dropped white pamphlets over the area. "The Japs were told that if they wanted to surrender, they would wave these pamphlets," Pulford says. "I remember when the planes came over to drop them." He believes it happened late in the afternoon. Although his first thought was that it happened on the day Schreiner was wounded, he isn't certain of that. But he is certain that Schreiner contacted the command post on his patrol.

"Being there at the C.P.," Pulford says, "I heard that Dave had called back to find out what to do. They dropped these pamphlets, and evidently Dave had seen Japs waving them. They were told to do that if they wanted to surrender. He was told to take an interpreter and crawl up there and see what he could arrange."

Who told Schreiner that?

"I imagine it had to be the commanding officer at the C.P., or it might even have been regimental," Pulford says. "Then shortly after that, we heard that he had crawled up there, and when he raised up to talk to them, they machine-gunned him." If survivors' memories are accurate, Schreiner went in and out of consciousness after he was brought back to the lines.

Private First Class Ed Liguori was in his foxhole. "Somebody said, 'The lieutenant's been hit!'" Liguori recalls. "I got out of the foxhole and walked over to where the medics were treating Dave. He was unconscious, breathing heavily, and it was so sad. He wasn't moving. He wasn't talk-ing. There might have been a moan. They were giving him plasma. They were giving him fluids through his ankle because the blood vessels col-lapsed. I didn't know anything about it at the time, being a young, dopey kid. But later, when I was teaching, I learned about these things. They couldn't find any blood vessels in his arm, so they were administering plasma in his ankle. I guess they found a vein down there."

Private First Class Vern Courtnage, a driver who did work for com-panies in the battalion, had transported Schreiner often, and he saw him right before he was loaded onto a jeep to be taken to an aid station. "He was on the ground, on a stretcher, with a covering over him," Courtnage says. "The corpsmen were working on him, and they loaded him into the jeep. My friend drove the jeep; his name was Duane Carey. We loaded him onto that jeep, and everybody was wishing him well, and he was con-scious. The last words he spoke, that I heard, anyway, were, 'If any of you guys think I'm crying, I'll get out of here and kick the shit out of you!' That stuck with me all those years. That was the last I saw Dave."

The men watched their lieutenant leave in the jeep. They had seen their buddies die, had crawled over bodies as if they were rocks, and were steeled to death, even as they knew it might come to them.

But, god, why Schreiner?

James Singley, the private first class in the weapons company who had served under Schreiner on Guam, was near Schreiner's company that day on Okinawa. He immediately heard one of the inaccurate stories about Schreiner's wounds.

"Word came down the line that Dave had gotten shot by a sniper right between the eyes," Singley says. "Now, when somebody who was well-liked got shot, we always passed the word down the line. Word came down that that's what happened. You never knew whether it's what happened exactly, but that's what came down the line about Dave."

Obviously, if that had happened, Schreiner would have died imme-diately. But it's illustrative of the way stories—often inaccurate ones—spread among the men.

Schreiner underwent emergency surgery at a field hospital. But there wasn't much hope. David Nathan Schreiner died the next day, June 21, 1945. He was twenty-four.

"Just a beautiful man died," Vic Anderson says.

The doctors let his buddies know that even if they had managed to save him, he probably would have been paralyzed because of where he was wounded. "I was told he was injured in such a way in the spine that he never would be able to do anything," Mark Hoskins says, the words catching in his throat.

The official dispatch makes no mention of a faked surrender. That raises the question: Why cover that up? If Schreiner died as he gave the benefit of the doubt to surrendering Japanese, that doesn't render his death less tragic than if he had been struck down by a sniper or a soldier emerging from a cave. In fact, in June 1945, such a tale of Japanese battlefield treachery would have been appropriate as the nation braced for an invasion of the Japanese home islands.

However, if Schreiner's death was the indirect result of being ordered to try to arrange a surrender, and the pamphlet drop ended up endangering Schreiner and others, there would be reason to create a more conventional battle scenario for Schreiner's death—it would save face for the officers who had ordered Schreiner to attempt to arrange a surrender.

George Feifer's book *Tennozan* discusses in depth the dilemma of American troops when deciding whether to accept surrenders, given the horrific fighting and barbaric Japanese tactics—and not just on Okinawa. Feifer doesn't claim to have discerned the actual numbers of Japanese and conscripted Okinawans who died after trying to give up, but he makes it clear that the number was significant. It is also clear that A Company added to that toll, and part of that was a response to rumors of how the popular Schreiner was mortally wounded. Again, it's important to note that Schreiner was hit on a day when Japanese and Okinawan surrenders were increasing. There were strategic reasons to accept surrenders if information about the location and strength of surviving Japanese defenders could be gathered. But that didn't mean that all those signaling an intention to surrender were sincere.

"There was a bunch of us mad," says William Ramey, the pharmacist's mate. "Everybody thought a lot of Dave. It made everybody so mad, they didn't take no more prisoners. That was the end of that outfit taking prisoners."

Charles Pulford adds, "Everyone was in shock. I remember that. And everybody was mad. I mean, mad. . . . We decided not to take prisoners. But we did let the civilians through."

Judy Corfield, Schreiner's niece, says that her late mother, Betty Johnson, attended a Sixth Marine Division reunion in Chicago in 1996. Johnson, Schreiner's sister, returned from the reunion and told her daughter that according to several members of Schreiner's platoon, he indeed had been accepting a surrender, under a white flag, from several Japanese. The story, handed down orally, was different from the version Charles Pulford remembers from being at the command post. Betty Johnson was told that Dave had been wary as the small Japanese party approached him, and when the Japanese soldier in front bowed, he had a rifle hidden behind his back. Johnson was told that a Japanese man reached forward and fired the rifle at Schreiner, and another tossed a grenade.

Constance Sherman Smyth, Schreiner's longtime friend from Lancaster, says the word in his hometown was that he was shot in the back.

So, there are conflicting stories about Schreiner's death, and they almost certainly will never be resolved. However he was mortally wounded, Schreiner's death on June 21 came hours before Major General Roy S. Geiger declared that organized resistance had ended and the island was secure. Geiger had succeeded Lieutenant General Simon Bolivar Buckner as commander of the forces when Buckner was struck in the chest by an artillery shell shard and killed on June 18. Geiger's declaration was premature, because isolated resistance and U.S. mop-up operations continued.

Lieutenant General Mitsuru Ushijima, commander of the Japanese 32nd Army, committed suicide on June 22.

Tenth Army commander Lieutenant General Joseph W. Stilwell declared the campaign over on July 2.

Bud Seelinger lost two teammates on Okinawa. Other Seelinger buddies were killed, too, but he couldn't help being more torn up by the deaths of Baumann and Schreiner. "He was just heartsick," says his wife, Mary Elaine Seelinger. "He was broken up."

He wasn't alone.

In the hospital on Tinian, Sergeant Gus Forbus was beginning his long recuperation from his leg wounds. A young Marine, another member of the 4th, came into his room.

"Sarge," he told Forbus, "I've got some bad news."

"Oh, shit," said Forbus. "Don't tell me Dave got killed."

"Yup."

Forbus broke down.

☆ ☆ ☆

Schreiner's final letter home arrived in Lancaster on June 25. He was already dead. His parents didn't know that as they opened the letter with his return address in the left-hand corner.

Lt. David N Schreiner
Co A 1st Bn 4th Marines
6th Mar. Div.
FPO—San Francisco

And they read their son's reassuring final line—the one about a company commander being in a relatively safe position.

★ ★ ★

A total of 2,938 Marines were killed or missing in action on Okinawa. U.S. Army dead and missing numbered 4,675. The combined number of wounded for both services was 34,116. In addition to Baumann and Schreiner, the Football Classic players killed were:

* Lieutenant Chuck Behan, the former Detroit Lion who had been the captain of the 29th Marines' team in the Football Classic game.
* Corporal Tony Butkovich, halfback, Illinois and Purdue.
* Captain Bob Fowler, center, Michigan.
* Corporal John Hebrank, tackle, Lehigh.
* Lieutenant Hubbard Hinde, tackle, Southern Methodist.
* Corporal Rusty Johnston, halfback, Marquette.
* Lieutenant George Murphy, end, Notre Dame.
* Corporal Johnny Perry, back, Wake Forest and Duke.
* Lieutenant Jim Quinn, end, Amherst.
* Private First Class Ed Van Order, tackle, Cornell.

Murphy, the 1942 Notre Dame captain, was killed in the mid-May battle for Sugar Loaf Hill. The Tenth Army's official Okinawa combat history, published three years later, said Murphy first ordered "an assault with fixed bayonets" against Japanese forces.

"The marines reached the top [of the hill] and immediately became involved in a grenade battle with the enemy," the combat historians wrote. "Their supply of 350 grenades was soon exhausted.

"Lieutenant Murphy asked his company commander Capt. Howard L. Mabie for permission to withdraw, but Captain Mabie ordered him to hold the hill at all costs. By now the whole forward slope of Sugar Loaf was alive with gray eddies of smoke from mortar blasts, and Murphy ordered a withdrawal on his own initiative. Covering the men as they pulled back down the slope, Murphy was killed by a fragment when he paused to help a wounded marine."

A Marine correspondent wrote of Murphy's death at the time, and that story was carried in many U.S. newspapers in May. It had Murphy making multiple trips to help carry the wounded to an aid station before he was hit as he rested. It added, "Irish George staggered to his feet, aimed over the hill and emptied his pistol in the direction of the enemy. Then he fell dead."

Forty-nine of the sixty men in Murphy's platoon were killed or wounded on Sugar Loaf Hill.

Bus Bergman, the former Colorado A&M star, was a platoon leader in the same Company D and earned the Bronze Star for heroics on Sugar Loaf Hill three days after Murphy's death. He had shared a tent with Murphy on Guadalcanal, and the two men ran around together and became close. He had met Schreiner at Quantico and played in the Football Classic with others who were killed, and he lost many other Marine friends on Okinawa as well.

"You look at it, and they were twenty-four-year-old guys who were never coming back," Bergman says. "I keep thinking about it a lot. I know how lucky I was."

★   ★   ★

The liberated Mark Hoskins returned to the United States on a ship, landed in New York, and caught a train to Chicago, where he was reunited with his wife. Mary was ecstatic to see her husband. "I got there before the train came in, and it was terrific," Mary says. She had known he had lost weight, but still she was shocked when she spotted him. "He was terribly, terribly thin." She also had to break something to him: His brother, Charles, the best man at their wedding, had been killed in Luxembourg shortly after the Battle of the Bulge while serving with an infantry regiment with Patton's Third Army. Mark's family had decided not to tell him about his brother's death in letters.

Mark met up with his surviving brother, Billy, at the Great Lakes Naval Training Station, and he and Mary took the Zephyr to Dubuque, where they visited his parents. Then Mark went to Lancaster, for a leave, and he and Mary stayed at his parents' home, by then the residential part of the city's funeral home.

★   ★   ★

On June 28, Jerry Frei flew the last of his sixty-seven missions in the P-38. After his squadron leader took the picture of him in the air on that final mission, and he landed safely, he wrote to his girlfriend, Marian, and his parents, George and Gertie, back in little Stoughton.

At some point in the near future, he was coming home.

★   ★   ★

Judy Johnson, Schreiner's niece, was three and a half years old. "I was visiting my grandparents, which I did regularly, because I wasn't in school yet," Judy (now Judy Corfield) says. "My mother would send me there to keep them busy. I would spend a lot of time going back and forth to the Hoskins home, too, which was only a block away, especially after Charles died and Had was imprisoned. That kept everybody busy, taking care of Judy."

It is one of her earliest memories.

The news arrived at the telegraph office the night of June 28, after the office was closed.

Everyone in Lancaster knew the Schreiners' habits. They were up every day at 5:30 a.m. The delivery boy arrived at the door a little after 7. He handed the telegram to Bert Schreiner. The proud father pulled the sheet out of the envelope.

```
70 GOVT
WASHINGTON, D.C.
8:41 P.M., JUNE 28, 1945

MR. AND MRS. HERBERT E. SCHREINER
216 SOUTH TYLER
LANCASTER, WIS.


DEEPLY REGRET TO INFORM YOU THAT YOUR SON FIRST LIEU-
TENANT DAVID N. SCHREINER USMCR DIED 21 JUNE 1945 OF
WOUNDS RECEIVED IN ACTION OKINAWA ISLAND RYUKU ISLANDS
IN THE PERFORMANCE OF HIS DUTY AND SERVICE OF HIS
COUNTRY. WHEN INFORMATION IS RECEIVED REGARDING BURIAL
YOU WILL BE NOTIFIED. TO PREVENT POSSIBLE AID TO OUR
ENEMIES DO NOT DIVULGE THE NAME OF HIS SHIP OR STA-
TION. PLEASE ACCEPT MY HEARTFELT SYMPATHY.

A A VANDERGRIFT GENERAL USMC
COMMANDANT OF THE MARINE CORPS
```

Judy Corfield remembers standing at the window and watching the delivery boy walk down the hill and head back to the telegraph station.

"The bad news has arrived," Bert Schreiner said.

He did the best he could to comfort Anne. Then, he called the Hoskinses and Carthews at their homes.

Doris Hoskins, Mark's mother, knocked on the bedroom door. Mark and Mary Hoskins were still asleep.

"You'd better get up," she said softly. "I have some bad news."

Both Mark's and Mary's parents had already been over at the Schreiners' home. When his parents told him about Schreiner, Mark cried.

Almost immediately, he was called to the phone. The caller was a shaken Harry Stuhldreher. The Wisconsin coach told Hoskins he was leaving for Lancaster immediately. Hoskins rushed over to the Schreiners'.

He still sobs years later, recalling the day.

★ ★ ★

The Madison papers put out extras.

Oh, god, not Dave Schreiner!

The *Wisconsin State Journal*'s front page headline:

> Dave Schreiner Dies
> Of Wounds on Okinawa;
> Fiancee flying here

The story said Ensign Odette Hendrickson, who had joined the WAVES and was stationed at Hunter College in the Bronx, was returning to Wisconsin.

The July 5 issue of the weekly *Grant County Independent* carried the entire Marine Corps dispatch, describing Schreiner's death, plus a boxed "In Memoriam" statement from Stuhldreher. The coach declared, "At Wisconsin, we called him 'Big Dave,' not because of his physique but because of his all-around makeup. His personality, modesty, unselfishness, and friendship all were big. His loss leaves a big vacuum—as big as Dave himself was in all ways—in all our lives."

★ ★ ★

In the *State Journal* on July 1, Henry J. McCormick wrote:

> If there was ever a better football player at the University of Wisconsin, I never knew him. If there was a better end who ever played football any place, I never saw him. And if there was a boy who wore his honors with more modesty than Dave Schreiner, I never knew him.
>
> It wasn't so long ago that Dave's father and I had a long talk. Naturally, he was worried about Dave, but he was philosophical.
>
> "Whatever happens," said Mr. Schreiner, "I know that Dave is doing what he wanted to do." Mr. Schreiner reflected a moment. "You know," he said, "Dave had a chance to be assigned as a physical instructor when he finished training, but he requested that he be given active duty. And that's the way it should be."

★ ★ ★

The Schreiners received a card from the Marines. As promised, it told them where Dave was buried.

```
GRAVE 789, ROW 32, PLOT A
SIXTH MARINE DIVISION CEMETERY, OKINAWA
```

Later, Colonel Alan Shapley, the 4th Regiment's commander and the former Navy football star player, wrote to Anne Schreiner. He called Dave "one of my very good friends. We all used to say, jokingly, in the 4th that Dave was not just an All-American football player, but an All-American boy in all respects."

Years later, Vic Anderson's words are eerily similar. "I can't say enough about both of them," he says of Schreiner and Baumann. "They were both outstanding men. Dave Schreiner was not only an All-American football player, he was [All-American] in every respect of the word."

Frank Kemp says, "They were wonderful men. They were good officers, and the men were just crazy about them. There are two Marines as good as I've ever known. They were a terrible loss to the Marine Corps, the country, their families, everybody else. We had never seen two better officers than those young men."

Clint Eastment calls Schreiner "a peach of a man. He was excellent as a soldier and as a person." Eastment, who was eight years older than Schreiner, paused before adding, "I'd love to have a son like him."

At Camp Pendleton, Elroy Hirsch composed a letter to Roundy Coughlin, and it later ran in the *State Journal*.

I really received a blow when I read about Dave Schreiner. I admired him more than any other player. Not only was he an All-American on the field but he was one of the best-hearted and most honest fellows I knew. In my room at home he has the top spot among my football pictures. I don't think he ever had an enemy. I never heard a bad word against him.

The Badgers had lost their leader.

TWENTY-EIGHT

V-J

The Badger V-12 Marines were scattered and still assuming they would be those expendable lieutenants at the edge of an invasion of Japan, when they got word of their teammates' deaths. An invasion was now nearly guaranteed, despite isolated hopes that the Japanese would surrender before U.S. troops came ashore on the home islands. The way the Japanese were fighting to the death in most cases, and Japanese authorities' call for people to give their lives for the emperor in a National Resistance Program, underscored both the invasion's inevitability and its likely fearsome toll. So did the actions of the kamikaze pilots, sacrificing themselves as they crashed their planes into ships—in many cases the wrong ships, since kamikazes, after all, couldn't stockpile experience, such as the visual identification of American ships. This was a nation unwilling to quit, with citizens willing to die.

Marine Fred Negus, the Badgers' 42 sophomore center, ended up stationed at a replacement depot in Hawaii. He understood what was to come, although he didn't know that President Truman on June 18 had approved Operation Olympic, a fall invasion of the island of Kyushu that was to involve three Marine divisions.

"There were about five thousand Marines there, and we were officers by that time," Negus says. "They'd come in every day and pull out certain groups. They'd call out the names and say they needed somebody out front. We thought we were going to go to Maui for training to hit the main island of Japan. They were going to put two new lieutenants to a platoon, and you knew the chances there were about 95 percent that you weren't going to make it. We knew it would have been ugly, but we were ready to go."

★ ★ ★

In the China-Burma-India Theater, '42 halfback Jim Regan, the Army man teaching the Chinese how to use Army vehicles, witnessed a transformation.

"When the big invasion of Burma came earlier, they had all the vehicles they needed, and thousands of Chinese were able to drive them," Regan recalls. "They couldn't drive before. We couldn't speak each other's languages, but they were good people. I liked the Chinese. They wanted to learn, and they wanted to help America. They used that word a lot, *America.*"

* * *

While waiting for orders to return to the States, Jerry Frei served as acting operations officer of his P-38 reconnaissance unit in the Philippines. The unit was preparing to move to Okinawa, thanks to U.S. forces who had taken the island. As he flew his missions, Frei often looked down and wondered about his friends on the ground. Then, in letters from home he got the one-two punch to the solar plexus: First, Bob Baumann, then Dave Schreiner. His fellow lineman, and then his revered cocaptain. Both dead. On the ground.

He knew that in later years he would tell everyone who asked that flying—while highly dangerous and certainly nerve-wracking—at least left a man at his own controls and sleeping in what could pass for a real bed. He knew that if he could go on to coach college football, as he hoped, he would remember Dave Schreiner as an inspiration. After what he and his teammates went through as young men, he knew he was never going to call twenty-one-year-olds "kids" or treat them like children or act as if winning was more important than teaching and nurturing. If that bothered some folks, the hell with them. He now knew what war was. And football wasn't it.

Soon he was on a troop transport, heading to San Francisco. When the ship was two days from the West Coast, its speakers blared the news about an atom bomb—whatever that was—and Hiroshima.

It was August 6, 1945.

* * *

Bob Rennebohm met up again with Fred Negus.

"I was taking over a mortar section, a replacement outfit that was going to hook up with one of the divisions and get ready for the invasion of Japan in November," Rennebohm recalls. "The last night we were in the states, I was putting my troops on board ship, and the four of us officers went into downtown San Diego to have a last beer in the country."

The news was spreading, via word of mouth and in extra editions of the newspapers. Rennebohm heard about the bombing of Hiroshima on the way back to the ship.

"So we got on the ship and sailed at 6 in the morning, and it was quite exciting," Rennebohm says. "We zigzagged over to Hawaii. We were supposed to go to Guam, but when the Japanese started making noises about surrender, [Marine brass] decided we would be better off at Pearl Harbor. We were at Pearl Harbor, and who was standing at the gangplank but Fred Negus. He said, 'I've got you all set up on the football team here.'"

Football sounded a lot better than an invasion of Japan, which is why the Badgers—and the other Marines of their generation—are incredulous about anyone second-guessing Truman's decision to green-light the use of atomic bombs on Hiroshima and, on August 9, Nagasaki.

On August 14, Emperor Hirohito ordered the Japanese to lay down their arms. Truman announced that Japan had acceded to the demands of unconditional surrender. The official Japanese surrender came on September 2, aboard the USS *Missouri* in Tokyo Bay.

"I've expounded on that every chance I get when people have very short memories," Rennebohm says of the atomic bombs. "The revisionists feel sorry that we did that. When you consider what they were doing to us, there was every reason in the world to drop the atomic bomb and get the thing over with. It's too bad it happened to the Japanese, but they started it. They beheaded a few of our people and shot a few prisoners and they wanted to play rough, so there certainly was no reason not to drop that bomb."

Jim McFadzean, the '42 reserve back and Navy man, was in Hawaii, waiting for enough LCTs to arrive before he headed to Japan.

"You may have people tell you Harry Truman was wrong to drop the bomb," McFadzean says, "but I thank him, because he saved my life. I still say that. When I look at it, we were very lucky."

* * *

John Gallagher, the V-12 Marine and quarterback from Eau Claire, was in San Francisco, about to head to the Pacific, when the fighting stopped.

"They were dancing in the street, every woman hugging every guy," he says. "I can remember it very vividly, because at night you always saluted the officer of the day as you came aboard ship. This guy pulled his gun and boom—he didn't mean it, but he was so excited, he pulled the trigger when he shouldn't have."

Fortunately, the gun was pointed in the air.

* * *

George Hekkers, the sophomore '42 tackle from Milwaukee and the veteran of A-26 fighter missions in Europe, was relieved to hear he wouldn't have to fly missions over Japan.

"We were on the train to pick up another aircraft and go over to the South Pacific," he says. The train was on the move in Northern California when Hekkers heard that the fighting was over.

"Everyone was celebrating, and I was wondering what the hell was going on until they told me," he recalls.

After leaving the train, Hekkers received a cable from the War Department telling him to report to Long Island for a secret "White Project." He reported to Hempstead and discovered that the "White Project" was the First Air Force football team, which was going to play games to promote the sale of war bonds.

★ ★ ★

After the war ended, P-38 fighter pilot Bob Omelina, the halfback from Cudahy, moved into Japan with his unit and spent about six months there. "That was a little hairy because we landed outside Tokyo at a place called Atsugi," he says. "We found that our ground echelon had not made it because they got caught in a typhoon. They were a couple of weeks late in getting up there, and we had to live on our own, so to speak. We had canned rations with us. We took the ammunition out of the nose of the P-38, and we had canned Spam and cheese and stuff like that. I had an air mattress I blew up, and I slept under a P-38. We did that for about ten days, and that wasn't much fun."

After the base at Atsugi was established, the fighter pilots lived in nearby Tokyo.

"I was at the Imperial Hotel until we got kicked out when the brass came in," Omelina says. "The funny thing is, when we walked down the street—and we walked right down the middle of the street, because we didn't like to be close to buildings—there wasn't a soul around. But after you walked by, you could just sense people looking out the door at you and checking. That went on for a couple of days, and pretty soon kids were coming alongside.

"I give the American soldiers credit for being tremendous diplomats, because it wasn't a couple of days [before] those kids were chasing them around and they were giving them candy bars, and the parents were trying to get them away. The kids just kept on following, and the Americans had their arms around the little kids, walking with them and teaching them how to say words and trying to pick up some words of their own in Japanese. I think that kind of broke the ice. Pretty soon people found out we weren't the ogres that apparently the Japanese hierarchy had told them we were."

Omelina's final duties were as a pilot of a P-51 fighter, flying patrol missions at the Russian border from Hokkaido, the northernmost Japanese island. The Americans were beginning to sense trouble in the relationship with the Russian allies. Omelina came home on a passenger liner being used by the military. "I ended up playing bridge for about eighteen or twenty hours a day, and I won a bucketful of money," he says.

★ ★ ★

Back in the states, AAF pilot instructor Otto Breitenbach also assumed that the Japanese surrender spared him from being sent to the Pacific to fly in combat. Like many instructors, Breitenbach was recruited to stay in the AAF after the war. He considered it. "But after giving it a lot of thought and talking with my wife, we decided it would be better if I went back to school," Breitenbach says.

★ ★ ★

Army man Jim Regan, weakened by his repeated battles with malaria, was brought home from China.

"Once I got back and stepped on land, I said, 'That's it, I'm home free and I'm going to do the best I can the rest of my life.'"

That was a common sentiment among the surviving Badgers.

★ ★ ★

The V-12 Marines had various duties in the fall of '45. "I went to Guam for a month, to Okinawa for maybe another month, and then they sent me to China," John Gallagher says. "I put in a year in China, repatriating the Japanese who had been in China."

Elroy Hirsch was given a choice: Occupation duty in China or playing football for the El Toro Marines in California, coached by former Northwestern coach Dick Hanley. He chose football.

Service football was popular at the box office, even before the war ended. After playing for the Great Lakes Naval Training Station in '43, Badger starting guard Evan "Red" Vogds had been sent briefly to a naval station in the Boston area. Then he was shifted to the West Coast, where he served as a physical trainer of WAVES and played for the Fleet City Naval team in '44 and '45. In the fall of '45, Fleet City beat the Second Air Force in front of 62,000 fans in San Francisco's Kezar Stadium. Pat Harder, the Marine roustabout, played football for the Marines in Georgia and never went overseas.

Rennebohm and Negus played for a Marine team in Hawaii after the war ended. "We went on the other side of the island and worked out and played the Army twice and played the Navy twice and got beat every time," Negus says. "They were all pros, and we were all college guys. When we went back into headquarters after football was over, they didn't like us. The brass got really upset. Marines aren't supposed to get the hell beat out of them."

Rennebohm laughs. "Back in California, Elroy Hirsch was a big star for the El Toro Marines," he says. "So we get the bright idea, 'Why don't we have a Marine championship between the Hawaiian Marines and the El Toro Marines?' And when they asked General Geiger about it, he said, 'Hell, what kind of Marines are they if they lose to the Navy and the Army! They don't get to go back to the states to play football, they get to go to occupation duty!' The first half of the alphabet got China, the second half got Japan. Fred and I both ended up staying in Hawaii, because we heard that a colonel was looking for a couple of men in his outfit in special services division. So we went in and interviewed with the colonel, and he got on the phone. He said, 'Pull Rennebohm and Negus off the Japanese assignment; they're staying here in my outfit.'"

While in the special services, the two men organized another football team, this time a touch team. "We had a couple of Purdue guys on our team, too," Negus says. "It was five- or six-man football. It was something to do, and we were winning. In fact, we won the island championship."

Negus suffered a broken nose in one game. Later, because of a chronic separated shoulder, he was sent home and assigned military policeman duty at the Great Lakes Naval Training Center. "I was officer of the guard one weekend, and four guys attempted to escape," Negus says. "They found one guy, and they told me, 'Lieutenant, would you mind turning your back for a second.' The guy wouldn't talk. They took a billy club and hit him a couple of times in the ribs, and he said, 'I'll talk.' That's how they found the other three guys. I had to stick around until the court-martial took place. All of a sudden, guys are coming back from overseas, and I'd meet them at the airport, and they'd give me a hard time. 'You aren't out yet?' 'No, I'm not out yet.' I didn't think I'd ever get out."

While waiting, he took a leave to join Rennebohm as the best men at the wedding of Elroy Hirsch and Ruth Stahmer. Finally, in the late summer of 1946, Negus was mustered out. Like the other Badger V-12 Marines who were primed for the invasion of Japan but didn't have to fight, Negus and Rennebohm thanked God—and Harry Truman—and then went on with their lives.

★ ★ ★

Private Charles Pulford, the 4th Regiment's runner, was mustered out of the Marines at the Great Lakes Naval Station, north of Chicago, on January 8, 1946. He says that when he was in the final stages of processing, he noticed an older couple approaching Marines and asking questions. The couple was directed to Pulford.

"They were Dave's mother and dad," Pulford says. "Evidently someone must have told them I was with the 1st Battalion, 4th Regiment. They said who they were, and if I could have crawled into a hole, I would have. I just felt so bad to have to even talk about this, to let them know what happened."

He says he told Bert and Anne Schreiner about the faked surrender.

"They were really, really upset," Pulford says. "Any parent who had a fine son like that would be, to know that he died through treachery like that. They didn't say much that I remember. They just thanked me for telling them."

The Schreiners apparently decided not to tell anyone else in the family about Pulford's description of Dave's death. It was already painful enough.

TWENTY-NINE

Badgers Again

The war was over.

Wisconsin Coach Harry Stuhldreher greeted more than one hundred candidates at varsity fall practice in 1946. Thirteen of them had played for the 1942 Badgers: ends Farnham "Gunner" Johnson, Hank Olshanski, and Bob Rennebohm; guards Ken "Roughie" Currier, Jerry "Toughie" Frei, John Gallagher, and Ralph Davis (winner of a minor letter in '42); center Fred Negus; quarterbacks Ashley Anderson and Jack Wink; halfback Jim Regan; and fullbacks Erv Kissling and Earl Maves. Plus, halfback Frank Granitz, who'd been ruled academically ineligible on the day of the 1942 opener, was back. Halfback Rod Liljequist and tackle Dick Loepfe, who both participated in 1942 spring practice before dropping out of school and entering the service, were on the roster as well.

There were occasional mentions in the newspapers that the players were "military veterans," and even that seemed to be an afterthought. It was as if they had been off plowing fields for three years.

"This squad may turn out to be as good as the 1942 outfit, but it can't be rated that high right now," Stuhldreher told Henry J. McCormick of the *State Journal*."In the first place, we knew what the 1942 squad could do because we had the boys in spring practice that year and because so many of them were boys we had for two previous varsity seasons."

The noticeable absences were Elroy Hirsch and Pat Harder. Both had college eligibility remaining, but Hirsch had signed with the Chicago Rockets of the new All-America Football Conference, and Harder had joined the National Football League's Chicago Cardinals for 1947.

Hirsch also got a baseball contract offer from the Chicago Cubs. "I wanted to get married," he recalled later. "I didn't want anyone else mov-

By the time they were the Badgers starting guards after the war, pals and AAF pilots Roughie Frei and Toughie Currier looked a decade older than they did when they showed up on campus in 1941.

PHOTO COURTESY OF THE UNIVERSITY OF WISCONSIN SPORTS INFORMATION DEPARTMENT

ing in on Ruth. The Rockets gave me a thousand dollars for signing and a contract for six thousand dollars. I was flush."

Also, many of the underclassmen from the '42 team either didn't return to school or chose not to play football.

The Badgers had a problem that was typical of college football teams in the '46 and '47 seasons. It was nothing calculated or even hostile, but the men who served in the wartime military felt as if they had little in common with the younger boys who hadn't.

"When we came back after the war, we were quite worldly, as you would expect most of the servicemen were," Rennebohm recalls. "It was a little bit hard to fit into the discipline of an undergraduate, after spending time in the service and being that much more mature. Some of us were starting to get some gray hairs.

"Right after the war, freshmen were immediately eligible for varsity football, so you had the combination of those of us right back from the service, and young kids who had just graduated from high school, seventeen-year-old kids, playing on the same team together. Their eyes would bulge out of their heads when they heard some of the language from some guy who had spent three years in the Marine Corps."

Most of the war veterans were married and were attending college on the G.I. Bill. Currier's young son, Charles, was a regular on the practice field. The veterans and their wives tended to hang out together socially, and even the single veterans—such as Kissling, whose knee still bore his battle scars—visited their married teammates for spaghetti dinners and card games.

"I was married then, had a child who was six or seven months old," says Gallagher. "I'm on the G.I. Bill, thank God, and I'm trying to make a living, working at the tavern again. I got my old job back. I was a bartender again, and I was much more mature with much more responsibility.

"There was good camaraderie with the fellows. You had seen so many things by then. When we got together, the stories would fly. It was more bullshit than anything else. It was fun. But we were worrying about trying to get in shape."

Recalls Negus, "I had the G.I. Bill, and I worked a little bit, but not too much. School was paid for. My wife worked in a department store on the floor selling high-priced clothes. That's where Harry [Stuhldreher] bought most of his clothes."

Regan, after having played for the baseball team in the spring of '46, was injured in the preseason football workouts and was finished for the season. But he continued to hang out with his teammates. "I don't think I had anything against the younger guys," he says. "I think the stranger thing was having that lackadaisical attitude that you're not going to get killed.

Two generations of football Badgers: Ken Currier with Charles Currier, who would grow up to letter as a starting Wisconsin lineman in 1964 and 1965.

Mark Hoskins, left, joined Anne Schreiner and UW Chancellor Edwin Fred when the university honored Dave Schreiner at a post-war game.
PHOTO COURTESY OF THE UNIVERSITY OF WISCONSIN SPORTS INFORMATION DEPARTMENT

Plus, I had the G.I. Bill and my [malaria] disability, so I felt rich!"

With Frei, Negus, Currier, and Maves in the starting lineup, and the rest of the '42 veterans all getting in the game, the Badgers routed Marquette 34–7 in the '46 opener. The '42 quarterbacks, Wink and Anderson, were rusty and couldn't crack the starting lineup.

Then the squad took the Badgers' first-ever airplane trip, journeying to Berkeley to face the California Golden Bears. Some of the nervous boys asked their older starting guards, Roughie and Toughie, if they had ever been on a plane.

Yes, said World War II pilots Jerry Frei and Ken Currier.

After the ride in the DC-4, the Badgers beat the Golden Bears 28–7. The season deteriorated from there, with Wisconsin going 2–5 in the conference and 4–5 overall.

"I enjoyed it as much then as I did before," Anderson says. "We didn't have a very good team, but I enjoyed it."

The 1947 team still included seven members of '42 squad—Rennebohm, Currier, Frei, Maves, Wink, Regan, and Olshanski. Frei suffered repeated concussions—the newspapers parroted Stuhldreher's assessment that it was "an acute sinus infection"—and team doctors ordered him to give up football after he started the first few games. The November 6 *State Journal* ran a huge mug shot of Frei on the front of the sports section and reported, "Possessed of tremendous competitive spark and a fine influence on the squad, Frei is certain to be missed. Giving up football was hard to take, but Jerry realized that it was the only thing to do."

The story was wrong.

Frei never gave up football.

The Badgers went 5–3–1 overall and finished second in the Big Ten, behind Michigan, with a 3–2–1 conference record.

The '42 Badgers were all through.

Epilogue

Now that you have made it this far, I will concede that *Third Down and a War to Go* would be a different book if I had started it sooner, when my father and more of the 1942 Badgers were alive.

I wasn't able to talk with Pat Harder about his Model A, nor with Paul Hirsbrunner about his heritage and scraped-up face. I couldn't ask Ken Currier about showing up on campus with only a few dollars and nowhere to sleep, or Jack Wink about those quarterback meetings with Harry Stuhldreher.

Ultimately I communicated with fewer than half of the members of the '42 team. The men I did find and interview were terrific, even if some memories were rendered foggy by the passage of sixty years and, in a couple of cases, the ravages of Alzheimer's disease.

It was inexcusable that I didn't take down or point to that team picture and say to my father: *Tell me about these guys. How did you meet Ken Currier and when did you know you had found a friend for life? What was it like to play in Camp Randall and Soldier Field?* (I didn't even ask him that when he was the Chicago Bears' offensive line coach, working in the same stadium.) *Was it fun to live in the firehouse? How about those card games in the Union? Tell me more about what Harry Stuhldreher was like to play for.* As I mentioned in the prologue, I remember many brief surface conversations and cursory examinations of his college years and his military experiences, but never anything of substance or illuminating depth—at least not until I was the newspaperman in search of a Veterans Day column. Even then, I concentrated on his service in the Army Air Forces and his missions in the P-38, leaving much territory uncovered.

Belatedly, in the summer of 2002 I traveled to Madison and began to learn about the '42 Badgers through both archival research and interviews. Over the next year, I was able to ask the teammates of that backup Badgers guard—the eighteen-year-old nicknamed Toughie—many of the questions I hadn't had enough wisdom to ask him. And as we talked about their youths and their lives, I felt enriched by the knowledge.

I toured Elroy Hirsch's memorabilia-filled basement with Crazylegs himself. I met Dick Thornally in San Antonio, when his alma mater was playing mine (Colorado) in the Alamo Bowl. (I lost the bet.) I sat with John Gallagher, Dave Donnellan, and Don Litchfield in an Eau Claire restaurant and noticed the waitress finding excuses to keep coming back and eavesdrop. I caught Ashley Anderson on the telephone the day after he shot his age—eighty-one—on the golf course.

I visited Lancaster and found Dave Schreiner's medals and Purple Heart in a file drawer at the Grant County Historical Society. I felt as if the selection of his letters available there—in particular, the December 11, 1941, note to his parents—was my first handshake with him and made me determined to get to know him better. Later I visited his niece, Judy Corfield, in Geneva, Illinois, and quickly became immersed in the family archives, including many originals and copies of Dave's letters that had been passed down. I went to San Diego and spotted Mark Hoskins, wearing his straw Panama hat, waiting for me on the sidewalk at his apartment complex to guide me to the correct parking spot. He showed me his prized framed picture of Schreiner and young Had Hoskins together as children in Lancaster. I noticed the catch in his voice when he talked about his friend and also heeded the gentle suggestions from both him and his wife, Mary, to avoid disrespecting Schreiner's memory by making him into something he wasn't—a saint, near-valedictorian, and prospective international statesman. Frankly, some of the portrayals of Schreiner over the years approached mythic caricature. I found the truth more compelling.

I met or spoke on the phone with other Badgers, with widows, with offspring, with nieces and nephews, and I walked away feeling I had learned about not just the '42 Badgers, but—in a strange way—about myself.

Yes, there are gaps in this work that research couldn't fill, because the men who could fill them were gone. And, because in some cases I couldn't locate the Badgers or their families, I acknowledge that there might be some compelling stories I have missed.

But I'm glad I decided to tell the Badgers' story.

I have read, in awe, many of the books about the World War II generation, including the unforgettable *Flags of Our Fathers* and the handful of works by the late Stephen Ambrose, a former Badger football player himself. Those books were about American men, most of whom were placed in threatening combat roles. Admittedly, the '42 Badgers were a cross-section group that in some ways illustrated the whims and capriciousness of the system that helped win the war. To call their willingness naïveté would be insulting. It was more about faith, in both the country and the fates.

As Dave Schreiner mentioned in his letter four days after Pearl Harbor, when the war was just beginning, the Badgers were typical college students. They had conflicting emotions, including, in some cases, a desire to postpone their military service as long as possible as they continued in college or even to avoid the military altogether if the American involvement was short. But as the war continued, as it became clear that service would be a virtually universal phenomenon for men their age, they both accepted and even came to eagerly await their chance to serve their country—wherever that took them and wherever it led.

That's what I mean by All-American.

As I learned more about these men, I was stunned by the fact that many of their "choices"—including my father's decision to try to join the Army Air Forces Reserve unit—were so happenstance or the products of unit locations or the suggestions of a football coach who, it turned out, didn't know what he was talking about.

They were willing, and, when called, they went. Whether that meant the China-Burma-India Theater or stateside pilot instruction or Okinawa, well, that was going to be the way it worked out. They all weren't heroic in combat, because not all of them were asked to be. If they needed to be, they were—or would have been, if it had come to that.

The V-12 Marines were spared combat service as they attended school and waited out the backlogs at boot camp and Officers Candidate School, but, as I tried to make clear, they were ticketed to help lead the invasion of Japan—and for Marine lieutenants that would have been a virtual death sentence. Other Badgers would have flown in or otherwise served in an invasion. As a conventionally liberal baby boomer who read John Hersey's *Hiroshima* and opposed the Vietnam War, I was once prone to decry the use of the atomic bombs against Japan. Long ago, I realized Truman was right, and this project only reinforced that view. As unfortunate as the unleashing of the atomic threat was, the decision—in the final accounting—saved lives among both Japanese and Americans.

Near the end of my research and early draft process, I received word from San Diego that Mark Hoskins had died of cancer at age eighty-one. At the urging of others who knew of his deteriorating health, I had sent him an early draft of this book. I'm glad he got to see it, and I'm proud that he called and said he enjoyed the manuscript. He did gently point out, though, that I had fouled up the words to the song he performed at the Empire Room in New York with the Badgers' "Singing Firemen Trio"

in 1940. I had the last line as "You can't get your finger in your nose."
No, no, no, he said. It was "You can't get your finger in *those*." I stand
corrected. But of this I always was certain, and I got it right: Mark Hoskins
was a gentleman.

It isn't just the Badgers who are slipping away from us, of course.
Shortly after I spoke with William Ramey, the corpsman who treated
Schreiner on Okinawa, I wrote him and other members of the Sixth Marine Division, thanking them for their help. The news came back from a
relative: Ramey had died shortly after our conversation. Sadly, as I write
this, I am assuming that others I interviewed will leave us between the
completion of the manuscript and publication.

Just before Hoskins's death, I visited my father's gravesite at Fort Logan National Cemetery in Denver during Memorial Day weekend. The
Cub Scouts and other volunteers were placing the flags on the thousands
of graves, and they had already been to Jerry Frei's. I looked around, again,
and as I do every time I go there, I wondered about the stories of the
men and women buried around my father. I hope their children discovered them in time.

Lives and Deaths

In 1941, University of Wisconsin artist-in-residence John Steuart Curry painted this tribute to UW football players, including Dave Schreiner, shown here catching a pass. For many years the painting hung in the UW Athletic Director's offices in Camp Randall Stadium; it currently hangs in the stadium's Mendota Gridiron Club.

PAINTING BY JOHN STEUART CURRY; PHOTO BY JOEL HEIMAN

80 SCHREINER, Dave E Sr. 6-2 198 Lancaster, Wis.

and

74 BAUMANN, Bob T Sr. 6-2 210 Harvey, Ill.

In March 1947, the University of Wisconsin renamed two residences inside the stadium structure the Bob Baumann and Dave Schreiner Residence Halls. Many of their 1942 teammates attended the dedication, including Mark Hoskins, who was enrolled in the UW law school, and several others who were back as undergraduates.

At the ceremony, Harry Stuhldreher said, "In all my experience in coaching, I met no finer examples of American manhood than these two fine gentlemen."

Then it was Mark Hoskins's turn to speak.

"We won't dwell on the fact that they aren't here today," he said. "It seems that they should have been." He called them "a symbol" of his generation's sacrifices in the war and repeated a hope that the deaths of his contemporaries—not just Schreiner and Baumann—would remain appreciated through the years, and would be worth it.

Bob Rennebohm, who was sidelined all that season with a bad ankle, was called on to represent the younger Badgers from the 1942 team who were students again. (He was destined to be a Badger captain in 1947.) In an eloquent tribute to his fallen teammates, he said he hoped memories of Baumann and Schreiner would inspire future Wisconsin students.

At the end of the ceremony, the Residence Halls Chorus sang "Varsity." The traditional draping of arms over one another and slow swaying to the song took on new meaning.

Varsity, Varsity,
U-Rah-Rah, Wisconsin,
Praise to thee we sing!
Praise to thee, our Alma Mater,
U-Rah-Rah Wisconsin!

Tears flowed, and so did the memories.

The stadium dormitories, quickly constructed for military personnel during the war, were closed in 1951. The space was later converted into athletic department and academic offices.

In 1945 the Badgers retired Schreiner's No. 80. No Wisconsin football player has worn it since.

Nearly four years after Schreiner's death, in May 1949, his remains were returned from Okinawa. After brief services at the First Congregational Church and at the home of his parents, he was buried in the family plot at Hillside Cemetery, on the outskirts of Lancaster.

Bud Seelinger, Paul Hirsbrunner, and Mark Hoskins were the pallbearers, along with three Schreiner pals from Lancaster—Ivan Kinney, Leroy Eastman, and Dick Phillips.

★ ★ ★

A heartbroken Bert Schreiner aged quickly. He died in 1950, at age seventy-one.

Anne Schreiner died in 1992 at age 105. Until she moved into a Lancaster nursing home at age ninety-nine, she kept Dave's room largely the way it was when he left for the Marines. She always talked about the Wisconsin Badgers as her "boys." And the endowed scholarship started by Bert Schreiner in Dave's honor put many football players through school.

As they went about their lives, Schreiner's and Baumann's teammates never forgot them.

22 ANDERSON, Ashley QB Jr. 5-11 182 Milwaukee, Wis.

After getting a degree at the University of Wisconsin in accounting, Anderson went to work for his father in Chicago at the family automotive store. They bought Army and Navy surplus, and the business thrived. He worked in the auto and truck parts industry for various companies, primarily in Milwaukee, until he retired. He lives in Cary, North Carolina, outside Raleigh.

54 BOORMAN, Harry   C So. 5-11 190 Chicago, Ill.

61 BOYLE, Pat   G Jr. 6-0 183 Duluth, Minn.

45 BREITENBACH, Otto HB So. 5-9 173 Madison, Wis.

Breitenbach, the young pilot instructor, didn't go out for football after returning to the UW campus. "I planned to play because John Gallagher was here, Fred Negus was here, all of them were coming back," he says. "But my wife was pregnant. And ninety dollars a month didn't go very far. Actually, the GI Bill was sixty dollars a month to start with, and then we got a raise.

"I went to work first of all as a student assistant trainer, because I got paid for that. It wasn't much. And then that fall of '46, I was asked to be an assistant coach at Edgewood High School," the local Catholic high school and Breitenbach's alma mater. Breitenbach moved on to coach at Chilton (Wisconsin) High School and later returned to Madison and became one of the state's most successful high school football coaches ever, at Middleton and La Follette. In 1973, he joined the University of Wisconsin staff as an assistant athletic director and later was associate athletic director; he also served as commissioner of the Western Collegiate Hockey Association. After his retirement from the UW Athletic Department, he was director of the Wisconsin State Games. He lives in Madison with his wife, Pat.

33 CALLIGARO, Len   FB Sr. 5-11 190 Hurley, Wis.

76 CRABB, Jack   T So. 6-3 210 Milwaukee, Wis.

Crabb, who survived both the Battle of the Bulge and rooming with Pat Harder, returned to the UW after his Army stint and concentrated on track and field. "By then, my knees were no good," Crabb says. He moved to Cheney, Washington, after graduation and got into high school coaching "for three or four years. But then we had so many kids—we ended up with seven—and I got into the insurance business and officiated in football, basketball, and baseball for years." Later he served as a district court judge and on the Cheney City Council. He still lives in Cheney.

64 CURRIER, Ken   G So. 5-10 190 Rice Lake, Wis.

Roughie Currier, the flight instructor, turned down a $4,500 contract offer for the 1948 season from the Green Bay Packers because—in a response common at the time—he preferred to seek more stable and long-term employment. He took a job as assistant football coach at Beloit Memorial High School, quickly became head coach, and had a handful of great teams before becoming an athletic director and teacher. He remained at Beloit until his retirement.

His son, Charles—the little boy who haunted the Badgers' practice field in 1946–47—was a standout Badger lineman from 1963 to 1965.

Ken's wife, Eileen, died in 1994. Roughie was plagued by diabetes later in life and died in 1998. He and Jerry Frei remained close until the day he died.

At Currier's funeral, Frei told the story of Ken Currier seeing a pretty woman on a train he was riding back to Rice Lake; Currier did handstands to get her attention. She was a very serious, studious musician, the polar opposite of Ken Currier. She was also his beloved wife for more than fifty years.

—DAVIS, Ralph

68 DEAN, Bob   G So. 5-11 193 Tomahawk, Wis.

Dean, the reserve guard who served at the communications station in Costa Rica, didn't go out for football again after the war. He attended law school and worked in the law school print shop and later practiced law in Black River Falls, Eau Claire, and Wausau. Venturing into politics, Dean became a state senator and minority floor leader and was a JFK delegate at the 1960 Democratic convention. He went on to become a county judge and an appellate court judge.

Dean suffered from Alzheimer's late in his life. His ex-wife, Katherine Ann Dean, recalls sitting in a doctor's office waiting room during the Desert Storm war against Iraq. "On the TV in the waiting room," she says, "they were showing a review of the troops in Desert Storm. They had the American flag on and then they played 'The Star-Spangled Banner.' This man who couldn't get his clothes on in the right order, who had to be reminded to swallow when he ate, who didn't recognize me as a wife of thirty-four years, this man stood up in this crowded waiting room, placed his hand over his heart and stood there and sang the words to the 'Star-Spangled Banner.' People looked at him, but no one laughed. It was quite a thing. It brought tears to my eyes."

He died in 1999.

23 DIERCKS, Bobby   QB Sr. 5-8 181 Antigo, Wis.

78 DONNELLAN, Dave   T So. 5-11 195 Eau Claire, Wis.

Donnellan, the mortar officer at the Battle of the Bulge, returned to school and played for the Badgers in '46 and '47. "I went to work at Presto [a cookware manufacturer in Eau Claire] in their cost-accounting department," he says, "and after six months, I decided they were going broke." He went into real estate and insurance, and Donnellan Real Estate signs still dominate the Eau Claire market. He still lives there with his wife, Jane, and continues to work in the real estate office.

65 FREI, Jerry   G So. 6-1 190 Stoughton, Wis.

Toughie Frei remembered how his tentmate and fellow P-38 pilot Don Garbarino raved about his hometown of Portland, Oregon. After graduating from the UW in 1948, Frei and his wife of nearly three years, Marian, loaded their belongings into their old car and drove to Portland. "Don Garbarino hadn't told me it rained a lot," Frei said later. He visited the Portland Public Schools office and was hired on the spot for a coaching and teaching job at Portland's Grant High School. He was an assistant to Ted Ogdahl when the Generals won the 1949 Oregon state championship and he later landed the head-coaching job at Lincoln High. Frei coached at Salem's Willamette University from 1952 to 1954 and joined Len Casanova's University of Oregon staff in 1955. He succeeded Casanova as head coach in 1967, was twice named United Press International's national coach of the week in 1970 (when the Ducks tied for second in the Pacific Eight Conference), and began his long NFL career as the Denver Broncos' offensive line coach in 1972.

He is buried among other veterans in Denver's Fort Logan National Cemetery.

24 GALLAGHER, John   QB So. 5-8 189 Eau Claire, Wis.

After playing guard at Michigan in '43 and then doing occupation duty in China, the V-12 Marine came back to the UW campus weighing 205 pounds. "We had a track around Camp Randall, and I had to work out every day to get my weight down," he says. "Hell, that was tough. You were drinking and smoking in the Marine Corps, and now you had to get in shape again. I didn't think I'd ever make it, but I did."

He played a lot at guard in 1946 and then graduated, still with a year of football eligibility he never used. He began as a high school coach at a small town in Northern Michigan.

"I'm sitting there talking to the superintendent at the interview," Gallagher says. "It's June, and I looked out the window and said, 'Mr. Peterson, that looks like snow.' He said, 'Yep, that's snow.' I said, 'When the hell does it stop?' He said, 'If you live here, you never know if it's going to stop.'"

Gallager made it back to his hometown, Eau Claire, as the head coach in 1950 and held the job for ten years before becoming the high school's principal. He retired in 1980 and still does part-time real estate work for his buddy Dave Donnellan.

83 HANZLIK, Bob   E Jr. 6-1 195 Chippewa Falls, Wis.

The V-12 Marine made it into the "Ripley's Believe It Or Not" newspaper feature in 1951 by playing for three different Big Ten programs — Wisconsin, Michigan, and Minnesota. Hanzlik planned on returning to Madison in 1946, but after he drove a car to Minneapolis to earn fifty dollars, he was waiting for the train home and ran into a Minnesota track coach, who recognized him and asked if he would consider attending the University of Minnesota.

Given his previous problems with Harry Stuhldreher, he had an open mind. He says the Gophers' offer was twelve tickets per home game and a job at First National Bank. "I got a buck and a quarter an hour," he says. "That was big money then. I ran securities down to different brokerage houses in downtown Minneapolis."

After college graduation, Hanzlik played briefly for the Philadelphia Eagles, and then he worked for General Mills and Mobil Oil. He retired as a Mobil section manager in the Portland, Oregon, area.

34 HARDER, Pat   FB Jr. 5-11 193 Milwaukee, Wis.

The roustabout fullback, who didn't return to Wisconsin for his final season of eligibility, had a seven-season career in the NFL with the Chicago Cardinals and Detroit Lions. As a kicker and back, he led the league in scoring in 1947, 1948, and 1949 and was named All-Pro all three seasons. He was briefly the Green Bay Packers' Milwaukee ticket manager and was a sales manager for Weyerhauser. His wife of forty-five years, Marge, says her husband "was never very happy" when not involved with football, "because football was his first love." He was best known to a later generation of fans as an NFL umpire from 1965 to 1982. He told an interviewer for a Milwaukee Athletic Club publication, "The Good Lord gave me the gift of being a football player by providing me with great natural ability. But I enjoyed officiating more because I had to learn that on my own." Harder died in 1992.

72 HEKKERS, George   T So. 6-3 197 Milwaukee, Wis.

Hekkers, the former pilot, didn't return to the Badgers. He signed with the Miami Seahawks of the All-American Football Conference and then played three seasons for the Detroit Lions.

"I was just kind of a run-of-the-mill type guy, and I asked myself, what the heck am I going to do for the rest of the year?" Hekkers says. "I was married by that time and had a youngster, and they didn't pay much to play ball. It was starvation. I went into the film industry, working on the lots, good physical work. I didn't like that, so I went into stage technician work in television and the legitimate stage, not motion pictures. I liked that and stayed with it."

He became the president of the stagehands union and retired in 1986. He lives in Burbank, California.

71 HIRSBRUNNER, Paul T Sr. 6-2 212 Darlington, Wis.

"The Indian" received a significant disability check for the rest of his life for the shrapnel wounds he suffered on Saipan with the First Marine Division. The injuries ruled out a return to the family endeavor, farming. After marrying his college girlfriend, Patricia, he started his professional life as a cheesemaker. "Cheesemakers were very well thought of where he came from, in southwestern Wisconsin," Patricia Hirsbrunner says. "I didn't see that as his way of life, but he had to give it a try." He moved on to teach advanced agriculture techniques to farm families in Lancaster, where he and Patricia occasionally had dinner with the Schreiner family. Over the years he was a field representative for a milk company, sold insurance, and worked as a water systems inspector for the state of Texas. He retired in the mid-1980s and died of cancer in 2000.

40 HIRSCH, Elroy   HB So. 6-1 185 Wausau, Wis.

After the All-American Football Conference's Chicago Rockets went belly-up, Crazylegs had a Hall of Fame career with the Los Angeles Rams as a receiver and starred in three movies, *Crazylegs, All-American* (1953), *Unchained* (1955), and *Zero Hour* (1957). He became the Rams' general manager in 1960 and was the University of Wisconsin athletic director from 1969 to 1987. After he retired, he and Ruth remained in Madison. Until declining health curtailed his activities, he was a highly visible ambassador for UW athletics. He died on January 28, 2004. "There has never been a more loved and admired ambassador for Wisconsin sports than Elroy Hirsch," Wisconsin athletic director Pat Richter said in a statement. "His charismatic and charming personality brought smiles to so many Badger fans. He loved life, loved people, and loved the Badgers."

11 HOSKINS, Mark   HB Sr. 6-1 185 Lancaster, Wis.

The former POW and Lancaster "Touchdown Twin" graduated from law school in 1948 and served six years as the Grant County district attorney early in his career. "That's what you did in a small rural community," he says. "I did that to get experience."

In private practice he specialized in estate law. He and Mary spent winters in San Diego many years before he retired and moved there full-time. For years, he and Mary lived a short drive from 1942 Ohio State captain George Lynn. Hoskins died in June 2003, at the age of eighty-one. He is buried in Lancaster's Hillside Cemetery, not far from Dave Schreiner's grave.

89 JOHNSON, Farnham   E So. 6-0 191 Neenah, Wis.

Like Elroy Hirsch, Gunner played briefly for the Chicago Rockets and then moved on to the Chicago Bears. Later, in the machinery business, he was considered a genius in the field of conveyor belts and traveled all over the world. He was living in Winfield, Alabama, the home of his employer Continental Conveyor and Equipment Company, when he died in December 2001.

—KING, Tom

16 KISSLING, Erv   G So. 5-8 187 Monticello, Wis.

Booby got into high school coaching, beginning his career at Sturgeon Bay, Wisconsin. "I stayed there three years, and I quit," he says. "I hated it up there. Everybody with twenty bucks in their pocket was a cherry-orchard millionaire, I called them." He moved to Adams-Friendship and then settled in at Oregon High School near Madison. He was the Oregon Panthers' athletic director and coach from 1953 to 1985, and he still lives in the little town. His son, Dan, was a four-year letterman for the Badgers, from 1986 to 1989.

67 KLINZING, Vern   G So. 5-10 187 Fond du Lac, Wis.

26 LITCHFIELD, Don   QB So. 5-11 184 Eau Claire, Wis.

B-17 pilot Litchfield went into the car business right after the war. Today he owns Litchfield Auto Sales in Eau Claire. "I've always been feeling very bad that I didn't get a degree from the university," he says.

52 LYNCH, Lawrence   C So. 6-0 187 Waukesha, Wis.

—LYONS, Pat   E Sr.   Horicon, Wis.

The senior end who had missed the first two games while juggling a heavy engineering class load went into the Navy in 1943 and was assigned to radar training school. He studied at Bowdoin College in Brunswick, Maine, and the Massachusetts Institute of Technology. He never was sent overseas, which he later told his children he regretted.

After the war, Lyons put his metallurgical engineering degree to good use in a long executive career in the manufacturing, electronics, and defense industries. He retired from Norris Industries in Southern California and was living in La Habra, California, still working as a consultant, when he died in 1994.

62 MAKRIS, George   G Sr. 5-10 185 Rhinelander, Wis.

As the head football coach at Bolling Air Force Base, Makris tutored quarterback Johnny Unitas. "He was a nice fellow, not difficult to coach," Makris says. "I recommended him to the pros."

Eventually Makris landed the head-coaching job at Temple University, where he had Bill Cosby on his roster. "He was more interested in entertaining," Makris says. "I guess he was funny, but he wasn't funny to me as a football coach."

After leaving coaching, Makris became a public relations and marketing executive. He lives in Medford Lakes, New Jersey.

35 MAVES, Earl   FB So. 5-10 187 Stanley, Wis.

Maves, the reserve fullback, died very young of Lou Gehrig's disease.

15 McFADZEAN, Jim   HB Sr. 5-10 178 Winnetka, Ill.

McFadzean's wife, Mary, was working in Madison when Jim left the Navy.

He enrolled in graduate school at the UW and was a graduate assistant coach for Stuhldreher. "I think I got one hundred dollars a month, and all I did was take roll for the guy who was head of the PE department," he says. He landed coaching work in the New Trier, Illinois, district and stayed at New Trier High his entire teaching and coaching career. He coached track and field, freshman football, and lacrosse. Jim and Mary live in Wilmette, Illinois.

53 McKAY, Bob　　C Sr. 6-0　192 Sioux Falls, SD

51 NEGUS, Fred　　C So. 6-2 201 Martin's Ferry, Ohio

Negus, the V-12 Marine, played three seasons for the Chicago Rockets and one year for the Chicago Bears. "I was going to play for a second year, but I got a job with International Paper Company selling corrugated boxes in Wisconsin, and I couldn't play football," he says. "I decided I could make more on a job than playing football. I waited until the day before they went to training camp, and I called up George Halas and said, 'George, I got a job, I can't keep it unless I quit playing football, so I decided to quit playing football and keep the job.' He said, 'Well, you have to do what you have to do, Fred.'"

Negus moved around in the packaging business and then, along with his son, Fred Jr., founded Fort Atkinson Packaging in 1986. He and his wife, Mary Alice, live outside Fort Atkinson, and Fred still visits the plant almost every day.

69 NEPERUD, George　　G So. 5-9 195 Chippewa Falls, Wis.

Neperud, the Navy flyer, worked for Northrup King and Co. and Honeywell in Minneapolis. He went to law school at night and then was in private practice in Litchfield, Minnesota, for thirty-five years. He flew Corsairs for the Navy Reserves until 1959. He lives in Litchfield.

86 OLSHANSKI, Hank　E So. 6-1　189 Wausau, Wis.

Elroy Hirsch's running mate and a V-12 Marine, Olshanski was a longtime prominent realtor in Madison. He died in 1996.

46 OMELINA, Bob　　HB So. 5-10 178 Cudahy, Wis.

Omelina, the P-38 pilot, turned down a test pilot job for Lockheed and returned to school. He didn't play football again. After graduating in 1948, he coached and taught at Cudahy High School, near Milwaukee, for two years. He then moved into public relations and sales for Ladish, a forge company in Cudahy. Ladish sent him to the Wharton School of Business, and he became the company's chief operating officer until retiring in 1989. He lives in Scottsdale, Arizona.

14 PFOTENHAUER, Don HB So. 5-9 185 Escanaba, Mich.

31 RAY, Bob   FB Sr. 5-11 187 Eau Claire, Wis.

18 RAYACICH, Dan   HB So. 5-11 178 Superior, Wis.

44 REGAN, Jim   HB So. 5-11 181 Berwyn, Ill.

After graduation, Regan, the Army veteran, briefly worked as a private detective. When he decided he didn't like the work, his uncle (a priest) helped him land a coaching and teaching job at a Catholic high school. He moved on to be a highly successful coach at two high schools in his hometown of Berwyn, Illinois. He retired in 1984 and lives with his wife, Rita, in Plainfield, Illinois.

87 RENNEBOHM, Bob   E So. 5-11 187 La Crosse, Wis.

Rennebohm, the V-12 Marine, attended the Detroit Lions' training camp in 1948 but decided pro football wasn't for him and walked out. He then went to work for a Chicago-based packaging company. Seven years later, he accepted the job as the head of the University of Wisconsin Foundation.

"Fundraising was relatively new at public schools, and I got together with my colleagues at Big Ten schools," he says. "We had conferences to talk about what we did and how we were going to do it. I spent thirty-five years as executive director, and then they changed the title to president."

He and Elroy Hirsch often visited Lancaster both as representatives of the university and as former teammates of Dave Schreiner, and they always took Anne Schreiner out to dinner. "She was a wonderful lady," Rennebohm says.

Rennebohm retired as foundation president in 1988 and served as a consultant until 1993. He and his wife live in a beautiful home on Lake Mendota in Madison.

75 REICH, Herbert　T So. 5-11 215 Chicago, Ill.

60 ROBERTS, John　G Sr. 5-10 185 Des Moines, Iowa

Harry Stuhldreher recommended Roberts, the former Army Air Forces pilot instructor, for the football coaching job at Stevens Point High School. He was there from 1946 to 1951 and later was head coach at what is now the University of Wisconsin–Stevens Point from 1952 to 1956. He was executive director of the Wisconsin State High School Athletic Association from 1957 to 1985 and championed the sport of wrestling. Roberts was Scholastic Wrestling magazine's man of the year in 1974. He and his wife, Janet, live in Stevens Point.

17 SCHROEDER, Bill　HB So. 6-1　190 Sheboygan, Wis.

43 SEELINGER, Bud　HB Sr. 5-11 178 Great Falls, Mont.

Seelinger, the sole surviving member of the Badgers on Okinawa, coached high school football for five years in North Dakota and his native Montana and then founded his own insurance agency in Havre, Montana. He retired in 1986, and he and his wife, Mary Elaine, moved to Whitefish, Montana. He died in 1999. Mary Elaine still lives in Whitefish.

84 STUPKA, Bob　E Sr. 6-0　181 Watertown, Wis.

77 THORNALLY, Dick　T Sr. 6-3　216 Chicago

Thornally, the former Marine, considered a career in coaching but signed on with Container Corporation of America as a sales trainee. "I wanted to be a coach so bad I could taste it," Thornally says. "My wife talked me out of it, and I guess it turned out all right. I loved selling. That was my life."

He worked for three other container companies and then started his own company, Commander Corporation. He eventually sold the company, worked for a time for the buyers, and finally retired in 1986. A widower since the death of his wife, former Wisconsin sorority girl Barbara Appleton, he lives in San Antonio, Texas.

—UTEGAARD, John

63 VOGDS, Red   G Jr. 5-11 194 Fond du Lac, Wis.

Vogds, the Navy physical instructor, played for the Chicago Rockets and Green Bay Packers and then returned to his hometown of Fond du Lac, where he owned a thriving insurance agency. "He did not talk about himself," says his widow, Bunny. "Everybody in town knew, and they were very proud that he had been a Badger and a Packer." He died in 1994.

70 WASSERBACH, Lloyd T Sr. 6-0 210 Bailey's Harbor, Wis.

25 WINK, Jack   QB So. 5-10 190 Milwaukee, Wis.

Wink, the V-12 Marine, began his teaching and coaching career at New London (Wisconsin) High School. He moved on to Wayne State in Nebraska and Stout Institute in Wisconsin and joined the staff of St. Cloud State in Minnesota in 1956. He was a football and hockey coach at St. Cloud for nearly thirty years, despite having multiple sclerosis. Lung cancer claimed him in 1995.

ANGUS, Robert (Manager)

Angus, the manager who had been a standout high school football player on a leg withered by polio, worked part-time for the *Wisconsin State Journal* while in college. He joined the Fort Atkinson, Wisconsin, paper, the *Union*, as a sportswriter and was the managing editor for nearly forty years before his retirement. A respected newspaperman, he died in 1995. He attended Badger team reunions and swore, time after time, that Pat Harder scored at Iowa.

FISCHER, Eugene (Manager)

Fischer, the team manager from Milwaukee, served as a flight clerk in the Army Air Forces during the war and returned to Madison to get his degree. He eventually worked in claims for Wausau Insurance in Kansas City for thirty-eight years. He still lives in Kansas City.

1942 Game by Game

Note: Statistics were haphazardly kept and often unreliable. In some cases, individual and team statistics don't add up. Published categories varied from game to game as well. Asterisks (*) refer to Completions-Attempts-Had Intercepted.

Wisconsin 7, Camp Grant 0

At Madison, September 19

Camp Grant	0	0	0	0 — 0
Wisconsin	0	0	0	7 — 7

Team statistics

	CG	W
First downs	6	11
Net yards rushing	73	201
Net yards passing	57	53
Total offense	130	254
Passing*	4-13-4	3-13-5

Individual Statistics

RUSHING
Camp Grant: Stasica 13 carries for 73 yards, Nori 5-4, Anderson 1-(-9), Westphall 2-0, Cary 8-15, Brandon 1-(-10).
Wisconsin: Hoskins 13-37, Hirsch 9-89, Seelinger 5-0, Calligaro 11-55, Regan 1-(-2).

PASSING
Camp Grant: Stasica 3 completions in 14 attempts, 42 yards. Nori 1-4, 15.

234

Wisconsin: Anderson 1-4, 7 yards; Wink 2-4, 46; Seelinger 0-1; Hirsch 0-3; Regan 0-1.

RECEIVING

Camp Grant: Anderson 1 reception, 7 yards; Nori 2-35.
Wisconsin: Hoskins 1 reception, 7 yards; Schreiner 1-28; Hanzlik, 1-18.

WISCONSIN PLAYER PARTICIPATION

Starters: Hanzlik, LE; Baumann, LT; Vogds, LG; Negus, C; Currier, RG; Hirsbrunner, RT; Schreiner, RE; Anderson, QB; Seelinger, LHB; Hoskins, RHB; Calligaro, FB.
Substitutes: Stupka, Thornally, Wasserbach, Roberts, Boyle, Boorman, Wink, Hirsch, Ray, Regan, Harder.

Wisconsin 7, Notre Dame 7

At Madison, September 26

Notre Dame	0	0	7	0 —	7
Wisconsin	0	0	7	0 —	7

Team statistics

	ND	W
First downs	14	7
Net yards rushing	226	128
Net yards passing	66	24
Total offense	292	152
Passing*	4-13-2	2-11-3

Individual Statistics

RUSHING

Notre Dame: C. Miller 4 carries, 12 yards; Livingstone 12-53; Early 12-29; Mello 26-112; T. Miller 1-6; Bertelli 1-(-10); Clatt 1-2; Piccone 1-2.
Wisconsin: Harder 11-10; Ray 2-3; Hirsch 11-37; Regan 1-4; Hoskins 2-22; Wink 2-2.

PASSING

Notre Dame: Bertelli 4-13, 66 yards.
Wisconsin: Hirsch 1-4, 10 yards; Hoskins 1-3, 14 yards; Wink 0-4.

RECEIVING

Notre Dame: Murphy 2 receptions, 17 yards; Livingstone 2-49.

Wisconsin: Harder 1 reception, 10 yards; Schreiner 1-14.

WISCONSIN PLAYER PARTICIPATION

Starters: Hanzlik, LE; Baumann, LT; Vogds, LG; Negus, C; Currier, RG; Hirsbrunner, RT; Schreiner, RE; Wink, QB; Hirsch, LHB; Hoskins, RHB; Harder, FB.
Substitutes: Wasserbach, Boyle, Anderson, Regan, Ray.

Wisconsin 35, Marquette 7

At Madison, October 3

Marquette	0	0	7	0 — 7
Wisconsin	0	28	7	0 — 35

Team statistics

	M	W
First downs	12	11
Net yards rushing	111	242
Net yards passing	112	179
Total offense	223	421
Passing	9-22-6	5-12-3

Individual Statistics

RUSHING
Marquette: Schuette 3 carries, 14 yards; Carlson 8-5; Strzykalski 16-66; O'Hagen 1-3; Capulis 3-2; Eigner 4-13; Johnston 5-6; Ruden 1-2.
Wisconsin: Harder 9-91; Ray 5-21; Hirsch 7-28 Hoskins 6-50; Calligaro 7-22; Regan 4-6; Anderson 1-10; Seelinger 1-(-10); McFadzean 1-9; Maves 1-2; Pfotenhauer 1-2.

PASSING (ATTEMPTS NOT AVAILABLE)
Marquette: Strzykalski 4 completions, 65 yards; Johnston 5, 24.
Wisconsin: Wink 2 completions, 102 yards; Hirsch 1, 41; Harder 1, 13; Anderson 1, 23.

RECEIVING
Marquette: Carlson 1 reception, 23 yards; Kuffel 1-26; Harrington 2-16; Vogt 2-30; Davis 1-3; Caldwell 2-14.
Wisconsin: Schreiner 4 receptions, 138 yards; Hanzlik 1-41.

WISCONSIN PLAYER PARTICIPATION
Starters: Hanzlik, LE; Baumann, LT; Vogds, LG; Negus, C; Currier, RG;
Hirsbrunner, RT; Schreiner, RE; Wink, QB; Hirsch, LHB; Hoskins, RHB;
Harder, FB.
Substitutes: Lyons, Stupka, Johnson, Olshanksi, Thornally, Wasserbach,
Hekkers, Donnellan, Boyle, Makris, Roberts, Frei, McKay, Boorman,
Calligaro, Ray, Seelinger, Pfotenhauer, Regan, Anderson, McFadzean,
Diercks, Maves.

Wisconsin 17, Missouri 9

At Madison, October 10
Missouri   2 0 0 7 — 9
Wisconsin   3 7 7 0 — 17

Team statistics

	M	W
First downs	16	13
Net yards rushing	122	289
Net yards passing	170	19
Total offense	292	308
Passing*	7-21-2	2-6-0

Individual Statistics

RUSHING
Missouri: Reese 6 carries, 22 yards; Steuber 13-43; Adams 6-10; Cater 2-
(-6); O'Hara 6-23; Bouldin 2-6; Pitts 1-0; Darr 5-0; Volz 1-4; Morton 2-14.
Wisconsin: Harder 7-17; Ray 12-42; Hirsch 22-174; Hoskins 5-23; Regan
3-12; Wink 1-2; Anderson 1-4.

PASSING (ATTEMPTS NOT AVAILABLE)
Missouri: Carter 2 completions, 50 yards; Steuber 3, 57; Darr 2, 63.
Wisconsin: Hoskins 1, 1 yard; Hirsch 1, 18.

RECEIVING
Missouri: Lister 2 receptions, 38 yards; Morton 3-54; Ekern 1-31;
Wren 1-47.
Wisconsin: Schreiner 1 reception, 18 yards; Ray 1-1.

WISCONSIN PLAYER PARTICIPATION
Starters: Hanzlik, LE; Baumann, LT; Vogds, LG; Negus, C; Currier, RG; Hirsbrunner, RT; Schreiner, RE; Wink, QB; Hirsch, LHB; Hoskins, RHB; Harder, FB.
Substitutes: Lyons, Johnson, Thornally, Hekkers, Boyle, Frei, McKay, Boorman, Makris, Roberts, Wasserbach, Donnellan, Stupka, Anderson, Diercks, Regan, McFadzean, Seelinger, Ray, Calligaro.

Wisconsin 13, Great Lakes 7

At Chicago, October 17

Wisconsin	0 0 13 0 — 13
Great Lakes	7 0 0 0 — 7

Team statistics

	W	GL
First downs	10	8
Net yards rushing	152	113
Net yards passing	17	104
Total offense	169	217
Passing*	2-6-4	6-19-4

Individual Statistics

RUSHING
Wisconsin: Ray 7-11; Calligaro 10-32; Hirsch 15-65; Seelinger 4-17; Regan 3-10; Hoskins 8-9; McFadzean 1-(-9); Wink 1-6; Anderson 1-(-2).
Great Lakes: Smith 14-44; McCullough 2-5; Sweiger 4-16; Kmetovich 3-2; Mucha 2-8; Belichick 5-30; Harrell 7-7; DeCorrevont 1-1.

PASSING (ATTEMPTS NOT AVAILABLE)
Wisconsin: Hirsch 1 completion, 6 yards; Hoskins 1, 11.
Great Lakes: Smith 2, 83; Popov 1, 1; DeCorrevont 1, 11; Harrell 1, 9; McCullough 1, 3.

RECEIVING
Wisconsin: Ray 1 reception, 6 yards; Calligaro 1-11.
Great Lakes: Preston 1 reception, 65 yards; McCullough 1-1; Mulleneaux 2-29; Hickey 1-9; Kmetkovich 1-3.

WISCONSIN PLAYER PARTICIPATION
Starters: Lyons, LE; Baumann, LT; Vogds, LG; Negus, C; Currier, RG; Hirsbrunner, RT; Schreiner, RE; Wink, QB; Hirsch, LHB; Hoskins, RHB; Ray, FB.
Substitutes: Johnson, Stupka, Wasserbach, Thornally, Boyle, Makris, Frei, Roberts, McKay, Boorman, Anderson, Seelinger, Regan, McFadzean, Calligaro, Harder, Maves.

Wisconsin 13, Purdue 0

At Lafayette, October 24

Wisconsin	0 7 0	6 —	13
Purdue	0 0 0	0 —	0

Team statistics

	W	P
First downs	18	5
Net yards rushing	245	35
Net yards passing	36	104
Total offense	281	139
Passing*	3-12-0	8-13-1

Individual Statistics

RUSHING
Wisconsin: Harder 25-99; Hoskins 8-13; Hirsch 12-50; Anderson 1-1; Seelinger 1-4; Ray 8-44; Regan 3-18; Calligaro 3-11; McFadzean 1-5.
Purdue: Buffington 1-3; Smock 5-13; Andretich 1-(-17); Stram 6-10; Berto 1-3; Bachmann 5-15; Chester 4-14.

PASSING (STATISTICS NOT AVAILABLE)

RECEIVING (STATISTICS NOT AVAILABLE)

WISCONSIN PLAYER PARTICIPATION
Starters: Hanzlik, LE; Baumann, LT; Vogds, LG; Negus, C; Currier, RG; Hirsbrunner, RT; Schreiner, RE; Wink, QB; Hirsch, LHB; Hoskins, RHB; Harder, FB.
Substitutes: Lyons, Stupka, Olshanski, Thornally, Wasserbach, Boyle, Frei, Makris, Roberts, McKay, Boorman, Anderson, Seelinger, Regan, McFadzean, Ray, Calligaro.

Wisconsin 17, Ohio State 7

At Madison, October 31

Ohio State	0	0	0	7 — 7
Wisconsin	0	10	0	7 — 17

Team statistics

	OS	W
First downs	15	12
Net yards rushing	230	242
Net yards passing	66	57
Total offense	296	299
Passing*	7-15-1	5-7-0

Individual Statistics

RUSHING

Ohio State: Fekete 20-65; Sarringhaus 13-55; Horvath 13-43; Lynn 1-1; James 7-57; Slusser 1-3; Frye 2-6.
Wisconsin: Harder 21-97; Hirsch 13-118; Hoskins 7-13; McFadzean 1-2; Wink 2-10.

PASSING (ATTEMPTS NOT AVAILABLE)

Ohio State: Sarringhaus 2 completions, 43 yards; Slusser 3, 26; Horvath 1, 13.
Wisconsin: Wink 1 completion, 15 yards; Hirsch 3, 39; Hoskins 1, 3.

RECEIVING

Ohio State: Horvath 2 receptions, 25 yards; Shaw 3-26; Fekete 1-25.
Wisconsin: Schreiner 4 receptions, 54 yards; Hirsch 1-3.

WISCONSIN PLAYER PARTICIPATION

Starters: Hanzlik, LE; Baumann, LT; Vogds, LG; Negus, C; Currier, RG; Hirsbrunner, RT; Schreiner, RE; Wink, QB; Hirsch, LHB; Hoskins, RHB; Harder, FB.
Substitutes: Lyons, Thornally, Wasserbach, Boyle, Roberts, Frei, McKay, Calligaro, Seelinger, Ray, McFadzean.

Iowa 6, Wisconsin 0

At Iowa City, November 7

Wisconsin	0	0	0	0 — 0
Iowa	0	6	0	0 — 6

Team statistics

	W	I
First downs	12	9
Net yards rushing	109	178
Net yards passing	61	44
Total offense	170	222
Passing*	7-18-3	2-6-1

Individual Statistics

RUSHING

Wisconsin: Harder 15-49; Ray 1-2; Hirsch 21-37; Hoskins 5-8; Ray 1-2; Seelinger 1-13.

Iowa: T. Curran 14-73; Farmer 7-21; Stauss 5-10; Ukness 14-43; Youel 3-2.

PASSING (ATTEMPTS NOT AVAILABLE)

Wisconsin: Hirsch 4 completions, 30 yards; Wink 1, 3; Harder 1, 18; Hoskins 1, 10.

Iowa: Farmer 2 completions, 44 yards.

RECEIVING

Wisconsin: Schreiner 2 receptions, 23 yards; Harder 2-13; Hoskins 2-15; Wink 1-10.

Iowa: Curran 1 reception, 22 yards; Burkett 1-22.

WISCONSIN PLAYER PARTICIPATION

Starters: Hanzlik, LE; Baumann, LT; Vogds, LG; Negus, C; Currier, RG; Hirsbrunner, RT; Schreiner, RE; Wink, QB; Hirsch, LHB; Hoskins, RHB; Harder, FB.

Substitutes: Lyons, Boyle, Roberts, Seelinger, Ray.

Wisconsin 20, Northwestern 19

At Evanston, November 14

Wisconsin	7	7	0	6 — 20
Northwestern	0	7	6	6 — 19

Team statistics

	W	NW
First downs	11	14
Net yards rushing	173	165
Net yards passing	54	94
Total offense	227	259
Passing*	5-8-0	10-21-1

Individual Statistics

RUSHING

Wisconsin: Hirsch 19-75; Harder 17-61; Hoskins 6-23; Ray 2-2; Anderson 1-(-9); Seelinger 1-21.

Northwestern: Graham 23-73; Ed Hirsch 15-79; Buffmire 6-13; Vodick 2-6.

PASSING

Wisconsin: Wink 1-1, 15 yards; Hirsch 2-3, 18; Anderson 0-2, 0; Harder 1-1, 15; Seelinger 1-1, 5.

Northwestern: Graham 10-21, 94.

RECEIVING

Wisconsin: Schreiner 1-14; Harder 2-10; Hoskins 1-6, Hirsch 1-21.

Northwestern: Motl 4-40; McNutt 1-10; Wallis 1-10; Vodick 2-16; Warren 1-6; Hasse 1-12.

WISCONSIN PLAYER PARTICIPATION

Starters: Hirsbrunner, LE; Baumann, LT; Vogds, LG; Negus, C; Currier, RG; Wasserbach, RT; Schreiner, RE; Wink, QB; Hirsch, LHB; Hoskins, RHB; Harder, FB.

Substitutes: Lyons, Makris, Anderson, Seelinger, McFadzean, Ray.

Wisconsin 20, Minnesota 6

At Madison, November 21

Minnesota	0	0	0	6 —	6
Wisconsin	7	7	0	6 —	20

Team statistics

	M	W
First downs	14	8
Net yards rushing	216	116
Net yards passing	41	82
Total offense	257	198
Passing*	2-11-5	3-5-0

Individual Statistics

RUSHING
Minnesota: Daley 15-89; Kulbitski 10-48; Lauterbach 2-17; Williams 3-10; Frickey 13-40; Luckemeier 2-12.
Wisconsin: Harder 11-43; Hirsch 12-43; Seelinger 3-9; Regan 1-2; Hoskins 7-9; Ray 5-4; Schreiner 1-1; Anderson 2-5.

PASSING (ATTEMPTS NOT AVAILABLE)
Minnesota: Daley 2 completions, 41 yards.
Wisconsin: Hirsch 2 completions, 61 yards; Harder 1,21.

RECEIVING
Minnesota: Hien 1 reception, 22 yards; Garnaas 1, 19.
Wisconsin: Schreiner 3 receptions, 82 yards.

WISCONSIN PLAYER PARTICIPATION
Starters: Hirsbrunner, LE; Baumann, LT; Vogds, LG; Negus, C; Currier, RG; Wasserbach, RT; Schreiner, RE; Anderson, QB; Hirsch, LHB; Hoskins, RHB; Harder, FB.
Substitutes: Lyons, Stupka, Thornally, Boyle, Frei, Makris, Roberts, McKay, Wink, Calligaro, McFadzean, Regan, Seelinger, Ray.

1942 Season Statistics

Rushing

	Attempts	Yards	Avg.
Hirsch	141	766	5.4
Harder	116	468	4.1
Hoskins	70	211	3.0
Ray	50	148	2.9
Seelinger	20	57	2.8
Regan	16	50	3.1
Wink	6	20	3.3
McFadzean	5	17	3.4
Anderson	7	9	1.3
Pfotenhauer	1	2	2.0
Maves	1	2	2.0
Schreiner	1	2	2.0

Passing

	Comp.	Attempts	Yards
Hirsch	18	40	226
Wink	9	24	210
Harder	4	7	66
Hoskins	5	10	41
Anderson	4	12	30
Seelinger	1	7	6

Receiving

	Receptions	Yards
Schreiner	16	350

(additional information unavailable)

1942 Badger Lettermen*

Major W

Players: Ashley Anderson, Bob Baumann, Pat Boyle, Len Calligaro, Ken Currier, Bobby Diercks, Jerry Frei, Pat Harder, Elroy Hirsch, Paul Hirsbrunner, Mark Hoskins, Farnham Johnson, Pat Lyons, Jim McFadzean, George Makris, Bob McKay, Fred Negus, Bob Ray, Jim Regan, John Roberts, Dave Schreiner, Bud Seelinger, Bob Stupka, Dick Thornally, Red Vogds, Lloyd Wasserbach, Jack Wink.
Managers: Eugene Fischer, Robert Angus.

Minor W

Harry Boorman, Otto Breitenbach, Jack Crabb, Ralph Davis, Bob Dean, Dave Donnellan, George Hekkers, Tom King, Erv Kissling, Vern Klinzing, Don Litchfield, Lawrence Lynch, Earl Maves, George Neperud, Hank Olshanski, Bob Omelina, Don Pfotenhauer, Bob Rennebohm, Dan Rayacich, Herb Reich, Bill Schroeder, John Utegaard.

---

* Major and minor letters (W) were awarded by Wisconsin coach Harry Stuhldreher, who in some cases withheld letters out of spite.

Sources and Credits

Dave Schreiner and Schreiner family correspondence, clippings, records, and photos

Grant County Historical Society, Lancaster, Wisconsin
Wisconsin Historical Society, Madison, Wisconsin
Judy Corfield, Geneva, Illinois
Ellen D. Goldlust-Gingrich and Kurt Gingrich, Madison, Wisconsin
(authors of "An All-American in All Respects," *Wisconsin Magazine of History*, 87:1, Fall 2003)

Other archival sources

Madison Public Library
University of Wisconsin Library
Columbus Metropolitan Library
Wisconsin Historical Society; Margaret Dwyer
Schreiner Library, Lancaster, Wisconsin; Joanne Halferty
University of Wisconsin Sports Information Department; Director Justin Doherty

Newspapers and periodicals

The Capital Times (Madison, Wisconsin)
Chicago Daily News
Chicago Tribune
Columbus Citizen
Columbus Dispatch

The Daily Cardinal (University of Wisconsin–Madison)
The Denver Post
Milwaukee Journal
Milwaukee Sentinel
Orange County Register
San Francisco Chronicle
Wisconsin State Journal (Madison, Wisconsin)

Author interviews

Ashley Anderson, Cary, North Carolina
*Victor Anderson, Brookfield, Wisconsin
Scott Angus, Janesville, Wisconsin
*Walter "Bus" Bergman, Grand Junction, Colorado
Otto Breitenbach, Madison, Wisconsin
Tom Butler, Madison, Wisconsin
*Bill Carroll, Westlake, Oregon
Judy Corfield, Geneva, Illinois
*Vern Courtnage, Hayward, California
Jack Crabb, Cheney, Washington
Charles Csuri, Columbus, Ohio
Charles Currier, Janesville, Wisconsin
Kay Dean, Wausau, Wisconsin
Dave Donnellan, Eau Claire, Wisconsin
*Clint Eastment, Rocky Point, New York
Gene Fekete, Columbus, Ohio
Eugene Fischer, Kansas City, Missouri
*Gus Forbus, Fallon, Nevada
Marian Frei, Lakewood, Colorado
John Gallagher, Eau Claire, Wisconsin
*Chuck Ganger, Cherokee, Iowa
*Frank Glancey, Bordentown, New Jersey
Bob Hanzlik, Portland, Oregon
*Jim Harwood, Odessa, Missouri
George Hekkers, Burbank, California
Patricia Hirsbrunner, Corpus Christi, Texas
Elroy Hirsch, Madison, Wisconsin
Mark Hadley Hoskins, San Diego, California

---

* Sixth Marine Division

Mary Hoskins, San Diego, California
Mark Hadley Hoskins, Jr., Lancaster, Wisconsin
*Melvin Kabik, Baltimore, Maryland
*Frank Kemp, Denver, Colorado
Erv Kissling, Oregon, Wisconsin
*Ed Liguori, Lakeland, Florida
Don Litchfield, Eau Claire, Wisconsin
*Robert Lowe, Denver, Colorado
George Makris, Medford Lakes, New Jersey
Jim McFadzean, Wilmette, Illinois
*John McLaughry, Providence, Rhode Island
Arlie Mucks, Jr., Madison, Wisconsin
Fred Negus, Fort Atkinson, Wisconsin
George Neperud, Litchfield, Minnesota
Bob Omelina, Scottsdale, Arizona
*Larry Parmelee, Brookfield, Wisconsin
*Charles Pulford, Punta Gorda, Florida
*William Ramey, Kernersville, North Carolina
Jim Regan, Plainfield, Illinois
Bob Rennebohm, Madison, Wisconsin
John Roberts, Stevens Point, Wisconsin
Mary Elaine Seelinger, Whitefish, Montana
*James Singley, Green City, Missouri
Constance Sherman Smyth, Littleton, Colorado
Dick Thornally, San Antonio, Texas
Bunny Vogds, Fond du Lac, Wisconsin

Other interviews

Elroy Hirsch interview by Barry Teicher. Tape recording, 1995. University of Wisconsin–Madison Oral History Project, University of Wisconsin Archives.

Betty Schreiner Johnson interview, June 25, 1992. Wisconsin Women during World War II Oral History Project, Wisconsin Historical Society Archives.

---

* Sixth Marine Division

Books and publications

Clipped Wings, the story of Stalag Luft III, a yearbook published by R.W. Kimball, "narrated" by O. M. Chiesl, 1948. Courtesy Mark Hoskins.

Spies in the Sky, a self-published booklet about the 26th Photo Recon Squadron, 960th Topographical Engineers, and the 3rd Emergency Rescue Squadron, by Don Esmond, Clyde Patterson, and William Wynne.

Alling, Charles B. *A Mighty Fortress: Lead Bomber over Europe* Havertown, Pennsylvania: Casemate, 2002.

Ambrose, Stephen E. *The Wild Blue.* New York: Simon and Schuster, 2001.

Belote, James H., and Belote, William M., *Typhoon of Steel.* New York: Harper & Row, 1970.

Butler, Tom. *The Badger Game.* Madison, Wisconsin: William C. Robbins/Straus Printing Company, 1991.

Cavanaugh, William C. *A Tour of the Bulge Battlefield.* South Yorkshire, UK: Leo Cooper, 2001.

Daughterty, Leo J. *Fighting Techniques of a U.S. Marine, 1941–45.* St. Paul, Minnesota: MBI Publishing Company, 2000.

Deane, Ronnie. *Crazylegs, A Man and His Career.* Madison: Montzingo & Gustin Advertising, 1987.

Gunn, John. *The Old Core.* Costa Mesa, California: J&J Publishing, 1992.

Leckie, Robert. *Okinawa: The Last Battle of World War II.* New York: Viking, 1995.

Morison, Samuel Eliot. *Victory in the Pacific, 1945.* Boston: Little, Brown and Co., 1960. Reprint: Castle Books, 2001.

Murray, Williamson and Millett, Allan B. *A War to Be Won: Fighting the Second World War.* Cambridge, Massachusetts: Belknap Press of Harvard University Press, 2000.

Rottman, Gordon L. *Okinawa 1945: The Last Battle.* Oxford, UK: Osprey Publishing, 2000.

Stuhldreher, Harry A. *Knute Rockne, Man Builder.* Grossett and Dunlap, 1931.

Stuhldreher, Mary. *Many a Saturday Afternoon.* D. McKay Co., 1964.

Zeiler, Thomas. *Unconditional Defeat: Japan, America, and the End of World War II.* Wilmington, Delaware: SR Books, 2003.

Index

Page numbers in *italics* refer to illustrations; page numbers in **bold** refer to mention in lists, such as rosters and game statistics.